IRISH INTELLECTUALS AND A

To my parents

IRISH INTELLECTUALS AND AESTHETICS

The Making of a Modern Art Collection

MARTA HERRERO

IRISH ACADEMIC PRESS
DUBLIN • PORTLAND, OR

First published in 2007 by
IRISH ACADEMIC PRESS
44, Northumberland Road, Dublin 4, Ireland

and in the United States of America by
IRISH ACADEMIC PRESS
c/o ISBS, Suite 300, 920 NE 58th Avenue
Portland, Oregon 97213-3644

WEBSITE: **www.iap.ie**

British Library Cataloguing in Publication Data
An entry can be found on request

ISBN 0 7165 3327 8 (cloth)
ISBN 978 0 7165 3327 6
ISBN 0 7165 3328 6 (paper)
ISBN 978 0 7165 3328 3

Library of Congress Cataloging-in-Publication Data
An entry can be found on request

Typeset by Carrigboy Typesetting Services.
Printed by Antony Rowe Ltd, Chippenham, Wiltshire.

Contents

Acknowledgements

I AM PARTICULARLY indebted to Hilary Tovey for supporting this project from the very beginning. Her ideas have always been an intellectual stimulation, and her patience in revising the text at various early stages helped me clarify my ideas and arguments. Phillip McEvansoneya was also extremely supportive in his thorough revision of chapter 2. I also thank Brian Torode and Ron Eyerman for encouraging me to write this book, and Alison Anderson and Matthew David for their help with the final draft.

A number of people have helped in different ways to make this book possible. I want to thank all my interviewees, and the staff at the Irish Museum of Modern Art who participated in this research, particularly Catherine Marshall. The staff at the Lecky Library in Trinity College, Dublin, especially Paul and Sean, were always extremely helpful in responding to my various requests to find material, usually at very short notice. I am particularly indebted to my friend Marty Whelan for all his help. My thanks also to the Institute for International Integration Studies, Trinity College, Dublin where I completed the final manuscript, and to Brendan Dempsey at Visual Services, for his advice on how to handle the images in this book. Thanks also to the library staff at the National Gallery of Ireland and the National Library of Ireland. Finally, I am indebted to my friends, who have always supported me, and reminded me how important it is to have fun! Thanks to Carme, Claire, Helen, Joyce, Ken, Lana, Michelle, Phil, Susana, Teresa, Tina and Virpi.

This research was carried out with the support of funding from various sources: a postgraduate scholarship from the Irish Research Council for the Humanities and Social Sciences; the Ussher International Fellowship Award and a postgraduate bursary both from Trinity College, Dublin.

Part of chapter 2 originally appeared in (2002) 'Towards a Sociology of Art Collections: Modernity, Intellectuals and Art Collections', *International Sociology*, 17 (1): 57–72.

Aspects of chapters 2 and 5 were discussed in a book chapter (2003) 'El arte moderno en Irlanda: la negociación de la modernidad y la postmodernidad' (Modern art in Ireland: negotiating modernity and postmodernity) in Lorente, J.P. (ed.), *Museología Crítica y Arte Contemporáneo* (Zaragoza: Prensas Universitarias de Zaragoza).

List of illustrations

Introduction

THIS IS A BOOK about art collections. It deals primarily with the collection at the Irish Museum of Modern Art (IMMA) in Dublin, and, in a historical context, it explores the origins of Ireland's first modern art collection, gathered for the Municipal Gallery of Modern Art in 1908. The study applies sociological approaches to intellectual practices – the formation of knowledge and expertise – to the practices involved in the making of art collections.

A study of art collections in the Irish context may seem to go against the grain, given the paradoxical status of the visual arts in Ireland. They are the poor relations of a century of Irish writers with a global reputation – James Joyce, Samuel Beckett, Oscar Wilde and, more recently, Nobel Prize-winning poet Seamus Heaney. The discrepancy between Ireland's literary and visual culture is poignantly expressed in the comment made by Irish art critic Brian Fallon (1994: 11): 'Irish painting and Irish sculpture are known only to a minority of scholars and cognoscenti, museum curators and a handful of salesroom addicts. And even these few rarely have any overall view or "picture" of Irish art and its line of development'. Fallon's pessimistic view is not to be taken lightly, but it also suggests the valuable task public institutions, museums, art galleries and other exhibition venues can play in encouraging greater public awareness of developments in the visual arts, and Irish art in particular. A number of initiatives have demonstrated a move in this direction, and have helped create an exciting, stimulating art world in the Irish capital. The development of Dublin's cultural quarter, Temple Bar, and the opening of IMMA, to commemorate Dublin's tenure as European city of culture in 1991, as well as the Millennium Wing of the National Gallery of Ireland in 2002, are some clear examples.

The empirical study offered in this book was carried out between 2000 and 2002, and explores a small field within Dublin's institutional art world: the field of modern art collecting. My main concern is to offer a focused exploration of Ireland's main national institution for the collection and display of modern art – the Irish Museum of Modern Art – by looking at the first decade of its collecting practices.[1] However, an underlying proposition in this book is that the making of any one art collection (in this case IMMA's) does not take place in a vacuum; rather, it is situated in a context, a network of collecting and exhibiting venues – the Royal Hibernian Academy, the Douglas Hyde Gallery, the Hugh Lane Municipal Gallery of Modern Art[2] – alongside other state and commercial players. This context is a fundamental aspect of this study, because it is where the works of artists who will make their way into IMMA's art collection are first promoted, exhibited and collected.

SOCIOLOGY AND ART

The academic sub-discipline informing this book is the sociology of art. Its general perspective is to analyze art in relation to the social context of its production, mediation and consumption. An approach widely used by sociologists is that of 'studying the art object sociologically' (Zolberg, 1990: 53) by analyzing art worlds. Sociologists use empirical research to identify the ways in which artworks are given public recognition in the artistic realm (Becker, 1982; Crane, 1987). The aim here is to offer a direct challenge to a predominantly Western conception of artistic creation, which sees it as the sole outcome of the artist's distinctive genius, by positing a 'practical theory of mediation' (Hennion, 2003: 81) in its place. The work of intermediaries – museums, art galleries, auction houses and art dealers – as well as audience' responses, is brought to the fore to illustrate the role they play in validating artistic reputations and styles. In this context, sociologists who have treated art museums as mediators look at how their activities – the making and display of their collections – contribute to the formation of artistic canons and reputations for artists; as well as examining the impact changes in museum funding make on the type of artworks which become part of an artistic canon (Alexander, 1996).

The making of collections occurs in the midst of negotiation and conflict amongst actors working in museums, such as trustees and curators, and external trends such as art market activity and the emergence of new funding sources (Zolberg, 1981). These conclusions (Zolberg, 1981; Alexander, 1996) derive from a sociology of organizations perspective, which pays particular attention to the interaction between museums as organizations and their environment. This book explores these aspects of museums and their collections; it explains the ways in which museum collections are made, who the individuals involved in the process are, and how collecting involves a negotiation between formal collecting policies and the individual tastes of museum personnel. However, its analysis of art-collecting practices is not situated within the confines of a sociology concerned with how changes in sponsorship affect the museum organization, its policy and activities.

Rather, it explores the role of museum professionals in formulating aesthetic categories of perception, such as 'modern art' and 'postmodern art', as well as the ways in which artworks can articulate modern and postmodern worldviews. Zygmunt Bauman's and Pierre Bourdieu's writings on intellectual practices provide a set of methodological tools, which are critically discussed, and then applied to the study of collecting practices. Collecting practices, those involved in the making of art collections, are interpreted here as a form of intellectual practice to the extent that they create knowledge about aesthetics – modern and postmodern – and the social world – modernity and postmodernity. But Bauman's work in particular also poses an interesting theoretical question which this book seeks to answer through a historical analysis of art collecting: can we argue that at the level of intellectual, collecting practices there has been a transition from modern to postmodern?

My emphasis on the study of institutions and what they do means that this book does not offer an analysis of the content of individual artworks. Some explorations of collections have given attention to the art object, although with a more general aim: to explain differences in taste (Haskell, 1976), the emergence of a taste for modern art (Bailey, 2002), or to illustrate the historical development of collecting as a specific behaviour (Alsop, 1982). One might object to the lack of attention given to the art object itself, and some might argue that any study ignoring it is merely reductionist. This type of critique would not, however, be a novelty – in fact, it applies to all sociological studies which emphasize the social context of the production and consumption of art.[3] But it is also part of a broader debate on disciplinary differences. Traditionally, the social sciences, on the one hand, and art history, on the other, have been characterized by their different analytical orientations: the former studies the context of art, while the latter evaluates art's internal characteristics. The difference between these, also called externalist and internalist approaches respectively, has shaped an ongoing debate (Wolff, 1981, 1983; Zolberg, 1990; Hennion and Grenier, 2000) which asks whether sociologists should focus on the study of art, and how they should carry out this task.

For some, though, this debate is a lost battle. Even when sociological explorations are noted as making valuable contributions to the understanding of art, they are, in the last instance, judged in terms which echo art history's ethos: 'Sociology of art remains unable to give a fully satisfactory account of the constructive role of aesthetic form from within its own theoretical horizons' (Tanner, 2003: 22). In this case, the sociology of art's failure is built upon a representation of the discipline as solely concerned with the formulation of general laws, testing concepts in a positivistic fashion, and intent on the production of causal explanations (Herrero, 2005a). This 'general sociology of art' (Tanner, 2003: 25) is forever pitched at a macro level of analysis, describing, for example, the functional contribution of art to social processes, or its role in formulating 'ideal typical models' (ibid: 14, 24). Conversely, recent research in the sociology of art (DeNora, 2003; Hennion, 2003)[4] shows a different trend to the one portrayed here, one where the work of art is analyzed in terms of the uses individuals make of it; seen not as an abstract entity, but in its 'materiality' (Hennion, 2003: 83), which in turn shapes the ways in which people describe and experience aesthetic pleasure. Most importantly, this argument shows how sociologists are developing ways of analysing artworks outside the remit of art history's perspective. This book follows this new development, and argues that it is possible to produce research which, while it does not engage in the study of aesthetics, still retains a sense of how artworks play a role in generating interpretations of what constitutes 'good art' or a canon such as 'modern art'. For example, art-collecting practices involve using artworks in visual displays – exhibitions which are instrumental in producing knowledge about what art is, and ideas about the role of artists in society. These are ways of engaging with the artwork which will be explored in this book, and conceptualized in terms of a distinct sociological research agenda.

The chapters that follow are structured around different aspects of art collecting, and elaborate in detail the issues outlined in this introduction. Chapter 1 discusses the literature on museum collections, mainly within the discipline of museum studies, and, through an engagement with the work of Zygmunt Bauman and Pierre Bourdieu, reworks the notion of intellectual collecting practices. The chapter offers an analytical framework that will inform the remainder of the book, based on the study of fields and the role of modern and postmodern collecting practices. Chapters 2, 3, 4 and 5 address the making of modern art collections in an historical and contemporary context. The emphasis in chapter 2 is to trace the origins of modern art collecting in Ireland, focusing on the foundation of the Municipal Gallery of Modern Art (MGMA) in 1908; it also investigates the nature of modern intellectual practices. Chapters 3, 4 and 5 are based on an empirical study of Dublin's art world, and the collection at IMMA in particular. The material used is based on interviews with art world members, gallery and museum directors, and curators. Chapter 3 contextualizes the position of IMMA in relation to other institutions, while chapters 4 and 5 analyze IMMA's collecting and exhibition activities as examples of postmodern intellectual practices. The thrust of these chapters is to explore the kind of intellectual practices involved in collecting art. The division between collecting and exhibiting is instrumental in distinguishing how these different practices contribute to validating IMMA's collection: chapter 4 analyzes collecting practices based on interviews with staff and board members at IMMA, while chapter 5 explores the ways IMMA's collection is actually exhibited. More specifically, it introduces some of the conventions used in exhibition design in order to explore the ways in which the museum's exhibitions create particular ways of looking at and thinking about artworks. The book concludes by discussing how a sociological approach to art collections can expand our understanding of the making of aesthetic categories of perception, and the changing role of art-collecting practices in legitimating existing ways of thinking about society.

CHAPTER 1

Outline of a Sociology of Art Collections

MUSEUMS, COLLECTIONS AND THE MAKING OF KNOWLEDGE

MUSEUMS, COLLECTIONS AND knowledge are intricately linked. Museums house objects deemed to be 'paradigms of their kind' (Pearce, 1995: 387), but in order to become 'paradigms' in museum collections they need to undergo a process of interpretation, starting with their removal from their location or context of production to their subsequent positioning in a museum, where they are given meaning and value within frameworks of intelligibility or interpretation (Hooper-Greenhill, 2000: 8). An artwork will be exhibited according to the museum's exhibition policy, which is developed following the guidelines for collecting set up by the institution, and will need the approval of a board of directors prior to entering a collection. Thus the inclusion of objects in museum collections and their use in exhibitions rely on the activities of museum professionals, as well as those directly involved in the making of collections, and in these activities the use and making of knowledge is a key practice.

The relationship between collections and knowledge is a recurring theme in the literature on museums, looking at how they create meaning through their collections and displays (Hooper-Greenhill, 1992; Pearce, 1992, 1995), and how these activities are influenced by the 'intellectual rationale' of their time (Pearce, 1992: 89). Some studies have also looked at how visitors derive meaning from museum exhibits (Hooper-Greenhill, 1989), while a number of authors have explored how exhibitions convey meaning through the visual arrangement of objects (Duncan and Wallach, 1980). Finally, another strand of the literature has highlighted how museum workers can shape the knowledge and ideas presented by museum collections (Hooper-Greenhill, 1992; Pearce, 1992).

In general, the literature on collections draws particular attention to the limitations of dualist thinking in which objects and human beings are separate, part of a duality between an 'active, understanding human subject and a passive, inert object'. Instead, objects in collections are to be seen as being intricately linked to the construction of identities and perpetuation of ideological structures (Pearce, 1995: 18). For example, Hooper-Greenhill (1992) has adopted Foucault's notion of 'episteme' to explain how what counts as truth and knowledge at a particular time influences the meanings taken on by collection objects. Thus the value and purpose given to an object changes depending on the episteme to which it belongs, for example Renaissance, classical or modern:

> Thus a painting of a 'Madonna and Child' would be understood in the Medici Palace as both a magical and religious thing, something that could give protection against evil forces, and something that should be held in awe . . . [In] 'the cabinet of the world', a painting of a 'Madonna and Child' would be understood as part of the representation of the hierarchical structure of the world. It would be one thing among other things both old and new that were placed together in the cosmological picture, and it might possibly be linked to other things of very disparate nature through resemblance and signatures . . . [In] the 'disciplinary museum', the painting would be part of a constellation of objects that represented liberation from tyrants and oppressors. In being seen, it took its place among the technologies designed to create docile bodies, and to reform the population as a resource for government. (Hooper-Greenhill, 1992: 194–5)

This example shows how collections are important as the context in which objects can take on roles and meanings, which vary historically; and it suggests the need to treat 'collection value' in its specificity. In the case of private collections, this context articulates a 'scenario of the personal', where the collection is a way of articulating the collector's own taste and preferences (Stewart, 1993: 162). Conversely, as was said earlier, objects in public collections can reflect a variety of factors: the policies of the institution to which they belong, as well as the aesthetic preferences of the director or the members of an acquisitions committee. Once they enter a museum's collection, however, they are valuable in terms of what they are made to represent. The collection and exhibition of non-Western art as an object of beauty is one such example of a museological discovery (Clifford, 1988: 227), and was made possible by the role of key museums in the West, such as the Museum of Modern Art in New York.[1] In the art museum, art objects are situated within specific modes of classification, which designate them as 'original', 'beautiful', or at least 'inspiring'. In this sense, the activities of museums have been said to contribute to creating a repertoire of knowledge, or a set of socio-cultural values characteristic of their own time.

THE INTELLECTUAL PRACTICES OF COLLECTING

The work of museums – formulating art policies, collecting and exhibiting artworks – must be seen as a knowledge-making intellectual practice which shapes how people think about what is valuable and important. Museum practices create knowledge about the world of which they are part, and assign value and meaning to objects in collections.[2] Moreover, collections constitute 'a unique domain, whose history cannot be consigned to the narrow confines of the histories of art, the sciences or history itself' (Pomian, 1990: 5). The expression 'unique domain' points to the need to go beyond a study of collections as representations of existing fields of knowledge, and explore them in their historical specificity and distinctive uniqueness. This means formulating questions, that can help reveal the rationale for their formation such as '[w]hen and how was the collection formed?', '[w]ho formed it?' and '[w]hy did this person/these people choose to assemble these objects?' (Pearce, 1992: 116).

Various authors have started to answer these questions, and argue that museum collections are instrumental tools in formulating ideas about the social world they inhabit (Pearce, 1992; Bennett, 1995; Fyfe, 2000). The distinction between modern and postmodern collections serves to illustrate the different role collections are said to have, and how this has changed historically. Pearce (1992: 139) argues that modern museum collections have been instrumental in creating a 'meta-narrative of the modern world', and have articulated a discourse 'through which objective realities and eternal truths could be defined and expressed' (ibid: 2). In this scenario, objects were displayed to represent a division of the world into types, each part of a sequence of development. For example, objects from Western and non-Western countries were exhibited in ways which made explicit the existence of a linear development, according to which peoples, states and civilizations were illustrated in terms of their being less or more advanced (Bennett, 1995: 76).

A different museological practice is that of postmodern collecting, which is said to reflect the characteristics of today's 'postmodern' world. The term postmodern is used here to describe how the boundaries between physical objects and what they mean have dissolved. Existing, modern notions of classification and value judgements have been subverted; what prevails now is a form of 'idiosyncratic assemblage' (Pearce, 1995: 149) which follows no external point of reference. A clear example of postmodern assemblage can be seen in the first exhibition of the museum's collection at IMMA in 1991, particularly the display of a work by Richard Long, *Green Quartz Circle*, next to a painting of the West of Ireland by well-known Irish artist Paul Henry (1858–1978). The museum's aim was to challenge viewers to decide – or question – which art form they preferred as a representation of nature. The exhibit caused considerable controversy, positioning the work of Henry, one of Ireland's most admired painters, next to what was seen as 'a load of old rubbish'.[3]

But the notion of a shift in the nature of collecting raises the following questions: if collecting practices are constitutive of meta-narratives which have been subjected to change – as from modern to postmodern – what happens to the notion of practice itself? When museum professionals are no longer involved in the making of modern meta-narratives, but are, rather, trying to deal with a postmodern world, what implications does this scenario have for collecting practices? There is a need to explore whether a change in the type of knowledge being produced through collections runs parallel to a shift in the nature of collecting practices. In other words, we need to develop, firstly, a theoretical model of intellectual practice, which pays attention to changes at the level of practice. Only then will we be able to explore empirically, with a study of both historical and contemporary collecting practices, the extent of the shift presented here. Is art collecting a way of representing something distinctively postmodern, while the practices that constitute it are modern? Or were postmodern practices involved in the representation of modern meta-narratives?

The remainder of this chapter explores the work on intellectual practices by two leading sociologists, Zygmunt Bauman and Pierre Bourdieu, and identifies those aspects of their theories which can help build up a framework for a study of art-collecting practices. Although their work does not address the topic of collections, their arguments on intellectual practices, are especially pertinent. The main focus of the discussion is on the role of intellectual practices in the artistic realm, and on how these practices change.

ZYGMUNT BAUMAN'S THEORY OF INTELLECTUALS

Modernity and legislators

Bauman sets up a framework for his sociology of intellectuals in *Legislators and Interpreters* (1987), although he has also written about the topic on other occasions (1992a, 1992b, 1995). In his work, the terms modernity and postmodernity refer to a shift in the nature of intellectual practices, and two different contexts in which the intellectual role is performed (1987: 3). In modernity the ideal type of intellectual practice was that of legislator, whereas in postmodernity the prevailing role is that of interpreter (ibid: 3). Bauman wants to move away from defining intellectuals by way of their characteristics or professions, and proposes instead to explain the category in relation to the role intellectuals perform in the maintenance and development of the social order (ibid: 18). His project thus has a twofold aim from the outset: to explain modernity and postmodernity as two different types of intellectual practice, and explore their associated models of social order.

What Bauman terms 'legislation' is a practice that emerged in Western Europe during the transition from pre-modern to modern society; a process which acquired momentum in the seventeenth century, and was completed by the nineteenth (ibid: 51). In fact, Bauman's work is a 'history of modern intellectuals' (ibid: 97). He traces a development in intellectual tasks from eighteenth-century philosophers to the twentieth century's 'educated experts', giving special attention to the role played by the French *les philosophes* in the third quarter of the eighteenth century, as 'this modality stands behind the idea of intellectuals in our own time' (ibid: 23–4). The aim here is not to discuss the achievements of *les philosophes,* but to identify briefly those aspects of their work that caused the transition from pre-modern to modern society, as well as leading up to a distinctively legislating intellectual practice. Bauman mentions three aspects of this transition: the suppression of pre-modern culture and subsequent move towards what he calls a modern, 'garden culture'; the importance of education; and the appearance of the concepts 'culture' and 'civilization'. But the need to shape human conduct with the help of education and culture was a symptom of two causes associated with the birth of modernity: firstly, the redeployment of social power, and the redefinition of social order, from the hands of the church to the service of the state; and, secondly, the implementation of a discourse of modernity in what Bauman calls the knowledge/power syndrome (ibid: 38), which would be the key task of legislators. In short, the role of legislators was made possible by the emergence of a new form of social power: 'the role of an expert or of a specialist may only arise under conditions where a permanent asymmetry of power aims at shaping or modifying human conduct' (ibid: 48).

Modern intellectuals are crucial participants in the making and maintenance of modernity's social order. The combination of two developments enables this association: a new type of state power geared towards setting up a 'social system according to a preconceived model of order'; and the establishment of a 'relatively autonomous, self-managing discourse', that of intellectuals, 'able to generate such a model' (ibid: 2). Modern legislation entailed 'the attainment of truth, the arrival at valid moral judgement, and the selection of proper artistic taste' (ibid: 4–5) coupled with the making of 'authoritative statements which arbitrate in controversies of opinions' (ibid: 4). Legislators had access to superior (objective) knowledge, for example; they used 'procedural rules', a practice geared towards validating or invalidating beliefs, particularly those that could not be subjected to the control of reason (ibid: 5). In fact, the employment and formulation of these rules is what distinguishes the 'intellectual professions' from 'meta-professionals':

> The employment of such procedural rules makes the intellectual professions (scientists, moral philosophers, aesthetes) collective owners of knowledge of direct and crucial relevance to the maintenance and perfection of the social order. The condition of this being so is the work of the 'intellectuals proper' – meta-professionals, so to speak – to be responsible for the formulation of procedural rules and to control their correct application. (Bauman, 1987: 5)

The co-operation between intellectual legislators and the modern state led to the creation of a body of knowledge designed to produce and support a theory of social order. Legislation was carried out in areas such as ethics, science, psychology, history and the arts, while legislators created a theory of history that projected Western Europe in opposition to the rest of the world. Bauman accepts that there was disagreement over the many conceptualisations of modernity which projected a theory of history, but agreement prevailed on one crucial point:

> they all took the form of life developed in parts of the Western world as the 'given', 'unmarked' unit of the binary opposition which relativised the rest of the world and the rest of historical times as the problematic, 'marked' side, understandable only in terms of its distinction from the Western pattern of development, taken as normal. The distinction was seen first and foremost as a set of absences – as a lack of the attributes deemed indispensable for the identity of most advanced age. (Bauman, 1987: 111)

Bauman names a number of authors who have provided visions of modernity, among them Friedrich Nietzsche, Sigmund Freud, Karl Marx, Norbert Elias and Georg Simmel. In sum, their work shares three features: the assumption that the changes caused by modernity are irreversible; a notion of modernity as an unfinished project; and the fact that they were all 'inside' views of modernity. However, Bauman also seems to accept the fact that there may have been disagreements, critiques of these views of modernity:

> It is perhaps debatable whether the philosophers of the modern era ever articulated to everybody's satisfaction the foundations of the objective superiority of Western rationality, logic, morality, aesthetics, cultural precepts, rules of civilized life, etc. (Bauman, 1987: 119)

Bauman's examples are by no means unproblematic. It is particularly difficult to identify any social scientists fitting the role of legislators, 'modernists in Bauman's strong sense' (Outhwaite, 1999: 11). Moreover, it is possible that modern intellectuals operated within two opposed fronts: those 'critical and oppositional individuals opposed to injustice and oppression', and the 'producers of ideology who legitimated the forms of class, race and gender domination and inequality in modern societies' (Kellner, 1995: 427). And yet, Bauman has addressed the role of 'critical intellectuals' in his writings, though his understanding differs from Kellner's. Critical intellectuals are 'the "intelligentsia" of the civilizational periphery' (Bauman, 1995: 228). As mentioned earlier, legislators were in charge of mapping out a theory of history, as a result countries were classified according to the opposition between centre and periphery. Peripheral countries were defined as 'uncivilized', 'lagging behind', and thus needing to embrace foreign, civilizing patterns. The role of critical intellectuals was to implement modernity from and in its periphery:

> They positioned themselves, at least mentally, outside the native reality, and that mental distance condensed both the 'reality' and their own

> condition into 'objective' entities sharply opposed to, and at war with, each other. In this opposition, native reality was constituted as an object of thorough and deliberate transformation, and/or as an obstacle to such a transformation which needs to be broken if the desired transformation is to take place. (Bauman, 1995: 229)

Bauman's use of the term 'critical intellectuals' here shares a certain similarity with Kellner's notion of 'oppositional individuals' – intellectuals in the 'periphery' were critics of their own society, and thus they embraced its transformation from 'backward' to 'modern' and 'civilized'. This argument precludes the possibility of a struggle between intellectuals at the periphery and the worldview of modernity legislated from the centre. The dynamics of intellectual practices outside modernity's core countries is an issue deserving further attention and will be dealt with in chapter 2.

Legislating modern art

In the area of taste and aesthetic judgement legislators made decisions, pronounced statements, segregated and classified art from non-art (Bauman, 1987: 134). They exercised an almost monopolistic power, which remained particularly unchallenged: 'no other sites of power attempted to interfere with the verdicts proffered by those "in the know"' (ibid: 134). Modern artists and their critics and analysts seem to fit Bauman's earlier distinction between 'intellectual professions' and 'meta-professionals'. On the one hand, art critics met with 'tasks they could handle'; they could 'find many a development in modernist art a puzzle – but they knew that this puzzle had a solution, and they had the means to find it' (ibid: 133–4). On the other hand, modern artists were the 'intellectual professions'; they followed in their practice the 'procedural rules' of modernity, in this case modern art, which 'Shared fully and whole-heartedly in this era's search for truth, its scientific methods of analysis, its conviction that reality can be – and should be – subjected to the control of Reason' (ibid: 133–4).

In painting, the grid exemplifies the most radical and consistent attempt to represent the essence of modernity; it 'decodes the work of modern authority manifesting itself in dividing, classifying, categorizing, filing, ordering and relating' (ibid: 133). On a similar note, the work of Surrealists could be seen as an expression of modernity; here artists such as Salvador Dalí and René Magritte drew on the psychoanalytic theories of Sigmund Freud and Carl Jung to represent the world of the subconscious. Artists and intellectuals worked together to maintain the knowledge that underpinned modernity – and the belief that reality could be represented by artists, and analyzed by analysts and art critics:

> The modernist artists broadcast on the same wavelength as their intellectual analysts and critics. They confronted their analysts and critics with tasks they could handle well, and were accustomed to handle by their professional training and inherited, institutionalised aesthetics. (Bauman, 1987: 134)

The only threat to the aesthetic judgement of legislators was its necessary opposite – 'pretentiousness without foundation, taste without legitimacy, choice without right'. This was the case with an ascending middle class who had the financial means to invest in art, and who ignored the authority of aestheticians when deciding how to spend their money. But, in the end, the legislators won the battle. They condemned the existence of an artistic judgement outside of their own, one which they regarded as a manifestation of 'aesthetic incompetence' (ibid: 136). The monopolistic rule of legislators in the artistic realm remained unchallenged because modern society safeguarded their authority:

> [The] general structure of modern society, with its in-built cult of education, truth, science and reason (and respect for the authority of those who embodied such values) guaranteed a mechanism through which the potential threats to elitist judgement could be absorbed and thus neutralized. For all practical intents and purposes, superiority of sophisticated aesthetic judgement was never truly put in question, however often it was resented or disregarded. (Bauman, 1987: 137)

As said earlier, Bauman mentions the existence of alternative tastes, which seem to pose a threat to the rulings of legislators, but argues in fact that the presence of alternatives highlights the monopolistic power of legislators, who are not challenged by them. In this, Bauman does not give enough importance to the possibility of struggles between factions of intellectuals; as a result, we do not know whether various artistic forms or styles were, for example, competing for recognition. The legislation of modern art was even able to face up to the challenge posed by the work of Marcel Duchamp, whose *Fountain* (1917), a urinal signed 'R. Mutt', transgressed all the conventions of modern art, but was, nonetheless, amenable to modern criteria of aesthetic judgement:

> [What] Marcel Duchamp did was to present a new *definition* of art (something chosen by the artist), a new *theory* of artwork (cutting off an object from its ordinary context and viewing it from an unusual point of view . . .), a new *method* of artistic work (creating a new thought for an object) . . . it could be seen as [iconoclastic] because at that time definitions, theories and methods still counted and were perceived as the necessary conditions and paramount criteria of artistic judgement. (Bauman, 1987: 131)

Duchamp's work posed a challenge to those in charge of legitimating what counted as modern art when his art could not be legislated with the use of existing definitions, theories and methods of artistic judgement. Nonetheless, Duchamp's rebellious act was still susceptible to modern legislation. In fact, as Bauman argues, it was seen as iconoclast but only through the application of (new) definitions, theories, and methods, which were the usual tools of legislators.

Postmodernity: a theory of change

In the postmodern worldview, the legislating practice no longer applies – postmodernity has its own associated intellectual practice: interpreting (ibid: 2–5). The postmodern worldview stands for a way of looking at the world, a sort of 'vantage point' which enables a perception of modernity as 'an enclosed object, an essentially complete product, an episode of history, with an end as much as a beginning' (ibid: 117). This is not to say that the socio-economic and political transformations experienced by modern society are obliterated and reduced here to an analytical stance. Bauman insists that 'postmodernist discourse . . . is about the credibility of "modernity" as a self-designation of Western civilization, whether industrial or post-industrial, capitalist or post-capitalist' (ibid: 118). Thus postmodernity is not meant to exclude other changes, such as those explained by the idea of post-industrialism; in fact, they can be seen as occurring alongside each other. The issue, for Bauman, is how to theorize something the term post-industrial ignores: 'a questioning of the self-consciousness of Western society, and the grounds (or absence of grounds) for such consciousness' (ibid.). His project is to address the shift in our perception of modernity:

> Unlike the notion of a post-industrial society, the concept of postmodernity refers to a distinct quality of intellectual climate, to a distinctly new meta-cultural stance, to a distinct self-awareness of the

> era. One of the basic, if not *the* basic, elements of this self-awareness is the realization that modernity is over; that modernity is a closed chapter of history, which can now be contemplated in its entirety, with retrospective knowledge of its practical accomplishments as much as its theoretical hopes. (Bauman, 1987: 119)

But if we accept the idea of postmodernity as a form of perception, a self-awareness of modernity's project, this raises the question: whose self-awareness is being qualified in this argument? In other words, who, to begin with, were those individuals or groups associated with a change towards a self-consciousness of postmodern Western society? We know that postmodernity has brought with it a change in intellectual practices, but is it possible to say that postmodern interpretation is the practice responsible for the postmodern perception of modernity? These are questions which will not necessarily be answered here, but it is important to raise them because they suggest further research is needed into Bauman's work.

Ultimately, the legislator's fall was caused by the 'divorce between the state and intellectual discourse' (ibid: 2), and by the state relinquishing its role in the reproduction of domination. While the establishment of universal standards of truth, morality and taste were crucial to the project of modernity, in the postmodern context, the power of the state has been replaced with new forms of social control (Bauman, 1992a: 112). Seduction – the dependency of consumers on the market – has become 'the paramount tool of integration (of the reproduction of domination)' (ibid: 97–8). Non-consumers, for their part, are subordinated by repression, which targets those individuals at the 'margin of society who cannot be absorbed by market dependency' (ibid: 98). Some of the techniques of repression are 'surveillance, "correction", welfare supervision, "medicalization", or "psychiatrization", as well as the servicing of the general legal/penal system' (ibid: 15).

Apart from the separation between the intellectual's role and the state, a further development encouraging the advent of postmodernity is the emergence of a postmodern discourse. Postmodernism was first used to designate a rebellion against modern 'functionalist, scientifically grounded, rational' architecture (ibid: 118) – a new perspective exemplified, say, by the Pompidou Centre in Paris. But changes in architecture were also a precursor to a more general revolt that was to affect Western art. A revolt that was so radical that art became no longer susceptible to legislation. Moreover, the arrival of postmodernity has helped highlight the differing characteristics of modern art and postmodern art. Bauman notes how 'Postmodern art is indeed radically different from modernism. It is, from the perspective of this difference, only now, in the last decade or two, that the orderly nature of modernist art . . . has become fully visible' (ibid: 132). In the postmodern context, art's radicalism is pre-empted; it is no longer a vehicle for protest. The modernist avant-garde, with its attempt to challenge the limits of what constitutes art, was absorbed by an art market where the value of art is not related to its capacity to challenge the status quo, but to its financial value as a vehicle for investment (ibid: 132). In this way, the art world adopts and transforms art into a commodity, into something that can be absorbed, accommodated, legalised, marketed and profited from (ibid.). But as to what or who precipitates a postmodern self-awareness and emerging postmodern discourse, Bauman seems to suggest that it could be due to the intrinsic characteristics of postmodern art, which resist legislation:

> The puzzle presented by post-modernist art, on the other hand, is one which truly baffles its analysts. The feeling of bewilderment and being lost in the maze of new developments results from the absence of the comfortable conviction that the new is just more of the same, an unfamiliar form of the familiar, that it is only a matter of time for it to lose its strangeness, to be intellectually tamed, that the tools sufficient for the job are available and one knows how to apply them. (Bauman, 1987: 134)

There is an unresolved tension in Bauman's discussion of the end of legislating practices in the artistic field. Is it due to the nature of postmodern art itself, a puzzle that resists analysis? Or are the mechanisms of the art market, and consumer society, responsible for turning art into a commodity, and thus into something whose value is determined by its 'success' or financial profit? The distinction is an important one – we still need to know who is in charge of implementing the transition towards postmodernity. If Bauman is saying that postmodern art has contributed to the articulation of a postmodern viewpoint, which makes relevant the modernist nature of modern art, then it gives postmodern artists a role in the shift from modernity to postmodernity. Without the existence of artistic creations that expressed the changes in the sort of art being produced, and, consequently, the inability of legislating practices to carry on as before, the emergence of a postmodern viewpoint and a postmodern interpreting practice would not have happened, at least not in the same way. But if we follow the argument that the market is responsible for the validation of what counts as art, this still leaves unanswered the question of whose perspective precipitated the emergence of a postmodern discourse. The issue is a contentious one, particularly when Bauman adds that postmodernism opened the eyes of so-called 'intellectual observers' (Herrero, 2005b). They seem to be the holders of a postmodern vantage point. They became aware of the changes taking place, a lack of 'objective grounds', not only in art, but also in other areas such as the social sciences and philosophy:

> [Postmodernism] had opened the eyes of intellectual observers to those features shared by the transformations in contemporary arts and the fascinating shifts of attention, anti-traditionalist rebellion, and strikingly heretical philosophically informed social sciences. Eyes were opened to the similarity between the erosion of 'objective grounds' in art and the sudden popularity of post-Wittgensteinian and post-Gadamerian hermeneutics in social sciences, or the vitriolic attacks of the 'new pragmatists' against Carthesian-Lockean-Kantian tradition in modern philosophy. It became increasingly plausible that these apparently disparate phenomena were the manifestations of the same process. (Bauman, 1987: 118)

But this argument on the awareness of 'intellectual observers' continues to leave various questions unanswered. Did intellectual observers play any role in change? Are they articulating a postmodern intellectual practice? And who are they anyway?

Postmodern interpretation

Postmodern interpretation is the new intellectual practice of postmodernity. In postmodernity, the global order of modernity is split into many 'local, partial, functionally specific and privately policed mini-orders' (Bauman, 1992a: 89). Their validation is in the hands of the 'relatively autonomous set of practices' of interpreters (Bauman, 1987: 4), and facilitated by the criteria developed within particular traditions or communities where, 'upheld by the habits and beliefs of a "community of meanings" [this criterion] . . . admits of no other tests of legitimacy' (ibid: 4). Interpreters also take on a role as translators, translating statements made in different communities, with their different knowledge systems. Interpreters then are experts in 'preventing the distortion of meaning in the process of communication' (ibid: 5).

There is a distinction to be made between the role of interpreters and the validation of postmodern communities. For Bauman the interpreting strategy is aimed at validating each of the many models of order (ibid: 4). A key difference in his definition is that interpreting, as opposed to legislating, is not a strategy 'orientated towards selecting the best social order' (ibid: 5). Instead, the knowledge interpreters produce is only valid within their community. This point becomes clear if we compare it with the role of legislators. Theirs was an extra-territorial practice, which was 'not bound by localized, communal traditions' (ibid: 5). They created their own rules, which were employed in the selection of the best social order. This is why only legislators owned knowledge of crucial relevance to the maintenance of a social order called modernity.

But the legislating practices of modernity are not completely at odds in a postmodern context. Bauman argues that the intellectual type of modernity has not been 'conclusively superseded by the advent of postmodernity' (ibid: 6). Postmodern interpretation includes both a postmodern form of legislation, and the practice of translating between communities, but:

> It is vitally important to note that the post-modern strategy does not imply the elimination of the modern one; on the contrary, it cannot be conceived without the continuation of the latter. While the post-modern strategy entails the abandonment of the universalistic ambitions of the intellectuals' own tradition, it does not abandon the universalistic ambitions of the intellectuals towards their own tradition; here, they retain their meta-professional authority, legislating about the procedural rules which allow them to arbitrate controversies of opinion and make statements intended as binding. (Bauman, 1987: 5)

Postmodern legislation occurs within communities since '[systems] of knowledge may only be evaluated from "inside" their respective traditions' (ibid: 4). Only from within their own community are intellectuals able to 'assure the survival of certainty, the dominion of reason' because their criteria depend on its validation by one such tradition. In this role, intellectuals 'supply their criteria for criticism', and 'spell out the rules which decide who are the rational discussants and who are not' (ibid: 145). Outside postmodern communities there are no criteria, that is, external authorities, in charge of legitimating local practices. The survival of certainty is only validated 'by the strength of [the intellectuals'] own work alone' (ibid: 145).

But the idea that validation of intellectual practices only takes place within communities is problematic. Bauman has also argued that, in the cultural realm, intellectual messages have a commodity status; they depend on the authority of the market for their validation. The statements they make, and with which they seek to validate their own communities, are now part of a 'game'; and the rules of this game are the rules of the market, where what counts as valid or successful is measured in terms of terms of its saleability:

> [Intellectual] messages must vie for their "share of the market" (that is, the share of public attention) with other competitors, following common rules of the competitive game. Like other products, they need game experts (the specialists in advertising or "hard selling") to stand a chance of success. Like other commodities, they must pass the test of the market – demonstrate (win) their saleability. It is the passing of that test that weighs much heavier than any other conceivable trait on the destiny of the intellectual engagement with social reality. (Bauman, 1992b: 100)

But if intellectual messages are a commodity to be validated, how does the validation of communities occur? Is it really up to consumers who 'buy' and validate intellectual practices? We need more exactness with regard to the types of practices in which interpreters are engaged, as well as the sort of empirical reality a community is meant to represent. Kilminster and Varcoe have argued that postmodern interpreters 'can simply offer up their ideas to whoever will listen, so to speak, without strings' (1996: 231). In a similar vein, Frow (1995: 138) praises Bauman's model of a 'community of meanings' for its openness towards the value structures of different social groups. Communities are value systems that assert the 'validity and the local specificity of a plurality of practices and codes of valuation'. In so doing, he says, this model 'refuses to maintain the privilege of any one culture over any other'. And yet, Frow's argument is only valid if it can be supported by empirical analysis. In other words, only when the notion of community is put into practice by applying it to an empirical reality is it possible to argue whether postmodern intellectual practices do reflect an openness towards the values of different social groups.

BOURDIEU'S SOCIOLOGY OF INTELLECTUAL PRACTICES

Bourdieu departs from existing approaches to the study of intellectuals by positing the idea that intellectuals are symbolic producers who carry out their practices solely in what he calls intellectual fields. As he says, 'This or that particular intellectual, this or that artist, exists *as such* only because there is an intellectual or an artistic field' (Bourdieu and Wacquant, 1992: 107). A key consideration in his approach is that intellectual fields do not exist in isolation, but as part of cultural fields such as the literary, fashion, academic etc, which then mediate specific intellectual struggles over the production of legitimacy for cultural works. Hence we find struggles over 'who is an intellectual and what are specifically intellectual traits' (Swartz, 1997: 221), as well as struggles over the definition of cultural and artistic value. The location of intellectuals in cultural fields has led some to argue that '[for] Bourdieu, the sociology of intellectuals is in reality a sociology of cultural fields' (ibid: 221). However, investigations into Bourdieu's sociology of culture (Fowler, 1997; Robbins, 2000) have sometimes obscured the intricate relationship between intellectual practices and cultural fields. The relevance of Bourdieu's work to this study of art-collecting practices is clear – his theory of intellectual practices attempts to resolve the question of how art is valued, or how 'out of the undifferentiated and undefined mass of works which are produced and even published, there emerge works which are being loved, admired, preserved and consecrated' (Bourdieu, 1969: 100). This book addresses the question of value in the context of collections: how is the value of collected works produced? That is, what makes certain works valuable enough to be part of a collection, and how are they then given meaning within that context?[4]

A theory of practices

Bourdieu's theory of intellectual practices is a variant of his overall theory which he calls a 'general science of practices'. He tries to transcend the opposition between objectivism and subjectivism as a suitable framework for understanding human action. He wants to escape 'the objectivism of action understood as a mechanical reaction "without an agent" and a form of subjectivism which portrays action as the deliberate pursuit of a conscious intention' (Bourdieu and Wacquant, 1992: 121). Alternatively, he advocates a 'relational' or 'structuralist' model of thinking in which individuals' practices and their legitimation are defined in relation to the other elements of the same system, for example to other practices (Swartz, 1997: 63). One way in which Bourdieu attempts to transcend the subjective and objective divide is by reconceptualizing the relations between the symbolic and material dimensions of social life (ibid: 65), and by mapping out a political economy of symbolic power. In short, he focuses on the symbolic dimension of social relations and attempts to analyze all practices oriented towards the accumulation of material or symbolic profit (ibid: 66). Intellectual practices, as we will see, exemplify the symbolic character of practices.

Symbolic capital

Bourdieu uses the term capital to designate the resources upon which individuals and groups draw to maintain their position in the social order. Capital can take various forms: economic (money and property), cultural (cultural goods and services including educational credentials), social (acquaintances and networks), and symbolic (recognition, prestige). Actors who are in possession of capital are able to negotiate their position within the power relations in a given field – this is why capital becomes an object of field struggle. For example, intellectual practices are part of a struggle for recognition or the accumulation of symbolic capital. In a cultural field, even more important than having economic capital is to increase one's symbolic capital – to make a name for oneself:

> For the author, the critic, the art dealer, the publisher or the theatre manager, the only legitimate accumulation consists in making a name for oneself, a known, recognized name, a capital of consecration implying a power to consecrate objects (with a trademark or signature) or persons (through publication, exhibition, etc.) and therefore to give value, and to appropriate the profits from this operation. (Bourdieu, 1993a: 75)

Practices such as critiques of books or the evaluation of paintings endow individuals or groups with symbolic capital, but a key aspect of these practices is that they are recognised by other agents as being disinterested, and not geared towards gaining other forms of capital, such as economic. If individuals obtain symbolic capital when their practices are recognised as disinterested, their work gains in symbolic power or legitimacy as a result of being separated from material concerns. Bourdieu refers to symbolic power as a 'misrecognizable, transformed and legitimated form of other kinds of power' (Bourdieu, 1977: 117), which does not exist *per se*, not even in the ideas expressed by agents, but only in the belief of the 'legitimacy of the words':

> This means that symbolic power does not reside in 'symbolic systems' in the form of an 'illocutionary force', but that it is defined in and by a determinate relationship between those who exercise this power and those who undergo it – that is to say, in the very structure of the field in which belief is produced and reproduced. What makes the power of words to command and to order the world, is the belief in the legitimacy of the words and of him who utters them, a belief which words themselves cannot produce. (Bourdieu, 1977: 117)

Symbolic power is especially relevant to this study of intellectual practices because cultural institutions such as museums are involved in the production of a 'legitimate vision of the social world and its divisions' and art collections are key participants in this process. A case in point was the destruction of modern art in Germany and occupied countries during the Nazi regime on the grounds that its form and style was an expression, or symptom, of 'artistic, moral, "racial" and genetic "degeneration"' (Gamboni, 1997: 46). The destruction of art was both a physical and a symbolic act; it was a way of discrediting the political system in which it emerged. It was also, following Bourdieu, an exercise in creating symbolic power by re-envisioning the legitimacy of a given political regime.

Intellectual fields

Another key term in Bourdieu's theory of practices emerges from his vision of the social world as one structured in fields, spaces constituted by different kinds of capital. Bourdieu's views on the intellectual field in particular can be traced back to his article 'Intellectual Field and Creative Project' (1969) where he refers to its origins and outlines its main traits. He elaborates the relationship between cultural and intellectual fields in subsequent studies of the academic field (1988), the cultural field (1993a), the literary field (1996), and the field of fashion (1993b). Of particular interest here is the argument that intellectual practices take place in cultural fields, where the production of symbolic capital for artworks occurs.

Bourdieu situates the emergence of the intellectual field towards the end of the seventeenth century, when the right to legislate in cultural affairs was no longer in the hands of economic, political or religious authorities, as artists gradually liberated themselves from the patronage of the aristocracy and the church. Their role was taken up by authorities 'that were intellectual in the proper sense' (1969: 90).

Critics, publishers, art dealers and journalists became increasingly involved in the selection and consecration of art. Moreover, there was a proliferation and diversification of institutions of intellectual and artistic consecration such as academies and salons, 'publishing houses, theatres, cultural and scientific associations and the simultaneous extension and diversification of the public' (ibid: 90). In fact, the intellectual field created a new level of contest, and was governed by a competition for cultural legitimacy (ibid: 91). Bourdieu explores the participation of 'a body of properly intellectual professions' in the production of cultural legitimacy, in creating 'the *public meaning* of the work and of the author' (ibid: 100). Here the meaning of a work is seen as public because its '*ultimate* truth and value' (ibid: 104) resides not in the work itself, but in the sum of potential judgements of it formulated by members of the intellectual world. That is, in the 'belief in the value of the work' (ibid: 73) – the production of cultural legitimacy – which results from intellectual struggles within a given field. This is why artistic works are symbolic, because their significance and value derives from the judgements of those who receive them, agents in intellectual fields, as much as from the work of those who produce them (ibid: 97). But intellectual struggles over the legitimate definition of a work are also involved in the making of what Bourdieu calls a 'vision of the artworld':

> Among these are the producers of works classified as artistic (great or minor, famous or unknown), critics of all persuasions (who themselves are established within the field), collectors, middlemen, curators, etc., in short, all who have ties with art, who live for art and, to varying degrees, from it, and who confront each other in struggles where the imposition of not only a world view but also a vision of the artworld is at stake, and who, through these struggles, participate in the production of the value of the artist and of art. (Bourdieu, 1993a: 261)

Alongside intellectual struggles over the production of a legitimate vision of the artwork, the intellectual field is a site for the struggle over intellectual recognition. In fact, the struggle over the imposition of the legitimate mode of cultural production is inseparable from a competition amongst intellectuals to maintain or enhance their position in the field. Even the label intellectual is itself a form of symbolic capital whose value and possession are objects of struggle (Swartz, 1997: 222). A crucial factor in determining who can be an intellectual, or who can play the intellectual game, is the possession of certain types of capital. As Swartz puts it, it entails two conditions: it requires an intellectual disposition, 'that is able to bracket off from immediate concern the needs of everyday existence in order to work with ideas'; and the possession of cultural capital to engage in the struggles in the intellectual field (ibid: 233).

For Bourdieu, participation in fields of cultural production and the types of practices carried out classifies individuals engaged in the creation of symbolic capital for artistic works – critics, collectors and curators, for example – in various ways. One can differentiate those intellectuals or symbolic producers who tend to defend prevailing attitudes and beliefs, from those who are inclined towards strategies of subversion or even heresy (Bourdieu, 1993a: 73). These strategies, which create a source of differentiation amongst intellectuals, correspond to two different sub-fields of cultural production: the field of restricted production and the field of large-scale production.[5]

The autonomous pole, or the field of restricted production (FRP) has a dominating position in the field of cultural production; it is aimed at what is termed high art (classical music, the visual arts, 'serious' literature) and 'develops its own criteria for the evaluation of its products' (ibid: 115). In the FRP economic profit is normally disavowed; agents compete instead for symbolic profit. As in a 'game of "loser wins"' (ibid: 39) what prevails is 'a profit of disinterestedness, or the profit one has on seeing oneself (or being seen) as one who is not searching for profit' (Johnson, 1993: 15). This disavowal of economic profit does not occur in the heteronomous pole of the field of cultural production, what Bourdieu calls the field of large-scale cultural production (FLSP), which involves mass or popular culture (ibid: 16), and produces cultural goods for the public at large. As opposed to the FRP, it follows 'the laws of competition for the conquest of the largest possible market' (Bourdieu, 1993a: 115), and it is subordinated to the demands of economic capital.

Thinking about change

Having considered Bourdieu's concepts of intellectual practices, field, and symbolic capital, it is relevant to look also at how he explains change and evolution in intellectual fields and practices. In 'Manet and the Institutionalization of Anomie' (1993a) Bourdieu refers to the emergence of a modern painting movement in France, from 1870 to 1880, as a 'symbolic revolution'; an 'ethical and aesthetic subversion' brought about by Edouard Manet in particular, and later on by the Impressionists, which caused the emergence of a new autonomous field of production. This symbolic revolution changed the categories of perception and judgement used to produce and comprehend representations. The new field was caused by a shift in the mode of aesthetic production, perception and judgement; from academic art seen with an academic gaze, to Impressionist art and a pure gaze. But, most importantly, Bourdieu seeks to undertake a structural explanation of academic art, 'relating it to the institutional conditions of its production'.

At the end of the nineteenth century, France's École des Beaux-Art gave emerging painters training, and a career as masters with the help of a system of hierarchical awards given at the state-controlled Salon exhibitions. But if the École gave painters the necessary honours and training to legitimate their profession, it also requested their submission to the academic style it championed. Academic painting gave primacy to content and to the display of a literary culture, and thus its emphasis was on the creation of 'readerly' paintings, intended to be 'read' rather than 'seen' (ibid: 245).

An exception to the École's stylistic principles was the work of artits Edouard Manet, who criticized academic art, and was accused by his critics of not finishing his paintings. An academic reading of Manet's 'pure paintings' was impossible because the academic tradition was attentive to the meanings of a painting, while Manet's art was attentive to form (ibid: 249). Manet imposed on his work 'a construction whose intention is not to help in the reading of a meaning, Manet dooms the academic eye, used to seeing a painting as a narrative, as a dramatic representation of a "story", to a second, undoubtedly more fundamental, disappointment' (ibid: 248).

But 'academic painting', with its calmness, serenity and the presence of idealized figures, was not only a reflection of an external 'reality', it was also related to an 'academic order' which it sought to maintain (ibid: 246), a set of individuals and institutions involved in the production of its legitimacy. When Bourdieu says that the field went through a symbolic revolution, he means a rupture with both the academic style and the set of values and practices underpinning it. This monopoly no longer exists in the new autonomous field of competition, which is characterised by the 'institutionalization of anomie', or the inability to claim an absolute hold of the 'nomos' (ibid: 250) ruling over the production of legitimate images. The break with the École's monopoly started with the collapse of the network of beliefs it sustained: the painters' belief in the legitimacy of the jury and its verdicts, the state's belief in the jury's efficacy, and the public's belief in the value of the school's academic recognition (ibid: 251–2). The creation of the Salon des Refuses in 1863 – an art exhibition held in Paris for artists whose work had been refused by the jury of the official Salon – made this disregard for the authority and judgment of the École clear. At the same time, those other 'superfluous producers', who had been excluded from the status of producer as designed by the École, gradually succeeded in producing their own market, and the mechanism for its consecration:

> This is a truly far-reaching revolution which, at least in the realm of the new art in the making, abolishes all references to an ultimate authority capable of acting as a court of appeal: the monotheism of the central *nomothete* gives way to a plurality of competing cults with multiple uncertain gods. (Bourdieu, 1993a: 253)

Bourdieu's notion of symbolic revolution is valuable in explaining changes at the micro level of practices – for example, how the evaluation of Manet's work through an academic gaze led to it being derided for its 'mistakes' and 'defects'. It is also useful to see how the rupture with an academic style is more than a mere change in aesthetic, but a change in the means through which artworks are endowed with legitimacy. That is, the École des Beaux-Art's principle of vision was created in a context where the state had authority over the careers of painters, and the evaluation of what constituted good art. Bourdieu is theorizing a change in the purpose and orientation of intellectual practices: they serve to legitimate not academic art, but impressionist art. However, this line of argument does not reveal whether there have been any changes to the specific ways in which intellectual practices were carried out, which is something this book seeks to explore.

OUTLINE OF A SOCIOLOGY OF ART COLLECTIONS

Earlier in this chapter it was argued that two key issues prevail in the study of collections: the idea that collections are created by intellectual practices, which assign value and meaning to the objects displayed; and the fact that collections themselves shape narratives, ways of thinking about the social world – a role that, it was argued, changes historically. Further questions emerge from these premises: what practices underlie the inclusion or exclusion of artworks from public art collections? How do these practices contribute to the creation of meaning for the objects exhibited? What sort of value is attributed to artworks by art-collecting practices? The rest of this chapter aims to reconcile these questions with Bauman's and Bourdieu's theories of intellectual practices in order to build up an analytical framework for the empirical study of art-collecting practices in the remaining chapters of the book. Initially, three main aspects need to be discussed: first, identifying the role of intellectual practices in the making of art collections following Bauman's concepts of modern legislation and postmodern interpretation; second, treating art collecting value as an example of what Bourdieu calls symbolic capital; and, third, drawing on Bourdieu's use of field as the terrain where the intellectual practices of collecting are carried out.

Bourdieu's approach to intellectuals is said to provide a 'strongly *normative* vision of what intellectuals should be' (Swartz, 1997: 222–3). This is a valid point, particularly if we think about his typology of intellectuals as those who are defenders of the orthodoxy in the FRP and those who are inclined towards subversion, and are associated with the FLSP. And yet, an aspect that needs further attention in Bourdieu's account is the question of what it is that intellectual practices do. An answer to this necessarily entails shifting the focus of enquiry from the definition of intellectuals, finding out what their main characteristics are, towards a more pragmatic issue, as for example how intellectual practices operate within fields. In this book, field is used to designate a space where art-collecting practices take place and contribute to the creation of symbolic capital for collected artworks. The chapters that follow address a number of issues in field analysis: how a field's boundaries are set up, who the participants in a given field are, and the relationships between fields. Each chapter includes a discussion of analytical problems or perspectives; for example, how to reconcile Bauman's notion of postmodern community with Bourdieu's field (chapter 4).

Another core concern in Bourdieu's theory of intellectual practices is to envision their role in the making of symbolic capital, or the legitimation of artworks, seen in the creation of prestige or renown for artists and their work. However, the link between intellectual practices and the judgement of value in art is a matter of dispute in

Bauman's and Bourdieu's theories. According to Bauman, contemporary, postmodern intellectual practices no longer play a role in the judgement and criticism of art, while Bourdieu believes this practice has prevailed since the emergence of intellectual fields. However, what Bauman calls modern legislating practices were crucial in classifying and distinguishing what counted as value in art. And the argument that intellectual practices are no longer engaged in the judgement and valuing of art can be counteracted if we consider, for example, the importance given by the literature on museums to the practices of collecting. Purchasing and exhibiting objects are practices which affect the sorts of values that are represented by a museum collection, as well as their meaning. Thus there is room for a study of collecting practices which explores both their historical and contemporary role as examples of intellectual practice.

Bauman's ideal types of modern legislation and postmodern interpretation are applied here to the study of intellectual collecting practices both in their historical and contemporary context. However, this distinction between past and present practices is a source of contention in Bauman's and Bourdieu's theories. A gap in Bourdieu's account is precisely one of Bauman's strongest points: his way of thinking about change in intellectual practices. Bourdieu's theory of intellectual practices addresses both the macro and micro levels of analysis. In his explanation of the emergence of an intellectual field, he theorizes how structural changes – the decline of the church and aristocracy as patrons of the arts – led to the creation of a new collective of institutions and individuals engaged in the production of the 'public meaning' of artworks. At a micro level Bourdieu pays specific attention to outlining a methodology of intellectual practices, for example how the distinction between academic and pure paintings was underpinned by different sets of assumptions about the correct interpretation of aesthetic value. But there is an aspect which Bourdieu overlooks. In his account of Manet and the shift to a new form of aesthetic, which grows in acceptance as academic art is replaced by the work of Impressionist painters, the practices of intermediaries – art gallery directors, art dealers – prove crucial in helping to produce symbolic capital for Impressionist art. Although Bourdieu argues that there has been a change in the sorts of authorities involved in the validation of Impressionist art, this still raises the question: is it possible to argue that the practices of intermediaries have undergone a shift? They are still involved in the production of symbolic capital, and, since Manet's symbolic revolution, is there anything intrinsically different in what they do? Bauman's model of postmodern interpretation, for example, takes into account how a new social context has led to a transformation in the nature of intellectual practices. I argue that there is a need for a model that reconciles both approaches, a situated model of intellectual practice contiguous with a shift at the level of the social, but which also problematises the argument that intellectual practices are no longer involved in validating what counts as art. In this book, intellectual practices are qualified along Bauman's terms, as legislating and interpreting, in line with the historical periods in which they are carried out; but it is also necessary to work with a concept of intellectual practices which accounts for the fact that they operate, and struggle, against each other within distinctive art fields.

In Bauman's thesis, modern intellectuals were instrumental in the reproduction of modernity's worldview. I have pointed out two difficulties in relation to Bauman's notion of legislators. Firstly, that it does not allow for the possibility of other intellectual practices taking place, or even struggling against, those of legislators. Even his concept 'critical intellectuals' suggests a co-operative role between intellectuals in core countries and those in the periphery. Apart from rendering too much homogeneity to the practices of legislators, intellectuals in the periphery do not necessarily comply with the views of legislators. Secondly, modern art becomes an uncontested category, because even when new tastes come to the fore, legislators can ultimately impose their own view of aesthetic value. In effect, Bauman's distinction between modernity's and postmodernity's intellectual practices can be questioned for paying too little attention to the possibility of more continuity in the practices of legislators, which are eradicated in the shift to a new postmodern intellectual model.

A number of authors have questioned the validity of Bauman's typology of modernity and postmodernity. Seidman (1994: 339) accuses Bauman of not following his own preaching in his call for a sociology of postmodernity: 'Does not Bauman's typology of societies in terms of premodernity, modernity, and postmodernity reflect the categorizing, ordering, legislative reasoning of the Enlightenment that he detects?' He notes that this problem could be addressed by submitting the social position of the sociologist to scrutiny. Best (1998: 317) makes a similar argument when he says that Bauman's analyses of the postmodern are built upon 'modernity conceptions of the "social"'. A similar criticism can be used to question the argument that the legislating practice has led to a change towards postmodern interpretation. But before doing this, we need to explore how intellectual practices operate through an empirical analysis situated in the context of Dublin's art world. The chapters that follow will examine and discuss the intellectual practices involved in art collecting, based on the set of concepts and arguments introduced here, and which will be dealt with in more detail at the beginning of each chapter. Chapter 2 begins this task by exploring the role of modern legislating practices in the foundation of Ireland's first modern art collection.

CHAPTER 2

A Collection for the Municipal Gallery of Modern Art

THE FIELD OF MODERN ART COLLECTING

THE FIELD OF MODERN ART COLLECTING (FMAC) includes the only two institutions in Dublin responsible for the collection of modern art: the Municipal Gallery of Modern Art (MGMA), whose origins are explored in this chapter, and the Irish Museum of Modern Art (IMMA), which is looked at later. The FMAC is structured by the practices involved in the making of public collections of modern art. The events surrounding the foundation of the MGMA in 1908, and the making of its collection, can be seen as starting the FMAC, for although modern art had been exhibited in the Irish capital before then, the MGMA was the first public institution responsible for its collection and display in Ireland. The opinions in the Irish press over the role of the MGMA and the type of art suitable for its collection was part of a broader debate about the benefits modern art might bring to a national art school, and the specific artistic influences that could help that development. The episode selected illustrates an aspect of an existing Field of Irish Art (FIA), located in Dublin, and in which, by the middle of the nineteenth century, various institutions were already in charge of collecting, teaching and exhibiting visual art: the National Gallery of Ireland (1864),[1] the Royal Hibernian Academy (RHA) and the Royal Dublin Society (RDS). Other initiatives, like the creation of art clubs and societies, and the organization of public exhibitions, also played a formative role in the promotion of Irish art.

Discussion of the MGMA and its collection took place alongside a process of nation-building which had its origins in the eighteenth century, a reaction to British domination that had turned Ireland into a British colony since the seventeenth century.[2] The search for alternative models for Ireland's national economic, social and political development was articulated in two forms of nationalism: political and cultural (Hutchinson, 1987). Political nationalists campaigned for political autonomy from Britain, and saw self-government as the only means to achieve this end; but it was cultural nationalism, and its attempt to preserve a distinctive Irish culture, which helped inspire a public controversy over the benefits of developing a modern art collection. The Celtic Revival which emerged around the 1880s represented a third stage in cultural nationalism (Hutchinson, 1987). This was a process which sought to regenerate the Irish nation through a return to its creative source: Gaelic civilization. Various groups – Anglo-Irish, Irish nationalists and others – turned to the arts as an expression of a national Irish identity.[3] The MGMA was to add another, more outward-looking dimension to this search for national self-awareness.

STUDYING INTELLECTUAL COLLECTING PRACTICES

An analysis of the historical genesis of modern art collecting in Ireland provides a good starting point for the study of intellectual collecting practices focused on the making of modern art collections. The method followed in this book is field analysis. This entails, firstly, treating art collecting as an intellectual practice situated in an FMAC, which is also part of a wider field, the FIA. This chapter includes only a limited number of participants in the FIA, those concerned with the promotion of contemporary art; thus the National Gallery of Ireland is omitted from this discussion. Chapters 3 to 5 are designed to provide a more general overview of the various institutions involved in the FIA, and modern art collecting in particular. Secondly, field analysis is concerned with the study of how symbolic capital is produced, the practices whereby institutions in charge of the exhibition, collection and sale of art endow their artworks with value. We need to investigate the reasons for invoking certain traits – aesthetic quality, international reputation etc. – and not others. This approach is important because what may be considered 'good art' changes over time, and, to a large extent, is influenced by factors such as institutional support.

The study of art collecting as an intellectual practice also involves investigating whether the practices involved in the making of a collection for the MGMA articulate a form of modern legislation (Herrero, 2002). Chapter 1 discussed how the term applied only to intellectual practices in 'the West', which had a leading role in the formation of modernity (Bauman, 1995: 229). The distinction between colonial and colonized countries was supported by a theory of history which presented as 'natural' an ordered hierarchy of nations ranking from those regarded as most 'civilized' to those which were 'uncivilized' or lagging behind (Bauman, 1995: 228). But in classifying countries as more or less modern, intellectuals operating in these countries were also positioned within asymmetrical relationships of power. Intellectuals in 'core' countries legislated a modernity which projected their nations as the apex of Western civilization, but we still need to know the role and form intellectual practices took in countries outside these legislating centres of modernity. In *Life in Fragments*, Bauman (1995: 228) argues that the conditions for the estrangement of legislators from the ruling state and the 'self-assertion of intellectuals' first appeared in the 'periphery' of civilization, where their practices became a vehicle for social critique. And yet, his argument about where and how legislating practices came to an end leaves their role in the making of modernity unexplained. An enquiry into the intellectual practices of collecting in Ireland, one of modernity's 'peripheries', offers the possibility of asking further questions. How are collecting practices legislating a particular definition of Irish art? Are they involved in the making of modernity's worldview? And, if so, are they legislating a distinctive Irish modernity? As argued in chapter 1, an analysis of intellectual practices offers the opportunity to explore whether they can create change in a given field. Can we argue that the emergence of an FMAC led to a new form of art production or aesthetic perception?

THE FIELD OF IRISH ART AND THE ROYAL HIBERNIAN ACADEMY

At the end of the nineteenth century, the RHA was the main institution in charge of the teaching and exhibition of fine art.[4] Its *raison-d'être* goes back to the eighteenth century when the only institution in Dublin, apart from a number of private schools, offering teaching in the arts was the Royal Dublin Society (RDS). Founded in 1731 by members of the ruling Anglo-Irish ascendancy, the RDS was set up to improve husbandry, manufacture and the arts and sciences (Strickland, 1969: 579), and by 1750 it was running its own schools (Turpin, 1995: 8).[5] Dublin's artistic community, however, was in search of more advanced instruction, an academy where young artists and students could study painting under experienced and competent teachers. Their ambition was at the root of the concept of the RHA. Over a decade later, in 1764, The Society of Artists in Ireland was founded and became the principal exhibiting organization in Dublin (Turpin, 1995: 18), where it also provided the first custom-built exhibition space. It held its first exhibition of pictures, drawings, sculpture and designs in 1765 (Strickland, 1969: 596). After a series of exhibitions held from 1766 to 1774, and in 1777, the 1780 exhibition was the last to be held in Dublin for twenty years (Strickland, 1969: 597–9; de Courcy, 1986: xi).[6] Only in 1800 did a similar initiative take place, when The Society of the Artists of Ireland had its first exhibition; further exhibitions were held in 1801, 1802, 1809, 1810 and 1811 (Strickland, 1969: 600). The society underwent a series of divisions and amalgamations, and as a result artists moved their exhibitions to the RDS's premises, but when in 1819 the RDS disposed of its exhibition rooms it left the artistic community once more without a venue to display its work.

The establishment of the RHA by royal charter in 1823 was the result of Irish artists' struggle to establish themselves as an independent body with a recognized organization that would foster artistic excellence at a professional level (ibid: 603).[7] A building for the academy was finally completed in Abbey Street in 1826 (Turpin, 1991: 198), centrally located on the north side of the river Liffey which bisects Dublin. That year the RHA held its first annual exhibition (Strickland, 1969: 603), and laid out the academy's aims in the preface to the exhibition's catalogue: the promotion of fine arts in Ireland through an annual public exhibition, and the provision of teaching to young artists, chiefly in painting, but also in sculpture and architecture (de Courcy, 1986: xii; Turpin, 1991: 198).

The RHA received a number of donations, including its building and adjacent grounds, as well as other gifts such as books, drawings, prints and sculptures, but it relied on private funding for the running of its everyday activities, until 1832 when the British government granted it an annual sum of £300 (de Courcy, 1986: xii). The RHA's position as the only institution in charge of promoting fine art was facilitated by changes in the remit of the RDS. Since the middle of the eighteenth century, the RDS had been running drawing classes, specializing in figure, landscape and ornament, architecture and modelling. In 1849 its drawing schools were converted into a School of Design, with an emphasis on educating designers in applied rather than fine art.[8] This new venture was influenced by developments in art education in Britain dating from the 1830s, and which sought to challenge the superiority of continental schools of art, particularly those in France and Germany (Turpin, 1995: 134). The new RDS School of Design was meant to encourage the production of manufactures in Ireland so that the country would be able to compete in foreign markets. The change had beneficial consequences for the RHA. It became the only institution in Dublin devoted to the teaching of fine art and the education of painters, and was thus able to attract the most artistic and creative students to its schools (Barrett and Sheehy, 1996: 445).

The reconfiguration of the RDS also had drawbacks, as most funds from the Science and Art Department in London were devoted to its schools, which were seen as the basis of future development in art education. In addition to this, the onset of the Great Famine in 1845 left the country in a precarious situation, with little money being spent on the arts or art institutions. By the early 1840s the academy had been enjoying some prosperity, partly as a result of purchases at its annual exhibitions by the Royal Irish Art Union (RIAU). The RIAU had been founded before the Famine, in 1839, as part of a vogue for art unions in countries such as Switzerland, Germany and Britain. Its local purpose was to make up for the decline in RHA exhibition sales from the end of the 1830s. The RIAU operated a selection committee system, collecting a subscription fee from its members, which the committee spent on the purchase of works of art by living Irish artists, preferably based in Ireland. The artworks were then distributed amongst members by lottery (de Courcy, 1986: xii; Turpin, 1995: 96; Black, 1998: 140–1).[9] Despite these efforts, the academy's difficulties reached a crisis in 1857 when no exhibition was held and its schools were closed (de Courcy, 1986: xii). That same year the RHA became the subject of a public inquiry by the Science and Art Department, which suggested that the RDS and RHA schools should amalgamate,[10] with the RDS taking over the RHA's life art class because it had better facilities. The RHA objected to this on the basis of the differing aims of both institutions: the RDS was devoted to teaching industrial art and manufactures more generally, whereas the RHA was to be in charge of the education of artists, a task which should be directed by artists (Turpin, 1991: 199).

The RHA's school was re-opened in 1862. The role of the RDS school was redefined to promote the preliminary discipline of drawing, and only after attending the RDS were prospective painters allowed to transfer to the RHA.[11] The period between the 1870s and 1890s was the most successful since the RHA's foundation, with high attendance and sales figures for its exhibitions, and the provision of awards for artists. The Albert Prize was inaugurated in 1871 with a bequest of around £800 from the Prince Consort Memorial Fund, which Queen Victoria directed towards art education (ibid: 202). A number of established Irish painters received this award: Walter Osborne, Joseph Malachy Kavanagh, Roderic O'Conor and George Russell (ibid: 203). The academy had the privileged position of being the only institution capable of conferring the status of professional painter on its students. The ultimate form of distinction, or symbolic capital, the RHA was able to bestow on artists was the title of academician, assigned by existing members of the academy only: RHA for academician, ARHA for associate academician, HRHA for honorary academician, and RHRHA for honorary foreign academician (de Courcy, 1986: xxiii).

After the 1890s there was a decline of public interest in the RHA, its exhibitions and annual sales (de Courcy, 1986: xiv). One possible reason was the unsuitability of its premises. Barrett and Sheehy explain how 'The social and intellectual centre of gravity of the city had shifted to the south side of the river. Abbey Street had become run down and no one was likely to visit it' (1996: 475). The extent to which the location of the academy's building led to a lack of public interest in its work is difficult to ascertain; what is clear, though, is that the institution's finances were being affected. A 1901 report recommended the closing of the academy's schools, the integration of the academicians into the staff of the Dublin Metropolitan School of Art, and the relocation of the academy at the government's expense (de Courcy, 1986: xiv–xv). The history of the RHA until this point reveals that the academy was in the paradoxical position of being able to produce high amounts of symbolic capital for Irish art, by training artists, distributing prizes and distinctions, while suffering from a lack of financial funds. Whether the academy would have turned into a different type of institution had it enjoyed a greater source of income is an open question. But at the beginning of the twentieth century the terrain was ready to welcome new forms of patronage for the arts, and subsequently a new aesthetic. The organization of art exhibitions outside the RHA's walls initiated this process.

FOREIGN ART: A NEW AESTHETIC IN THE FIELD OF IRISH ART

The decades from the 1870s to the 1890s were generally favourable to the arts, as seen in the formation of many art clubs established during this period.[12] The activities of the Dublin Sketching Club (DSC), founded in 1874,[13] and the Dublin Art Club, founded in 1886,[14] included art classes, sketching expeditions and exhibitions of artworks by their members (Barrett and Sheehy, 1996: 449). In 1875 membership of the DSC was opened to painters. Nathaniel Hone; Dr James Moore, future President of the RHA; John Butler Yeats – father of Jack Butler Yeats and William Butler Yeats, and a painter in his own right –, Percy French and Sarah Purser were amongst those who had joined the club by its tenth anniversary in 1884. The DSC's annual exhibitions sometimes displayed works by members who had trained outside Ireland (Anderson, 1986b: 45), but its tenth annual exhibition caused a stir. The display of 318 artworks included twenty-six paintings by American artist James McNeill Whistler, whose work was being exhibited in Ireland for the first time.[15] Sculptor Frederick Lawless, together with John Butler Yeats and William Booth-Pearsall had organized the loan, although it is not clear why it was decided to include Whistler's work.[16] In any case, the initiative divided the club's members between those who supported Whistler's work and those critical of it. The press reflected the controversy caused by the inclusion of sketches and paintings by American artists, Whistler in particular. It was the beginning of a struggle over the definition and benefits of contemporary art in Ireland.

Despite an acknowledgement that Whistler's work was 'one of the main attractions of the exhibition',[17] there was a lack of agreement as to the merits of his art. A reviewer in the *Freeman's Journal* criticized his sketches as 'clumsily and carelessly painted, and not possessed of any artistic merit', but praised his paintings:

> With regard to pictures of figures, both large and small, there can be no diversity of opinion as to the fact that they should be described in an exactly contrary way. Almost all of them are boldly drawn, and the details and colouring are carried out in a really faultless style, and with great fidelity to nature.[18]

The value of Whistler's works was put more explicitly in a review in the *Dublin Daily Express*, which referred to the great merit of having the American artists exhibited. Titled 'American Artists at the Dublin

Sketching Club Exhibition', it admired in particular Whistler's technique and insisted that his work was a much better influence than any available in Dublin:

> [The] instructive advantage remains to the members being able to study at leisure work resulting from better technique, better tone, and better art influences that we can obtain in Dublin. All really interested in the fine arts ought to see this American work – so original, so sensitive, and so daring, and learn to appreciate the advantage of painting with a square and well-considered touch.[19]

Booth-Pearsall, one of the exhibition's organizers, wrote a letter to *The Irish Times* in response to an article in the same newspaper[20] which had criticized the exhibition for being neither a loan exhibition nor an exhibition of the club's own output:

> [No] other club or society, except the Dublin Sketching Club, takes any trouble to show their members and the public any of the current art of the day . . . And in regard to the merits of the paintings themselves . . . I have received many letters of thanks and congratulations from artists, literary men, musicians, and others in Dublin, from whom commendation is an honour at any success in affording them an opportunity of enjoying this great artist's work in Dublin.[21]

An anonymous member of the DSC, in obvious disagreement with Booth-Pearsall, questioned the usefulness of such an exhibition when the RHA's academicians were only too willing to exhibit contemporary works:

> [The] visitors to the Leinster Hall to-day will not bestow upon the club pictures anything like the attention they are entitled to, and which they would receive but for the alluring attractiveness of the great works [Whistler's] upon the opposite wall . . . when we have the Royal Hibernian Academy in our midst and its members willing and anxious to exhibit the current art of the day upon its walls, it might be safely left to the members of that institution to place there, as they so successfully did at their last exhibition, work by greater and more artistic minds than our own.[22]

The controversy continued in the DSC's ranks when a group of members called for the resignation of Booth-Pearsall, Yeats and Lawless. The motion was defeated, and with considerable success, as Whistler was made an Honorary Member of the DSC (Anderson, 1986b: 50). The Whistler controversy forms the beginning of a debate over the benefits of bringing art by foreign artists to the Irish capital, but the DSC exhibition also brought to the fore a redefinition of the categories of amateur and professional artist. In general, these clubs and societies were an outlet for amateur artists to produce and exhibit their work. In so doing, they articulated a distinction between amateur painters and professional artists. While the former exhibited their works in art clubs and societies, the latter trained at the RHA's schools, and displayed their paintings at the academy's annual exhibitions. The inclusion of professional artists in amateur societies (Crookshank and the Knight of Glin, 1994: 270), and the exhibiting of their works by members of the DSC, disrupted this differentiation. It opened up an alternative space to the RHA, one in which professional artists could not only exhibit their work but also participate in the organization of activities like the DSC's exhibition. It would take another fifteen years, however, before the value of foreign art was brought into question again.

1899. THE MODERN PAINTINGS EXHIBITION

Dublin's isolation from external artistic influences changed when the Modern Paintings exhibition opened on 1 April 1899. The label 'modern' was used to describe a compilation of eighty-eight pictures, including works by French, English and Dutch painters, as examples of the 'main tendencies of painting during the last half century'.[23] The works were all privately owned and had been lent with 'a laudable desire to promote the knowledge of art'[24] by, amongst others, Edward Martyn, a wealthy Catholic landlord, who contributed one Monet, two Degas and a Corot; poet and dramatist George Moore, who lent a Manet[25] (O'Byrne, 2000: 55); and Scottish entrepreneur and art collector James Staats Forbes, who provided thirty works, including six by Corot.[26] The origins of the exhibition, and the starting point of the debate it engendered on the benefits of modern art to art in Ireland, go back to George Russell's (AE) letter to the *Dublin Daily Express* in September 1898, when he referred to the need for a loan exhibition of paintings that would create a public taste and inspire art students.[27] For Russell, the paintings which would be displayed expressed the poetic, 'internal things, dreams, spiritual longings'. He linked the language of poetry and its expression of a distinct 'Celtic imagination' to this poetic aspect of modern art. Modern art, he argued, could encourage a distinct Irish 'national art':

> The subtlety of modern art has reached a point where it seems able to express things long left to the poet . . . The colours and forms of the visible world, long brooded over and transmuted in the alchemy of thought, have come to convey to many a dual significance, of which the least important for purposes of art is their reference to an external nature, and the more important is that they have become the symbols of internal things, dreams, spiritual longings, and the reveries of the soul. . . . To bring to our people an understanding of a language like this, so capable of expressing the spiritual characteristics peculiar to the Celtic imagination, might result in the creation of a national art.[28]

Russell is rather vague about what kind of modern art represents a poetic language, as well as what type of poetry is characteristically Celtic. His ideas do, however, attempt to promote a form of poetic, modern art as a suitable model for a national art. Another side of the debate is exemplified by a short article in *The Irish Times* on the day the exhibition opened, which welcomed the knowledge of foreign schools it brought, and suggested that the production of Irish art would be stimulated by the display:

> The highest instincts of Art arc always stimulated by comparison, and such an opportunity as this brings that essentially important influence into operation . . . We undoubtedly have suffered to no small extent from our almost absolute ignorance of the production of foreign schools. We know little or nothing of their methods. Even the names of painters, familiar upon the Continent as household words, are unrecognised at home. But such an Exhibition as this will serve to remove a reproach, and remedy a disability.[29]

Other reviews were less explicit about the benefits of foreign art, though the *Dublin Daily Express* felt that the exhibition would lead eventually to a national school – indeed, the author created an analogy between the Dublin exhibition and the Paris Salon held in the Louvre in 1824, which suggests something of the significance given to the event: the Paris display included paintings by British artists such as John Constable and the President of the Royal Academy, Thomas Lawrence, and from it the 'exquisite French school of Barbizon emerged'. Implicit here is the view that a distinct Irish school of art was ready to emerge too: 'The soil, of course, was ready and the season fair; but may we not hope it will be so in Ireland?'[30]

Apart from facilitating a debate on the influence modern art could have at home, the exhibition showed the willingness of a group of individuals in a wide range of professional occupations to lend their support to the event, either as part of the exhibition's committee or by lending their paintings for public display.[31] Only two of the contributors, Sarah Purser and Walter Osborne, were professional painters. George Russell, although he had studied at the RDS and RHA schools, and won awards, was also a poet. Other contributors (T.W. Rolleston, Sir Arthur Vicars and James Brennan) were involved in the decorative arts (Larmour, 1992: 73). W. Strickland and W. Armstrong belonged to the museum administration sector (both worked for the National Gallery of Ireland) (ibid: 50, 60). The variety of occupations of those involved in the exhibition offers an insight into the production of symbolic capital within the FIA. It was facilitated by individuals with an interest in art, not necessarily painters, but in possession, at least, of two types of capital: cultural capital, general knowledge about art; and social capital, in terms of contacts to help secure the loan of works. A case in point is Purser's contribution. The exhibition provided her with an opportunity to become a 'public promoter of modern painting' (O'Grady, 1996: 140), and indeed she was to organize the next public art exhibition in 1901. Overall, the exhibition helped pave the way for modern art to be welcomed as a new aesthetic in the FIA. It created recognition, symbolic capital, for modern art by making it an object of public display; the exhibition also mobilized the press, starting a debate about the stylistic influences that would benefit the development of Irish art.

1901. JOHN BUTLER YEATS AND NATHANIEL HONE ON DISPLAY

On 21 October 1901, an exhibition of pictures by John Butler Yeats and Nathaniel Hone opened in Dublin at the rooms of the Royal Society of Antiquaries. On display were twenty-eight landscapes by Hone and forty-four works, mainly portraits, by Yeats (Kennedy, 1991: 7). The exhibition ran for two weeks and was financed and organized by Sarah Purser to give recognition to the works of these two artists, neither of whom had so far had a substantial showing (O'Grady, 1996: 98). Although both painters were academicians since 1892 and 1880 respectively, and could in principle show their work at the RHA's annual exhibitions, they had experienced difficulty in having their work accepted by the academy. Hone, who was Professor of Painting at the RHA's schools from 1894 to 1917 (Turpin, 1991: 204), has been described as the creator of 'some of the finest watercolours executed in late nineteenth-century Ireland' (Crookshank and the Knight of Glin, 1994: 259). Yet he never exhibited his watercolours at the RHA, (and ultimately he left them, together with the oils in his studio, to the National Gallery of Ireland) (ibid: 259). Watercolours were not favoured by the academy, which relegated 'all but a few watercolours to an ill-lit back room' (ibid: 221). Yeats also had problems having his work accepted at the RHA's exhibitions. In 1900 his portraits were displayed only because the President of the RHA, Sir Thomas Drew, was trying to win a larger grant from the government; in 1901, all the portraits he submitted for the academy's exhibition were turned down (Murphy, 1978: 225). It is not clear from Yeats's biography why his work was rejected – the painter himself did not seem to be aware of the reasons why, other than to remark: 'It is long since they rejected all my things straight off. I was generally reserved for the final judgment' (ibid: 225).[32]

But Purser was not discouraged by the RHA's judgement of Hone's and Yeats's work, and sought to give maximum publicity to the exhibition. George Russell and Edward Martyn wrote reviews lauding the national element in the artists' work; they represented the 'seeds of an Irish genuine art',[33] 'the true character of Ireland'.[34] However, their views also differed considerably. For Russell, Yeats's paintings revealed the spiritual life of his sitters, 'a poetic illumination, and a revelation of character':

> Some earlier pictures show him attempting to paint directly the ideal world of romance and poetry; yet interesting as these are, they do not convey the same impression of mystery as the pictures of to-day. Indeed, the light seen behind or through a veil is always more suggestive than the unveiled light. It may be that the spirit is a formless breath which pervades form, and it is better revealed as a light in the eyes, as a brooding expression, than by the choice of ancient days and other-world subjects, where the shapes can be moulded to ideal forms by the artist's will . . . Mr Yeats . . . has probably chosen wisely, and has painted more memorable pictures than if he had gone back to the fairyland of Celtic mythology.[35]

The suggestion that Yeats's paintings were more expressive than portraits from Celtic mythology supports Russell's earlier views on the need for art to represent something beyond the external world – though Russell had then favoured the visual representation of a Celtic imagination, while he now discredited the use of Celtic subjects to achieve it. By contrast, Martyn was more concerned with the practical aspects of art, such as the creation of a school of religious art or stained glass. He referred to the disadvantaged position of Yeats and Hone, who had not received the recognition they deserved in the Irish art world, and suggested that any artist who wished to be appreciated turn to religious art, for which there was a demand. For Martyn, Yeats had the right talent for such purpose: 'Mr. J.B. Yeats, one of the exhibitors here, would seem especially gifted for such work, if it is possible to imagine anyone succeeding in approaching the great masters of religious art in the past'.[36] Even though Yeats did not represent religious subjects in his work, his use of technique made him, at least according to Martyn, particularly suited for this genre.

The exhibition reveals some of the dynamics involved in the production of symbolic capital for Irish art at the start of the last century. Exhibitions outside the RHA's walls, apart from those by clubs and societies, were becoming more frequent – two in three years was a high number by Dublin's standards. They were also a means of counteracting the judgement of the RHA, particularly in this case, when works previously rejected by the academy were now exhibited at the same time as the RHA's annual event was being held (O'Grady, 1996: 84). Purser, who was not even amongst the RHA's distinguished academicians,[37] organized a successful event which attracted significant exposure in the Irish press. By now the FIA was ready to welcome a new institution; an art gallery and collection that would initiate a new practice, the making of a public collection of modern art, and its corresponding field within the FIA, the field of modern art collecting. The remainder of this chapter explores these practices, starting with the two exhibitions organized by Hugh Lane prior to the foundation of the MGMA in 1908.

THE MAKING OF A MODERN ART COLLECTION FOR THE MGMA[38]

Hugh Lane, the founder of the MGMA, was a newcomer to Dublin's art world. His life and achievements have received considerable attention (Bodkin, 1956; Gregory, 1973; Dawson, 1993; O'Byrne, 2000), and some of his biographical details are relevant to contextualize this debate on modern art and collecting. Born in Ireland, Lane spent most of his life in London, where by 1901 he was a successful art dealer in Old Master paintings. He still had important family connections in Ireland; he was the nephew of Lady Gregory, playwright and co-founder with William Butler Yeats of the Irish

Literary Theatre. His involvement in the promotion of the Irish art scene started in 1901 after he visited the Yeats-Hone exhibition, when he commissioned a series of portraits by Yeats and purchased some of Hone's paintings. Lane's activity in the artistic field increased between the years 1901 and 1908, but in the process he made enemies as well as friends; some viewed his enthusiasm for Irish art with suspicion, even questioning his artistic judgement. This animosity could be attributed to the fact that Lane never settled in Ireland; he continued to work and live in London (Sharp, 2003: 35), even though he sought public recognition in Ireland on various occasions, as when he pursued an official appointment at the National Gallery of Ireland, where he was appointed director in February 1913 (O'Byrne, 2000: 199). But Lane's personal motives aside, the effort he and his supporters put into the creation of a modern art gallery cannot be underestimated. Their interest in this initiative can be seen as an attempt by a small minority, mainly the Anglo-Irish, to carve out their own distinctive identity within Irish culture.[39]

1902. AN EXHIBITION OF OLD MASTERS AT THE RHA

In early October 1902, Hugh Lane approached Sir Thomas Drew, President of the RHA, and offered to arrange an exhibition of Old Master paintings of the British and French schools, which would be borrowed from Irish country houses at his own expense. The exhibition hoped to help redress the academy's financial plight. Once Lane obtained permission to go ahead with his project, he wrote to the Irish press explaining the nature of his intentions. He wanted to provide a platform for artistic education, and believed that paintings from British and French Old Masters would encourage an interest in art as well as the production of modern painting in Ireland.[40] But Lane's artistic judgement was called into question when two members of the honorary executive committee – painter Walter Osborne and W.G. Strickland – resigned before the exhibition opened, on the grounds that a portrait attributed to Joshua Reynolds was a copy (O'Byrne, 2000: 44). Lane managed to refute this claim and restore his position as a judge of aesthetic value, but the incident showed a certain distrust of his judgement. Despite this, press responses to Lane's project were enthusiastic,[41] and from the outset focused on the need for a national art in Ireland. The *Evening Herald* put this point clearly: national art had to be encouraged, 'At a time when so much is being done for the revival of Irish literature, old Irish music and Irish industries'.[42] But what type of national art was to develop from an acquaintance with British and French Old Masters? And what kind of nation would a national art help determine?

A few weeks before the Old Masters exhibition closed in February 1903, Lane took another opportunity to publish his ideas in the Irish press. In a letter to *The Irish Times* he linked the exhibition's success to the public's interest in the revival of Irish art;[43] the exhibition had attracted a larger number of visitors than the academy's regular exhibitions, and ran several weeks longer than initially planned (O'Byrne, 2000: 44). Lane now suggested a series of reforms at the RHA: a new building, a grant to support the academy school, and 'a fine gallery filled with pictures by the great moderns'. This latter project he described as 'the most necessary of all', and shows how quickly Lane had amended his earlier views on the benefits of Old Masters as an inspiration for artistic education. Such a gallery – probably at this stage he thought of it as part of the RHA – would provide an opportunity to 'produce a school of painting equal in importance and in profit to any in the world'. The exhibition of modern pictures was outside the remit of the National Gallery of Ireland, whose collection was 'of too early a date to do more than train the eye to the possibilities of "colour"'. Conversely, a modern art collection would stimulate the work of Irish painters: 'We may have the best instruction in the world, and the finest building, but without having examples of the best work of modern painters to study and emulate it will be but slow teaching'.

Lane's use of the term modern was probably referring to the work of contemporary foreign artists. A gallery of contemporary artists, he insisted, would provide Ireland with an opportunity already afforded all provincial towns in England. 'Let us join together in this desire to refine the national taste, encourage mental cultivation, and give rational amusement . . . Ireland is able to produce the necessary genius, if given the same opportunities as all other great cities have provided for their people'. Lane's reference to a 'national taste', 'mental cultivation' and 'amusement' reflect a nineteenth-century ideal of public improvement through art exhibitions (Taylor, 1999: xiv); in this case, exposure to modern art would allow the public to participate and thus improve Ireland's artistic culture. But there were contrary views, particularly about the nature of art in an Irish school.

The day after the publication of Lane's views, an article in the *Irish Daily Independent* entitled 'Native art' praised his efforts to establish a genuine school of native art in Dublin, and agreed with him on the creation of a public arena for contemporary art to help such a school develop. However, it disagreed on the type of art that would help inspire a distinctly national style. Foreign modern art, as Lane had suggested, was not appropriate because it would make 'an Irish Art Gallery a kind of cross between a Theatre of Varieties and a Café Chantant'.[44] If an Irish school of painting were to exist, it would have to be built upon the representation of historical Irish motifs:

> If by it is meant some of the more recent productions of certain British, French, German, and Italian masters, we entertain no burning desire to have them exhibited in Dublin . . . The stones of Celtic legend and Celtic song, the dark but sometimes lightsome pages of the history of our country, afford many subjects for the brushes of skilful painters . . . We believe that what Ireland needs for the creation of a genuine school of native art is not the wholesale importation of works of alien painters, but the development of Irish artistic taste and skill on distinctly Celtic lines.[45]

The article went on to criticize Lane's vision of a gallery of modern art, as well as the type of art it was to house. This opposition is indicative of the time; since the 1860s the Celtic Revival had associated the arts and crafts with the expression of Celtic themes and nationalist ideals (Edelstein *et al*, 1992: xiii).

Another participant in the debate was Edward Martyn, who also focused on the relationship between 'art and nationality' in an article of that title in *The Leader*. Dublin had its own collection of pictures in the National Gallery, he argued, and thus if another gallery was needed it should be financed by private funds. His piece did not address the question of how funding for a modern art gallery could be raised, but asked instead for support for a School of Religious Art:

> But the foundation of a native School of Religious Art makes no demand upon the ratepayer. On the contrary it brings wealth to a large number of workers, and benefits the whole community by the home circulation of a vast sum of money, which has hitherto found its way out of this poor country into the pockets of foreign purveyors of miserably bad art.[46]

Martyn saw religious art as the essence of a national art tradition. His remarks were a reflection of his own personal interest – he and Sarah Purser initiated a project for the teaching of stained glass at the

DMSA, which led to a generation of Irish stained-glass artists (Larmour, 1992: 91) – but his intervention was more than an expression of individual taste; it was part of a debate about the artistic sources that might inspire a national Irish art. Would it be the works of great moderns, Celtic themes, or religious images on stained glass?

An article in *The Leader*, signed 'Chanel', attributed the success of the exhibition to its novelty, adding that 'when the pleasure of newness has worn away it will meet with no better fate'.[47] For this contributor the difficulty of developing a distinct art tradition lay not in the form it should take, or the sources that might inspire it, but in the lack of development of Irish art itself. Added to this was a scarcity of financial resources, due to 'the smallness of the assistance we can get from the Irish aristocracy'. The author suggested, in line with Martyn's views, that Ireland needed to produce a national religious art: '[If] there is to be a true development of Irish art at all, this seems to be the only avenue open to it'.

1904. TOWARDS AN INTERNATIONAL AESTHETIC FOR IRISH ART

The debate over the gallery's role and the type of art suitable for its collection did not end there, but acquired a new dimension in 1904, when Lane organized his next public event, an exhibition at the RHA with a collection that was to form the nucleus of Dublin's future gallery.[48] The display included a large selection of paintings by nineteenth-century French artists on loan from the collection of Scottish entrepreneur James Staats Forbes,[49] a small number of Impressionist works on loan from the Paris dealer Paul Durand-Ruel, and a collection donated in support of Lane's cause by leading Irish and British artists (Sharp, 2003: 32). Amongst the Impressionist works were those by Edgar Degas, Claude Monet and Camille Pissarro.[50]

One outstanding feature of this exhibition was the inclusion of French Impressionist paintings, which were a novelty to the Dublin public, not seen since the display of works by Degas, Manet and Monet in the 1899 exhibition. What distinguished the 1904 exhibition from its predecessor, though, was the resolution that Ireland now needed a gallery and a collection of modern art, including foreign art, in order to allow a distinct Irish school to emerge. However, this new project, and the picture-buying campaign organized by Lane, did not always receive the support it needed. Lane's idea of a public modern collection was ahead of its time – indeed, his decision to exhibit French Impressionist art was something of a novelty for the dealer in Old Masters himself. Lane's awareness of more recent developments in French art probably started after the 1902 exhibition. On holiday in France with his friend William Orpen (O'Byrne, 2000: 53), during a short stay in Paris in September 1904 they visited art dealer Paul Durand-Ruel.[51] Following Orpen's advice, Lane first borrowed and then bought works by Edouard Manet, Claude Monet and Camille Pissarro for the Dublin collection. It is unlikely that he was ignorant of Impressionism, but in the company of an informed enthusiast like Orpen, Lane's interest in this new art had grown (O'Byrne, 2000: 55).

An editorial in *The Irish Times* on the day the exhibition opened offered Lane the newspaper's support. Recognizing that the standard of Irish art had fallen lamentably low, it argued that this decline could be arrested if Irish artists were given an opportunity to appreciate the work of their European counterparts:

> [The] exhibition which opens today in the rooms of the RHA marks an epoch in artistic education in Ireland . . . Without the inspiring examples of the great contemporary art of Europe, it is almost impossible for our native students to rise out of the slough in which they have been for so many years . . . the modern student has more to learn from contemporary art than from the art of the past.[52]

John Butler Yeats, writing in the *Dublin Daily Express*, fully supported the art gallery project. It would help painters develop the skill of 'having eyes that see everywhere natural beauty', a talent that could only be acquired by looking at paintings. Dublin was once an artistic city, Yeats recalled, the 'Paris of the British Empire', while now it was the only city of the kingdom without a gallery of modern pictures.[53] Yeats set himself against the attitude of 'looking backward'; rather, he favoured Lane's curiosity and desire to look forward and embrace new artistic tendencies. 'He is the sort of critic who will welcome the painter who will throw on the canvas any daring novelty in colour or form. The bold innovator seeking to break up some well-established convention can count on his support', Yeats said favourably.

Lady Gregory, who made a public appeal through *An Claidheamh Soluis* for funds to buy some of the Impressionist paintings on display, wrote in similarly enthusiastic terms about the gallery: it would be a source of 'dignity' to the Irish nation, and a contribution to its heritage.[54] In an earlier article in *The Irish Times*, she insisted that if French art was secured for Ireland, 'London will become a mere provincial town, and Dublin the capital of the British Isles as far as modern art goes . . . Dublin will become a place of pilgrimage for devotees of modern art'.[55] (London did not have a public collection of modern, international art until 1926, when an extension to the Tate Gallery was opened (Taylor, 1999: 146)). A month later, Lady Gregory invoked the same internationalist rhetoric in an article in the *Freeman's Journal,* making a connection between the merits of French Impressionism and the positive effects it would have on Ireland: as 'the best representation of art outside Paris' the collection supposed 'an advance in the dignity of our country in its place among nations, a worthy building-stone laid upon its wall'.[56]

Another contribution in *An Claidheamh Soluis* acknowledged the lack of prominence given to the visual arts in the Celtic Revival, a situation that would change when the arts were ready for it: 'There will come, no doubt, in this country a revival of art, but we may be certain it will not come until it is sure of a welcome'.[57] Irish art could participate in the country's cultural revival, but before it could help found a national identity, it needed to be able to reflect 'an ideal national life':

> We should, then, labour to develop such precision of instinct and of good taste as will enable us, as often as possible, to catch whatever reflection there may be of the Eternal Beauty. We should labour to increase the comeliness and beauty of what exists in the home, in the street, in the market places, in the class-rooms, that so we may establish a more serene atmosphere, more indestructible foundation.

More than that, the inspiration of foreign art was vital if Irish art was to reflect this new identity. 'We have . . . fallen behind . . . Painting demands study of standards . . . We must have schools, and we must, to adapt Arnold's phrase "See the best the world has done"'.[58]

Others disagreed. A letter in the *Dublin Daily Express,* signed 'Philistine', asked whether there was any evidence 'that loan collections of pictures help in any way our resident artists'. The author dismissed the collection as a range of 'grotesque specimens of the works of cranks and faddists of the modern Impressionist school'.[59] A correspondent in *The Irish Times,* 'Viator', questioned the high prices being asked for the paintings. Claiming a 'long experience of modern pictures and prices', 'Viator' thought the exhibition lacked any pictures of first-rate importance – 'some are not even second-rate in subject and treatment'.[60] 'Viator' might have been Lieutenant-Colonel George Plunkett, then director of the National Museum and a virulent opponent of modern art (O'Byrne, 2000: 65). Similarly, a report in the *Evening Herald* was particularly critical of the French paintings, accusing them of 'false sentimentalism and realism often of a grossly sensual kind'.[61]

References to Dublin as 'the capital of the British Isles' and 'the Paris of the British Empire' emphasize the importance many gave to the future MGMA as a means to outrival London. In January 1905 a circular was issued in *The Irish Times* by a group of Irish writers, including Lady Gregory, William Butler Yeats, Douglas Hyde, Edith Somerville, Emily Lawless and George Russell, calling for the purchase of works by French artists who were deemed 'essential to a study of modern art'.[62] A formal approach was then made to Dublin Corporation. The Public Libraries Committee was asked to prepare a report on the feasibility of such a gallery for Dublin; meanwhile, in February 1905, the Municipal Council authorized the Estates and Finance Committee to provide the sum of £500 to maintain the gallery. The Committee accepted the report, which stated that the paintings offered by Lane were of a high standard and worthy to be housed in an art gallery, and in June it authorized to hire and maintain temporary premises until the erection of a permanent building. The Public Libraries committee, under the chairmanship of Sinn Feiner Thomas Kelly, became involved in the search for new premises, and chose an eighteenth century mansion in 17 Harcourt Street. In September 1907 the Corporation accepted the proposal, and the formal opening of the gallery took place on Monday, 20 January at 17 Harcourt Street. A sub-committee was then formed to run the gallery, including four members of the original supporters' group, two RHA members, and two National Gallery governors. Lane was offered and took the post of Honorary Director (Carden, 2001: 118–20).[63]

1908. THE OPENING OF THE MUNICIPAL GALLERY OF MODERN ART

The MGMA opened its doors to the public on 21 January 1908. On display was its collection of 300 works, including 285 paintings by Irish, British, Dutch and French painters, as well as fifteen sculptures. According to the catalogue, the collection was divided into seven rooms and other exhibition spaces (an entrance hall, staircase and sculpture gallery are also mentioned) which showed works by Irish painters[64] (the term Irish was used to encompass both artists born in

Ireland and those of Irish descent), British schools,[65] portraits of contemporary Irish men and women,[66] French Impressionists, the French Barbizon School, and three rooms devoted to drawings, drawings and watercolours, and etchings and lithographs, as well as a sculpture gallery. Despite the emphasis given to the French Impressionists in the discussion so far, they were a minority in the MGMA's collection, where the highest number of works were by Irish and British painters. The collection was compiled from works presented by individuals, artists, and Lane himself; most of the Impressionist paintings were from his collection, among them Edouard Manet's *Le Concert aux Tuileries* (1862) and *Eva Gonzales* (1870), Camille Pissarro's *Printemps, Vue de Louveciennes* (1870), Pierre Auguste Renoir's *Les Parapluies* (1882–3), and Edouard Vuillard's *The Mantelpiece* (1905).[67]

The *Sinn Féin* magazine sang Lane's praises, adding that 'If every Irishman in his own sphere acted in the same spirit, Ireland ten years hence would be a country of self-reliant men and women'. The gallery was an achievement, a success in providing a cultural institution not reliant on Britain – for its funding, at least; the collection included works by British artists. Nonetheless, it was a new beginning in the artistic life of Ireland:

> The opening of the Municipal Art Gallery on Monday was the opening of an art epoch in Ireland. It is a noble thing for the capital of Ireland to possess the finest modern Art Gallery in Europe, but it is a greater thing for Ireland that she has now within herself the power to evolve a school in Art which will enable her to rank amongst the distinctive nations.[68]

The MGMA, *Sinn Féin* went on, would help give Ireland a school which would produce art equal in status to the art of 'distinctive nations', namely Britain, Holland, Italy and France. The emphatic claim that the MGMA was the 'finest modern Art Gallery in Europe' could probably be related to the inclusion of Impressionist works in its collection.[69]

The English editorial of *An Claidheamh Soluis* also linked the gallery to a new beginning, a new epoch, a manifestation of the new life 'commencing to surge through the veins of Ireland'.[70] The symbolism of Ireland as a body coming back to life is explicit; the gallery, too, was perceived as having almost a miraculous effect, reviving something, a new artistic identity which had long been lost. The newspaper thought the MGMA would help Ireland 'to put herself into communion with her own past', and referring to Hugh Lane, the article continued:

> He has made it possible for young artists so to educate themselves here at home in Ireland that their message of beauty may be delivered to Irish ears in accents which they shall understand, their secrets whispered to Irish hearts in tones which shall stir their inmost chords . . . there will grow up in our midst a school of painters and sculptors whose work will be an authentic expression of the soul of Ireland, because it will be the creation of artists who are in a genuine sense Irish.[71]

Although it was assumed that a gallery and collection would provide a platform for artistic education, and thus an Irish school of art, there is no suggestion as to what sort of aesthetic would develop from absorbing the work of foreign painters. The rhetoric of international prestige, however, was emphatic: it was assumed the collection could bring Dublin a status enjoyed 'nowhere else in Europe save in Paris and (to a lesser extent) in London'.[72] Ellen Duncan, who would be appointed the first curator of the gallery (Boylan, 1996: 100), wrote in similarly enthusiastic terms in two articles published in the *Irish Independent*. Describing the collection as 'a tour de force in selection', she insisted it would attract foreign art connoisseurs to Dublin, and, under the beneficial influence of foreign art, help Ireland 'take its place in the world':[73]

> This Gallery will enrich the country directly and indirectly. Indirectly, because a cultivated people, whose minds are awake to the intellectual tendencies that are stirring in other lands, is better fitted to take its place in the world, better equipped for the struggle for existence, than one which is ignorant of those influences. Directly, by bringing the foreign artist, the critic, the connoisseur, the wealthy visitor to Dublin. The superb collection of foreign masterpieces in modern painting and sculpture now in Dublin will attract attention all over the civilised world.[74]

Another supporter of the gallery's beneficial influence on Irish minds was the *Dublin Daily Express*, which felt the 'collection of French art' in particular would be a crucial inspiration to help Irish people adopt 'another attitude towards life'.[75] Presenting Ireland as a place that had remained isolated from developments in other countries, the arts being one such example, the writer concluded:

> [It] is more suitable to think over the possible advantages of this new gallery to us, to wonder if this collection of French art will influence the Irish intellect, stirring it to another attitude towards life . . . The Irish mind has looked at life from the same point of view century after century . . . France, who has always been the herald of new ideas, has blown her clarion in vain, Ireland never heeded the call. Perhaps – who knows, the unexpected always happens – Manet and Monet and their friends will bring about the change.[76]

The Irish Times praised the collection as one of the most representative and educative in the whole world. The international status of the collection was invoked again: the gallery 'had not been founded for the exhibition of modern Irish art only; there is no parochialism in art, and the aim of the Dublin gallery will be to illustrate modern art generally'.[77] To have such a collection housed in Dublin had important consequences: it would help Ireland re-position itself; a colonized country, the 'Cinderella of the nations', might aspire to becoming a wealthy art capital, with a collection that was one of a kind. As the writer put it, a 'jewel of singular beauty and distinction'[78] had been hung about the image of the city.

Lane's statement in the exhibition's catalogue was equally specific about the benefits of the MGMA:

> Till to-day Ireland was the only country in Europe that had no Gallery of Modern Art. There is not even a single accessible private collection of Modern Pictures in this country. That reproach is now removed.[79]

It is significant that Lane saw the MGMA as helping Ireland achieve a similar status to its European counterparts, at least as far as modern art collecting was concerned. It must be pointed out that the MGMA was, indeed, ahead of its time, because the inclusion of French Impressionist works differed from a European trend of setting up galleries to display works by national, living artists. The catalogue also carried a statement by United States President Theodore Roosevelt, whose comments reinforced Lane's views: '[the gallery] would be an important step toward giving Dublin the position it by right should have'.[80] In other words, Dublin was a capital with artistic talent, and the gallery was no more than emphasizing the status that Ireland as a whole should have.

Alongside the controversy over which kind of art would best encourage an Irish art school was the question as to the kind of nation a national art was to help determine.[81] The opinions expressed on the opening of the MGMA suggested that art would give Ireland a chance to articulate its own identity, one which would no longer see it defined as a colonized nation. While British colonial domination was to continue, the opinions about the gallery projected Dublin as an outward-looking European capital, ready to embrace foreign art, both in the formation of an artistic tradition and in helping Irish people open up their horizons to stylistic tendencies from abroad. This opinion was formed usually with exaggerated claims about the gallery's position vis-à-vis other European capitals, but the argument still applies: the MGMA was seen as a much appreciated resource that would help lowly Ireland become a better European nation.

The rhetoric of international prestige, and the notion that foreign art would help develop a national art, hardly coincides with the Revivalist emphasis on reconnecting the country to its Celtic past, drawing on its language, mythology and visual culture. These are, however much opposed in their means, two sides of the same debate. The need to revive the arts by looking back on Ireland's Celtic past co-existed with the wish to have an Irish school of art which would be outward looking, and inspired by the example of foreign artists with well-established art traditions.[82]

CONCLUSION

The empirical exploration of the MGMA and the context in which it emerged serves to answer two theoretical questions: firstly, whether the creation of an art collection for the MGMA was a legislative practice, and if so, how was legislation involved in the creation of an Irish modernity? And, secondly, did the intellectual practices involved in the making of Ireland's first modern art collection lead to any form of change in the judgement and perception of art? In other words, was the emergence of the FMAC paralleled by a shift in art appreciation or judgement?

The study of various exhibitions has illustrated the institutions and mechanisms which were involved in the production of symbolic capital for Irish and foreign art. The RHA's annual exhibitions and the organization of exhibitions outside the academy's walls were the predecessors of the MGMA, and the emergence of a new field, but it was Lane's arrival on Dublin's art scene, and the three exhibitions that he put together, which precipitated a debate over the future tendencies to be embraced by Irish artists. The opinions presented illustrate the workings of legislative practices: the making of aesthetic judgements, distinguishing and classifying what types of art were appropriate models for an Irish art school, are examples of what Bauman calls modern legislative practices. In the process, modern Irish art became a contested category. For some, 'good art' was a form of Irish art inspired by Celtic motifs; for others, it was most likely to emerge from a combination of foreign art, mainly French Impressionism, and Irish talent.

However, French Impressionism arrived in Dublin only after it had been publicly exhibited in Paris, where Impressionist exhibitions were held from 1874 to 1886. Moreover, Impressionist works had been part of a French public collection since 1890, when Manet's *Olympia* was accepted as a donation by the Luxembourg Gallery in Paris (Denvir, 1993: 179). The advocates of an Irish school of painting inspired by Impressionism were thus supporting a form of aesthetic already validated within the French art world, which was then to be given a distinctively Irish style. Similarly, the project of setting up a gallery of modern art was not originally Irish, but followed a European model which had started in 1818 when Paris became the first European capital to have a museum for works by living artists, the Luxembourg Gallery; a trend followed by the Neue Pinakothek (1853) in Munich, and Berlin's Nationalgalierie (1867). What was a novelty was the exhibition of a collection of foreign art, displaying artists of different nations, at a time when museums of living art had a nationalist emphasis (Lorente, 1998). Collecting, as a legislative practice in Ireland, was trying to emulate existing institutional and artistic models, while at the same time attempting to create something unique.

But to say that these collecting practices were a form of modern legislation does only explain one aspect of this type of practice. The making of a modern art collection, and the founding of a gallery of modern art, were also attempts to negotiate Ireland's relationship with modernity's intellectual project – a project which defined Ireland as 'inferior', 'lagging behind' modernity's advantaged nations. The debate surrounding the MGMA articulated a form of intellectual intervention; an attempt to re-conceptualize Ireland's disadvantaged status in modernity's hierarchy of nations, projecting it as a thriving European art capital which might even surpass London, where it would take another few years for the Tate Gallery to start buying French Impressionist works.[83] The representation of Ireland as a European capital exemplifies a form of legislation from the periphery;

an intellectual struggle against those legislating practices which portrayed colonized countries as 'naturally' inferior.

Finally, can it be argued that the emergence of an FMAC led to a shift in art appreciation and judgement? And if so, what form did it take? Initially, the MGMA challenged the RHA's position in at least two ways: it became the only leading institution for the promotion of modern art in the FIA, and it facilitated the emergence of new ways of thinking about an Irish school of art, inspired by and based on French Impressionism. Thus, the MGMA started what Bourdieu calls a 'symbolic revolution' to the extent that it endorsed modern art, as a new emergent aesthetic category, a type of art suitable to become part of a public collection.

However, despite its optimistic start, the MGMA became the victim of a series of events which stopped modern art from becoming a dominant aesthetic in the FIA. The internationalist school of Irish art never emerged, at least not in the way Lane projected it. Tired of waiting to find an adequate building for the gallery, Lane donated his collection of Impressionist paintings to the National Gallery in London. His untimely death in 1915 precipitated a long controversy with the gallery over Lane's donation.[84] In the meantime, those artists who choose to adopt aspects of modernist art – Jack Butler Yeats, Mainie Jellett, Evie Hone, Harry Clarke, to name a few – did not rely on the works in the MGMA's collection for inspiration, but travelled to countries such as France to learn new artistic tendencies at a time when Cubism and Fauvism had replaced Impressionism as cutting-edge artistic styles.[85] Thus, Irish artists were instrumental in bringing about a change in aesthetic in the FIA by embracing foreign artistic movements and incorporating them into their work.

However, despite these new influences on some Irish artists, Dublin continued to be dominated by the academicism of the RHA, and isolationist approaches to the arts which counteracted the city's expression of internationalism. Although the quest for a national identity in the visual arts prevailed, when those artists who adopted modernist tendencies tried to exhibit in Ireland they suffered the incomprehension of both art critics and the RHA. In the visual arts, and painting in particular, national art came to be seen as the expression of life in the west of Ireland (Kennedy, 1991: 22). This view was linked to Ireland's new status, freed from British rule and, since 1922, established as the Irish Free State. After 1922, Irish governments pursued isolationist policies promoting, almost exclusively, 'the ancient and pastoral culture of Gaelic Ireland to the exclusion of almost all other influences' (Kennedy, 1991: 21).

In sum, the story of the MGMA gives a valuable insight into the role intellectual collecting practices can have in creating emergent fields, and new categories of perception and judgement, such as modern art. However, maybe we need to re-think who key players in symbolic revolutions are: institutions, debates on aesthetics, or the practice of artists themselves? In this case, I suggest, history teaches us that artists are key agents in their potential to create change in artistic fields, by bringing new art forms, even if any art form needs the support of institutions, as well as a politics favouring a particular type of practice. In the conclusion I will return to the issue of change in relation to IMMA, exploring further the contribution of art-collecting practices to shifts in categories of perception and the creation of new fields. For now it will suffice to say that the MGMA succeeded in starting a new field, and a short-lived appreciation for Impressionist art.

CHAPTER 3

Dublin's Art World

AFTER THE MUNICIPAL GALLERY OF MODERN ART

AFTER THE FOUNDATION of the MGMA in 1908, it would take over eighty years for another major public art institution – the Irish Museum of Modern Art (IMMA) – to emerge in Dublin. The emergence of IMMA in 1991 took place in the midst of a series of transformations.

While the 1980s were characterised by economic recession, unemployment and emigration the 1990s saw the arrival of the Celtic Tiger, which made Ireland the fastest growing economy in the world in the last years of the twentieth century. As a result, the Republic became, primarily, an urban society with just 10 per cent of its work force employed in the agricultural sector. Parallel to this, the country started to reflect European demographic norms, changing attitudes towards the family and birth control, with the availability of contraception and legislation of divorce; all these changes facilitated an increased role of women in the labour force (Ferriter, 2004: 666).

During the 1990s, particularly under the leadership of Charles Haughey, Ireland benefited from the government's involvement in the arts. For the first time, the arts were included as part of governmental policy, supporting and sustaining individual creativiy. For example, in 1981, the Arts Council established Aosdána — an affiliation of artists that recognised the role of those artists who had made a significant contribution to the arts in Ireland (Ryan, 2003: 90). Another aspect of the government's policy was to encourage public access to the arts by means of public performances, theatres, music, opera, galleries, and exhibitions. The establishment of an Irish Museum of Modern Art in 1991 can be seen as an integral part of the government's proactive policy for the arts and culture.

In the period between 1908 and 1991 the FIA was shaped by a number of initiatives: the Irish Exhibitions of Living Art (IELA), the

Rosc exhibitions – Rosc: Irish word for 'the poetry of vision' –, the emergence of commercial galleries, the Friends of the National Collections, the start of corporate collecting by Irish banks, and the role of public organizations such as the Arts Council and the Office of Public Works.

This chapter continues to study the creation of symbolic capital with a focus on the FIA, and is followed by chapters 4 and 5 which return to the FMAC with an analysis of IMMA's collecting practices. In contrast to the chapters dealing with IMMA, and the preceding study of the MGMA, intellectual collecting practices are not the focus of analysis here – rather, this chapter's concern is to identify the players involved in the FIA, their position in the field, and their capacity to generate symbolic capital, in order to provide a context for IMMA's collecting practices. There are more agents in the FIA than those addressed here, such as the National College of Arts and Design, the main institution in charge of teaching fine art, but this is omitted from the analysis, as are statements from contemporary artists. Moreover, the FIA, as it is used here, only includes those institutions in charge of the promotion, exhibition, display and collection of contemporary and modern art; this is why the National Art Gallery of Ireland has been excluded.

THE IRISH EXHIBITION OF LIVING ART

In the 1940s, outlets for the exhibition of visual art were limited. The RHA's annual exhibition was the most prestigious in Ireland (Hartigan, 1987: 58), but during this period another line of artistic practice started to take shape when a generation of Irish artists who had studied abroad – such as Nano Reid, Norah McGuinness, Mainie Jellett, Evie Hone and Louis le Brocquy – incorporated into their work artistic developments which were current in Europe. The RHA's rejection of *The Spanish Shawl* by Louis le Brocquy for its annual exhibitions of 1942 and 1943 (Hartigan, 1987: 58) made the academy's opposition to the work of more modernist artists quite explicit (Kennedy, 1991: 114). It led to the beginning of the Irish Exhibition of Living Art (IELA) in 1943, a different exhibition space 'to make available to the public a comprehensive survey of work, irrespective of School, by living Irish artists' (Coulter, 2003: 87). This annual event became an alternative outlet to the RHA's exhibitions, and embraced a pluralistic aesthetic, including works following an academic tradition, as well as more modernist or avant-garde tendencies:

> While the IELA was an alternative to the RHA, the two were not mutually exclusive and many people exhibited work in both, even though each represented a different point of view. The RHA maintained what it believed to be the tradition, while the IELA brought to the attention of the Irish public the fact that there were Irish painters and sculptors whose work reflected the artistic concerns of the Continent. (Hartigan, 1987: 58)

The IELA provided the FIA with a means of creating symbolic capital for contemporary Irish art in at least two ways: firstly, through the initiative and organizing skills of artists who ran the exhibitions; and, secondly, because it sought to embrace a variety of artistic styles.[1] However, the exhibition was there most of all to impact on the public at large: 'perhaps the greatest achievement of the Living Art exhibitions was in demonstrating irrefutably that, despite the tenor of the times, Irish art was not immune to the mainstream of European intellectual endeavour' (Kennedy, 1991: 146). The international aspect of the exhibition was reinforced with the passing of a motion in 1944 favouring the inclusion of non-Irish artists (Coulter, 2003: 85).

The symbolic capital originated by the IELA is all the more important because the other major player in the FIA, the MGMA, was not playing an active role in promoting living artists either. During the 1940s and '50s, the committee responsible for acquisitions at the MGMA rejected *The Christ and the Soldier* by French Expressionist artist Georges Rouault, offered to the gallery in 1942 and 1952 (Walker, 1997: 24). Similarly, *A Family* by Louis le Brocquy was turned down in 1952, even though a group of art lovers were prepared to purchase it for the MGMA's permanent collection (ibid: 38).[2] These rejections by the MGMA throw the gallery's original project into a new light – they seemed to go against all that the gallery was set up to be. The work of foreign artists or Irish artists embracing foreign tendencies now had to overcome the verdict of an acquisitions committee unlikely to support such purchases. The gallery also ignored the positive reception given to le Brocquy's work, which had been exhibited and represented in Ireland and abroad. *A Family,* for example, had been shown at the Gimpel Fils Gallery in London in June 1951, and later on that year at the Waddington Galleries in Dublin; in 1956 it was awarded an international prize at the Venice Biennale (Russell, 1981: 9). Even so, le Brocquy's *A Family* did not find its way into the MGMA's collection.

THE EMERGENCE OF COMMERCIAL ART GALLERIES

The emergence of commercial art galleries supported IELA's profile. The first gallery was set up in Dublin in 1925 by Victor Waddington, and stayed in business for over thirty years (Walker, 1997: 31), until Waddington moved to London in 1957, where he also became a leading figure in the art world. In 1944 Leo Smith opened the Dawson Gallery, which closed in 1977 and re-opened as the Taylor Galleries in 1978. The David Hendricks Gallery was founded in 1956 and ran until 1988; the Oliver Dowling Gallery was opened in 1976. Apart from bringing an art trade to the FIA, these galleries played an important role in introducing audiences to artistic styles which posed a challenge to the art shown at the RHA's annual exhibitions. The Waddington Galleries and the Dawson Gallery sold work by academicians and artists influenced by artistic movements outside Ireland. The Dawson Gallery in particular played a role in 'undermining the stranglehold of the RHA, offering an opening for independent opinion and trade' (Walker, 1997: 31). The Waddington Galleries also contributed to this process by showing the work of many leading English and Continental artists, including Pablo Picasso, Pierre Bonnard, Henri Matisse, Georges Braque, Georges Rouault, Ben Nicholson, Ivor Hitchens, Henry Moore, Barbara Hepworth and André Masson (Fallon, 1998: 242). Moreover, in 1966 the David Hendricks Gallery organized an exhibition of Kinetic art, which introduced international figures such as Victor Vasarely, Jesús Rafael Soto, Julio le Parc, Carlos Cruz Diez, François Morellet, Bridget Riley, Peter Sedgley and others (Lambert, 1983: 23).

Commercial galleries promoted work by Irish artists, and, most importantly, brought art from the artist's studio to Dublin's emergent art market. In so doing, they not only created symbolic capital, in the recognition they gave to the work they represented, but they offered an alternative, and very much-needed space in the FIA for those who did not follow the aesthetic promulgated by the RHA. Fallon's (1998: 239) description of the annual RHA exhibitions as relying 'heavily on dull, semi-official portraiture, laboured genre pieces, and tritely "picturesque" landscape' is suggestive of the academic-realist style they represented (Walker, 1997: 21). It is important, too, to point out the connection between the IELA exhibitions and the workings of commercial art galleries. Art exhibitions gave artists and their work a public profile, but commercial galleries were a much-needed support mechanism to help both Irish and non-Irish artists sustain themselves financially:

> The Living Art exhibitions might exhibit modern Irish art publicly, James White [art critic][3] might publicise it verbally, a coterie of Dublin snobs might patronise it socially, but Waddington performed the essential service of selling it. (Fallon, 1998: 241)

This emerging art world created a fertile ground for usually wealthy individuals to invest in the visual arts, some of whom would become important donors to IMMA. For example, Vincent Ferguson, who bought the Hendricks Gallery in the early 1980s, donated an important set of works to IMMA's collection in 1997.[4] On a similar note, commercial galleries brought international art to collectors such as Gordon Lambert, willing to purchase the latest artistic trends. As will be seen in chapter 4, Lambert's donations are the backbone of IMMA's collection.

ROSC EXHIBITIONS

Another concerted effort in the realm of exhibitions was the founding of Rosc; from 1967 to 1988 a total of six exhibitions were organized in an attempt to lift Ireland's profile in the international art world, as well as to improve artistic production at home. All the exhibitions followed the same pattern, with a display of around 150 works by international artists, as well as an ancient section.[5] The inclusion of two Irish artists in 1977, seven in 1980, and ten in 1984 offset the initial absence of local representation. This inclusiveness towards Irish art suggests an increasing awareness of the high standard achieved by certain artists, who could rightfully be displayed alongside the best examples of international art. In short, the Rosc exhibitions are another example of the emergence of new initiatives to compensate for the lack of institutions to display art, and hence for the need to devise alternative ways of creating symbolic capital within the FIA. This idea is put clearly by Dorothy Walker, chairman of Rosc '80:

> Rosc has a twofold aim: a foreign policy and a domestic policy. The domestic policy arises from the regrettable fact that there is no National Museum of Modern Art in Ireland and that the Irish public in consequence is deprived of the experience of great twentieth-century art. So the Rosc exhibitions act as a quadriennial Museum of Modern Art for the Irish public, and they are still attempting to catch up on major artists from abroad whose works have never been seen in Ireland.[6]

Although Walker here refers to a venue for exhibiting international art, as opposed to a collecting institution, her words also reaffirm the MGMA's lack of success in creating a collection of renown, as Hugh Lane had intended it. In the meantime, the Rosc exhibitions mobilized economic capital through public and corporate sponsorship in support of the arts – from Aer Lingus, the Arts Council, and Carrolls and Co, the tobacco manufacturers. In 1981, the international aviation leasing company, Guinness Peat Aviation, sponsored the GPA Awards, worth £25,000 each, to help young and emerging artists (Walker, 1988: 137). The prize lapsed after the takeover of GPA in 1993 (Walker, 1997: 183),[7] but the awards offered an initial source of public recognition to Irish artists, some of whom are now leading figures in the FIA: Felim Egan, Kathy Prendergast, Willie Doherty, Dorothy Cross and Alanna O'Kelly to name a few (Walker, 1998: 137–41).

COLLECTING AND CORPORATE COLLECTIONS

Another important source of creating symbolic capital in the FIA is collecting. Being part of a corporate or a public collection is a sign of prestige for artists and their work. Many initiatives have been set up to support public collections. In 1924 the painter Sarah Purser (who was mentioned in chapter 2 in her role as a patron of Irish art) founded the Friends of the National Collections of Ireland, to purchase works for public collections both North and South. Its establishment was prompted by the realization that the emergent Irish state was not in a position to acquire works for Ireland's public collections – even through the 1960s the MGMA had no purchasing fund, and it was only in 1970 that Dublin Corporation contributed towards an acquisition, £300 to the sum of £2,700 for a Josef Albers' painting, *Aglow* (Gordon Bowe, 1999: 27). In 1951, the Arts Council was established with the task of stimulating public interest in and practice of the arts in Ireland (Kennedy, 1990: 224). Under the directorship of Fr Donal O'Sullivan, the council set out in 1960 to build up a permanent collection of contemporary Irish art (Walker, 1997: 56), at a time when no other public institution was buying work by living artists – the Friends of the National Collections' policy was to buy works by deceased artists only. To help fill the dearth of purchases of works by living artists, Sir Basil Goulding founded the Contemporary Irish Art Society in 1962 to buy works for the

MGMA. The society still exists to purchase, loan and donate works, not only for the MGMA, but more generally for their display in public galleries and institutions.[8] Between 1962 and 1974 (in that year Dublin Corporation allocated a purchasing fund to the gallery) the society donated a total of thirty-seven paintings and sculptures to the MGMA.

Corporate collecting has enjoyed the support of public funding from the Arts Council since 1973, when it set up the Joint Purchase Fund (originally called the Hotels Scheme) to encourage public and private institutions such as universities, banks and hotels, to buy works at half their price, while the council paid the remaining half. The scheme only lasted six years but it helped develop some corporate collections, like the Office of Public Works'[9] and the Bank of Ireland's. The latter is Ireland's longest-established corporate buyer; its collection started in 1970, while Allied Irish Banks (AIB) started collecting in 1980. Similarly, the Carrolls collection was built up in 1967 under the supervision of the architect Ronald Tallon (O'Kane, 2000: 39). A related development was the foundation of COTHU ('promotion'), the Business Council for the Arts, in 1988, to act as an information agency advising and guiding business on arts expenditure (ibid.).

An indication of the degree of expertise and seriousness attached to corporate collecting is the appointment of art advisers by the Bank of Ireland and the AIB to select and purchase works for their collections. The practice of collecting is complemented by the organization of exhibitions in Ireland and the printing of art catalogues, as in the case of the AIB and the Office of Public Works, to give wide exposure to their collections.[10] Statements in catalogues vouch for the seriousness of their endeavour; for example, in *AIB Art* (1995) Lochlann Quinn, chairman of the AIB group, referred to the bank's collection as 'unique in terms of the depth and scope in which it traces the development of modernism in Irish art' (1995: 3). The introduction to the catalogue by art adviser Frances Ruane continued this line of argument:

> When AIB first decided to put together an art collection in 1980 the ambition was to acquire works that would trace the development of Irish art, beginning with the period that signalled the birth of modernism around 1880 and continuing right up to the present. Fortunately the Bank resisted the urge to find a quick solution to covering the bare wells of its new corporate headquarters, opting instead for a more long

> term approach. Now, fifteen years later, we are still acquiring artworks that will flesh out the historical dimension of the collection, although there has been a shift in emphasis towards the support of living artists. (Ruane, 1995: 5)

The AIB collection is presented here as reflecting a specific period in the history of Irish art, tracing its development, and continuing this task in the present with purchases of works by living artists. Invoking the role it plays in representing Irish art legitimates the collection's symbolic value. Corporate collecting is a distinct practice and works at a pragmatic level, filling a gap in the FIA's historical collection of works by Irish artists. None of the public institutions have a representative collection of Irish art from the 1940s and 1950s, though this type of art is included in the AIB and Bank of Ireland collections.

THE FIELD OF IRISH ART NOW: DUBLIN'S COMMERCIAL AND PUBLIC ART GALLERIES

The remainder of this chapter introduces the present configuration of the FIA, focusing on its commercial and public galleries. It offers a brief description of their role and activities as an introduction to an analysis of the various processes in which they create symbolic capital in the FIA. The material used is largely based on interviews with the directors of seven commercial galleries and four public institutions, who articulate the core practices of collecting and exhibiting contemporary and modern art in Dublin. With regard to commercial galleries, whenever possible gallery owners were interviewed, or alternatively directors or managers; in some instances gallery owners also act as directors. Seven galleries were selected as representative, for their participation in the Irish Contemporary Art Gallery Association (ICAGA). The identities of those interviewed and their gallery affiliation have been kept anonymous to ensure the confidentiality of the statements included here. Only the identity of public gallery and museum directors who speak on behalf of their institution has been kept.

COMMERCIAL AND PUBLIC ART GALLERIES

Dublin's commercial galleries are relatively young – the oldest was only established in 1978 and the youngest in 1999. Most of the galleries are located in Dublin's city centre, and although they represent a variety of artistic tendencies, they share a set of common practices. Most of these galleries work with a stable of artists, most of them Irish, but they also include a number of non-Irish artists. Overall, they represent a core group of fifteen to seventeen artists, and hold between ten to fifteen solo shows per year, each lasting about three weeks, including two group exhibitions during the summer and Christmas seasons. Almost all galleries interviewed have represented their artists at international art fairs, and have their own websites to help them keep an international profile. Along with their exhibition programme, some galleries offer a consultancy service advising companies and individual collectors on their purchases. As far as public art galleries are concerned, apart from the National Gallery of Ireland, Dublin has four main institutions: the Royal Hibernian Academy (1823), the Douglas Hyde Gallery (1978), the Hugh Lane Municipal Gallery of Modern Art (1908), and the Irish Museum of Modern Art (1991).

Douglas Hyde Gallery

The gallery is situated in Trinity College and is one of Ireland's leading contemporary art galleries. Its exhibition programme includes exhibitions by emerging and well-established artists from Ireland and abroad. Although opened in 1978 at its present location in the Arts Building in Nassau St, its history goes back to 1959 when a group of students set out to create the College Gallery, an initiative that also led to the start of an art history course in Trinity College and a temporary exhibitions hall (Walsh, 1991: 21). The aim of the College Gallery during the 1960s, '70s and '80s was 'to promote interest in visual arts in college, particularly amongst students, and to do so by building up a comprehensive collection of pictures, either original paintings and prints or reproductions, to decorate students' rooms and, later, offices' (ibid: 21).[11] In 1967 the newly built Berkeley Library provided a suitable space as a temporary exhibitions hall.[12] This changed in 1978 when an opportunity arose to locate the gallery in the new Arts and Social Science Building in Nassau St. An agreement was then reached between Trinity College, which was responsible for incorporating the gallery into the new building, and the Arts Council, which would provide funding for its exhibition programme. The new venue was named after Douglas Hyde, the first President of Ireland and a Trinity College graduate (Dawson, 1987: 40). In 1984, and with the appointment of a new director, the gallery changed its exhibition policy from an emphasis on 'catching up on the backlog of twentieth-century art' to a focus on documenting younger Irish artists (ibid: 23). In March 1991, only a few months before IMMA opened, the gallery appointed a new director, and later that year opened a new space, 'Gallery 2', funded by a grant from the Arts Council. The Douglas Hyde Gallery is currently funded by the Arts Council, Trinity College and various friends and patrons of the gallery. Website: www.douglashydegallery.com

Hugh Lane Municipal Gallery of Modern Art

The Municipal Gallery of Modern Art added 'Hugh Lane' to its title (HLMGMA) in 1975 to commemorate the sixtieth anniversary of Lane's untimely death aboard the *Lusitania* in 1915. The gallery is located in Charlemont House, in Parnell Square, at the top of Dublin's main thoroughfare, O'Connell St. It offers an exhibition programme as well as an ongoing display of its permanent collection. Some of its exhibitions have included artists such as Alice Maher (1999), Vivienne Roche (1999) and Brian Maguire (2000), as well as emerging artists such as Catherine Owens (1999). The collection represents developments in Irish art in the twentieth century, including a collection of stained glass. Apart from direct purchases by the gallery, the collection has benefited from donations by the Friends of the National Collections of Ireland and the Contemporary Irish Art Society. One of the most celebrated additions to the collection is the donation by John Edwards of the *Francis Bacon Studio*, which was accompanied by an exhibition of Bacon's works (2000). The HLMGMA is entirely funded by the local authority, Dublin Corporation. The Friends of the Gallery help support its education and outreach programme, in which artists work with schools and community groups throughout the city. In 2006, the gallery has plans to open an extension including a new exhibition space with thirteen galleries, a space for education workshops, a lecture room, as well as an archive and storage area. Website: www.hughlane.ie

Irish Museum of Modern Art

The Irish Museum of Modern Art is Ireland's leading national institution for the collection and presentation of modern and contemporary art. It was opened to the public in 1991 in the restored Royal Hospital building and grounds in Kilmainham, about two miles from Dublin's city centre. The museum offers a dynamic programme of exhibitions and other activities, which include exhibitions of work from the museum's own collection, projects by its education and community department, and its exhibition department. In terms of activities, the museum's artists' work programme – open to artists in all disciplines and of all nationalities – sees artists meeting visitors and sharing their insights into the process of art making. The museum's national programme lends exhibitions of group and individual artworks from the collection to centres outside the capital. The museum has launched a friends and patrons scheme to raise funds for the long-term development of its programmes and activities. It offers a wide range of benefits for individuals and companies.[13] Website: www.modernart.ie

Royal Hibernian Academy

The Royal Hibernian Academy has undergone a transformation since its foundation in 1823, although its main objectives still prevail: it continues to be artist-based and artist-orientated, dedicated to developing, affirming and challenging the public's appreciation and understanding of traditional and innovative approaches to the visual arts. The academy has an education programme which includes lunchtime talks and tours, lecture series on contemporary art and Old Masters, and a schools programme offering guided tours. The Friends of the RHA was established in 1997 to support the development and upgrading of facilities, the production of exhibitions, and the academy's educational initiatives. It offers several membership modalities: individual, family, patron, benefactor and corporate. The benefits enjoyed vary, but include invitations to all exhibition openings, free entry to the RHA annual exhibition and to educational events. The academy is located in the centre of Dublin, at 15 Ely Place, a building which consists of four galleries distributed on two floors. The three on the first floor are: the Gallagher Gallery, or main gallery, dedicated to curated exhibitions of Irish and international art, and Galleries II and III. On the ground floor is the Ashford Gallery, which was inaugurated in 1999 for the use of academicians and associate academicians. It is also available to non-academicians who do not have commercial gallery representation in Dublin (in this case exhibitions are limited to one presentation), and is designed to introduce artists to the collecting public in order to prove their commercial viability. The Arts Council, fundraising initiatives, the revenues from its annual exhibition, and the support of benefactors, patrons and friends fund the academy. Website: www.royalhibernianacademy.com

COMMERCIAL AND PUBLIC ART GALLERIES AS A MARKET FOR SYMBOLIC GOODS

The last part of this chapter explores the practices of individuals working in commercial and public art galleries. These two groups have different roles in the FIA. Contemporary art galleries are the closest intermediaries between the artists' output and the public promotion of their work. Once a work is produced, and the artist wants to follow this particular route, it goes into a commercial gallery. Public galleries occupy a secondary space within the FIA, in that they usually promote the work of artists who are or have been represented by commercial galleries. The term 'secondary' is not intended to suggest that public art galleries produce a form of symbolic capital of less legitimacy than the capital articulated by commercial art galleries. Both are instrumental in the creation of symbolic capital for artists and their work, but it is important to understand that they also occupy different types of space in the overall FIA. The criteria of public galleries for exhibiting and buying works of art are built upon, to a great extent, the legitimacy these have previously acquired in commercial galleries. The decision to narrow this grouping of institutions to two is meant to highlight only those practices that play a direct role in public collecting, which is the main theme of this book. Commercial art galleries provide artworks for museums and their collections, while public institutions with similar functions to IMMA, in charge of either collecting or displaying mainly contemporary art, can help shed light on their position vis-à-vis IMMA and in the FIA more generally.

Commercial and public galleries are referred to here as two different sub-fields within the FIA. The term sub-field draws on Bourdieu's distinction between two poles in cultural fields. As seen in chapter 1, the autonomous and heteronomous poles refer to the ways producers achieve cultural recognition within a given cultural field. The autonomous pole, or field of restricted production (FRP), is aimed at 'high art' (classical music, the visual arts, 'serious' literature) and 'develops its own criteria for the evaluation of its products' (Bourdieu, 1993a: 115). In the FRP economic profit is normally disavowed. The competition between agents is geared towards obtaining symbolic profit, that is, 'a profit of disinterestedness or the profit one has on seeing oneself (or being seen) as one who is not searching for profit' (Johnson, 1993: 15). The disavowal of economic profit does not occur in the heteronomous pole, in what Bourdieu calls the field of large-scale cultural production (FLSP). This field involves 'mass' or 'popular' culture (ibid: 16), and produces cultural goods for the public at large. As opposed to the FRP, it follows 'the laws of competition for the conquest of the largest possible market' (Bourdieu, 1993a: 115). Yet Bourdieu himself warns his readers of seeing 'more than a limiting parameter' (ibid: 127) in the opposition between these two modes of production, which can only be defined in relation to one another:

> What is most important is that these two fields of production, opposed as they are, co-exist and that their products owe their very unequal symbolic and material values on the market to their unequal consecration which, in turn, stems from their very unequal power of distinction. (Bourdieu, 1993a: 128–9)

The rest of this chapter seeks to enlarge the explanatory potential of the 'market for symbolic goods' model by examining the practices of the sub-fields of commercial and public art galleries in Dublin.

THE SUB-FIELD OF COMMERCIAL GALLERIES

The sub-field of commercial galleries occupies a space between the autonomous and heteronomous poles described by Bourdieu. On the one hand, the galleries' main task is the creation of both symbolic and economic value for art – and their first priority is to endow the work they represent with prestige, namely symbolic capital. On the other hand, the creation of symbolic capital does not entail a disavowal of economic profit, as Bourdieu suggested in his theoretical model. Galleries in this sub-field depend on the sale of work to sustain their businesses. The interviews included in this chapter suggest, however, that a leading principle of this sub-field is the creation of symbolic capital, as opposed to the mere accumulation of economic capital. It is difficult to assess to what extent obtaining financial profit prevails over the creation of symbolic capital; both practices are closely linked. Commercial galleries need to promote their artists before they can reap any financial profits. This twofold task is highlighted in an article in the Irish art magazine *Circa*, which describes the specifics of the gallery business as follows:

> [The] bottom line is that commercial galleries are not cushioned, like publicly funded institutions, from hard commercial reality . . . and they have to sell work to survive. But to define them in terms of an exclusively commercial function is a distortion of the role they actually play . . . Such a definition is in fact to concentrate on one level of analysis at the expense of all others. The others might include the significant fact that gallerists are usually engaged in a passionate way with art rather than profit. (Dunne, 2000: 13)

Dunne's comment underlines the idea of commercial galleries as producers of two types of capital, economic and symbolic, and thus the need to take into account the link between these two practices in any analysis of the sub-field. But there is another key distinction to be made with regard to both sub-fields. In their reliance on sales, commercial galleries are unlike public cultural institutions, which are allocated a large part of their budget from public money, even if this may not necessarily be sufficient. Public galleries also enjoy a certain renown or reputation as a result of their position in the FIA – they represent the nation (IMMA); the city (MGMA); or work within the confines of a tertiary educational institution, such as Trinity College (DHG). However, this does not mean to say that the sub-field of public galleries is closer to the FRP than the sub-field of commercial galleries. Although the public galleries' finances do not depend on the sale of works, they still need to obtain their own funds, for example by organizing 'friends of' initiatives. Moreover, they rely upon the public for recognition; a large attendance at exhibitions is a sign of success, which is one of the principles operating in the FLSP. Hence both sub-fields occupy different positions, which are important to outline here as a way of situating the following analysis of the sub-fields' autonomy. Bourdieu (1993a: 115) describes a field's autonomy as 'the power to define its own criteria for the production and evaluation of its products'. One way of exploring the workings of autonomy is to look at the capability of galleries to develop or draw upon an existing type of art which they wish to represent, exhibit or collect.

AUTONOMY AND THE CREATION OF AESTHETIC VALUE

It has been argued that the making of aesthetic value is a practice that follows no rigid canon or school. Contemporary art practices are 'devoid of any normative aesthetics', as they stand in the middle of a period of 'aesthetic anomie' (Moulin, 1994: 9–10). An extreme example is philosopher Danto's view (1997: 16) on contemporary art: 'For art to exist there does not even have to be an object to look at, and if there are objects in a gallery, they can look like anything at all'. However, these arguments raise a number of questions: if anything can be art, why do only a few artists achieve international success? How can we explain the need for artists to be represented by commercial galleries? On what grounds do gallery owners and directors assess value when anything goes? For Bourdieu, being able to distinguish 'good art' is the result of having an aesthetic disposition (Bourdieu, 1993a: 8); a 'distinctive expression of a privileged position in the social space' (Bourdieu, 1984: 56). This argument also applies to the interviewees in this research. Their aesthetic disposition enables gallery owners to enter the sub-field of commercial galleries; it is a much-needed skill if they are to be accepted as legitimate players. The following quotes provide an insight into how the interviewees representing the various Dublin galleries define their ability to distinguish 'good art':

> In here we sort of know what we like and what sells, and what our clients are going to want to see, as well, so you sort of know when you see it. It's hard to say, it's just a feeling . . . when you see the images, you know. When they are posted into you or somebody brings a painting, you know straight away whether it is for us or not. I can't describe why – you just know. (G3)

> Well it's a bit of an instinctual thing, there is no real formula because the work is going to be original; I've never seen it before in some cases. So it's a personal response to what I think is very powerful for whatever reason to do with the material, concept. (G5)

> You'll always be able to tell. There's always that little bit extra, and you can tell by the work, but never with a name. (G2)

> Part of the appeal of art is that it speaks to you, so that's the emphasis. (G6).

> I have a certain eye for the aesthetic. I know for a fact that I'm very good at looking at stuff, and know whether I like it or not, and why. I've always had that. If there is one thing that I have, it's a sense of looking at something from an aesthetic point of view and knowing if it is good or what it's saying. Whatever that is, is a big help in here. (G4)

> It's something that you see and it works for you; it speaks to you and you're happy with it. (G7)

The use of phrases like 'you just know', 'an instinctual thing', 'it speaks to you', express a high degree of individual autonomy in the way galleries define aesthetic value; an autonomy that seems to be built on the innate qualities of those who look at artworks. This suggests an equal degree of autonomy in the articulation of an 'aesthetic disposition'; a disposition without which the field could not function because it is the very ability to distinguish what constitutes a work of art. In the quotes above, aesthetic dispositions are built upon the positioning of aesthetic value as a residual category, embodying all that cannot be apprehended or quantified through rational terms (e.g. following the principles of art history). Yet, even the appreciation of art quality does not take place in a vacuum. As Bourdieu notes (1993a: 257), 'the aesthete's eye which constitutes the work of art as a work of art' is created in the field itself.

In the study conducted, having an 'aesthetic competence' is not necessarily related to having a particular education.[14] Of the seven interviewees, only three had a background in art history. According to one of them, not having this type of knowledge was beneficial: 'I have no baggage as regards art history, what's good, bad, art education, and that's an advantage to run an art gallery', and added that assessing good art 'is a learning experience'. Another director did not have such a background either, but had long experience of working in galleries. A third interviewee said that, despite having attended art college, the gallery business had more to do with experience. These responses suggest, as Bourdieu indicated, that an aesthetic disposition is not merely the result of an instinctual process. Rather, it is related to education and experience. But there is another conclusion to be drawn here. Autonomy in the creation of aesthetic value is not something innate but comes into being in the sub-field itself. The sub-field provides individuals in the gallery business with the learning experience necessary to distinguish works with aesthetic value.

SCARCITY AS A FORM OF AUTONOMY

For Bourdieu (1993a: 117), autonomy is related to the field's capacity to generate 'a specifically cultural type of scarcity and value irreducible to the economic scarcity and value of the goods in question'. The more autonomous a field, the more capable it is of operating as 'a specific market', a market for symbolic goods. Scarcity is a principle of the Dublin sub-field of commercial galleries in various ways. One way of introducing the issue of scarcity in the sub-field is by reference to the Irish Contemporary Art Gallery Association (ICAGA).

THE IRISH CONTEMPORARY ART GALLERY ASSOCIATION

In the early 1990s, when commercial galleries in Dublin were going through an economic recession, they set up the ICAGA to help the gallery business. Its aim was to create more favourable conditions for the trade so that commercial galleries could keep their outlets open. An added concern was to gain recognition and support for the role commercial galleries played in the promotion of contemporary Irish art in Ireland and abroad. ICAGA set about obtaining recognition for galleries in two ways. Firstly, by lobbying the government, the Arts Council and the Minister for Arts to obtain a better tax regime to stimulate the purchase of art – lowering the VAT rate, for example – which so far has not happened. In fact, gallery owners felt that the government did not pay as much attention to commercial galleries as it should. As one interviewee put it:

> [The government is] more interested in museums and community art groups and things like that. But they don't seem to understand that the visual art scene is inextricably tied to the commercial galleries, and without artists selling work they are not going to survive. So they don't seem to understand that galleries need some help for survival. (G3)

Secondly, the association helped set a certain standard in the business. Its members would, for example, invite experts on tax issues to help gallery owners and directors deal with their tax. In so doing, galleries sought to improve their self-image, which was particularly important so that artists could 'trust gallery association members' as carrying out their business 'in a professional manner'. Established by six leading galleries – another gallery has since joined – ICAGA plays a less prominent role at present than when it was founded in 1993, due to the favourable economic climate the gallery business has enjoyed in recent years. Originally, galleries met every month, whereas now they try to meet about once a year. One important task of the association remains the publication, every four months, of the 'Dublin Gallery Guide', a directory of all public and commercial galleries in Dublin. The guide specifies which galleries are members of the association.

ICAGA helps create scarcity in the sub-field because not all commercial galleries in Dublin can be part of the association. Out of a total of around fifteen galleries, only seven belong to it. The right to be included is dictated by various criteria. Membership is open to galleries who have been operating full time in Ireland, North or South, for at least two years. They have to be commercial and privately funded, and more than 80 per cent of their business must be devoted to contemporary art. Existing members of the association second new members, who must have attained a standard of excellence to be eligible. While these criteria are a way of setting up the sub-field's boundaries, it is also possible to see how the maintenance of this boundary, and thus of the field's scarcity, is itself a source of struggle (Bourdieu, 1993a: 42). The *droit de suite*, or artists' resale right, is a case in point. A couple of years ago, members of ICAGA lobbied against a resale law, a form of legislation currently implemented in some European countries giving artists a commission every time their artwork is sold – at present, artists only get a commission when they sell their work for the first time. The problem of the *droit de suite* for commercial galleries is the threat it poses to the sub-field by forcing a large amount of art dealing outside the gallery sector:

> We were just worried. We have no problem with the artists making money out if it, but we were worried that it was going to force a lot of dealing underground. It was going to cause a lot of problems, like a black market, because people wouldn't want to pay the artist, so it was going to force that thing underground. So we were worried whether people would start to take their business and sell their pictures in the US or outside of the EU. Buyers and sellers wouldn't want to be paying the commission bit, so they would deal outside of the EU, so we were worried it was going to affect our business. (G3)

PROMOTING ARTISTS IN 'THE LONG RUN'

Another way of thinking about scarcity is to look at it in relation to the number of artists represented by each gallery. Initially, the field generates scarcity because it is not capable of representing all those artists who seek to be promoted by commercial galleries. Consequently, achieving commercial representation becomes a struggle for artists. In turn, scarcity is a situation that benefits galleries because it gives them the autonomy, freedom and choice to select those artists they want to work with. Given that the main practice of galleries is the selection and promotion of a stable of artists, my concern is to explore the practices involved in maintaining the relationship between artist and gallery. This can help clarify how galleries produce symbolic capital for their artists, as well as how the accumulation of this capital creates symbolic value for commercial galleries. The galleries' main interest is to establish relationships that will generate high levels of symbolic capital. In doing so, scarcity becomes a site of struggle and negotiation over the optimum relationship between them and 'their' artists. The achievement of an 'ideal' relationship reproduces the field's autonomy, and, in this, time plays a crucial role.

Invariably, all interviewees said they were only able to represent a limited number of artists. Generally galleries work with a core of fifteen to seventeen artists, and organize from ten to fifteen solo exhibitions a year. Shows can last from two-and-a-half weeks to a month, so galleries can offer exhibitions by the same artist every two years. Group shows are another form of exhibition, very common during the Christmas and summer periods. Solo shows are usually with artists from the gallery's core group, while artists participating in group shows may only work with galleries on an occasional basis. A gallery director comments on his situation as follows:

> When we started we had already about twenty-four artists, an ideal number to deal with because you could have one exhibition every two years by each of the artists. Unfortunately, I added a few immediately, and then after that quite a few, in fact far too many. So we have so many artists at the moment that we can't take any more, we can't create a space for them. (G7)

Another director refers to his struggle to reduce the number of artists on his books:

> I've tried to keep it together and had to reduce the number of artists, and have to do that again. I think it will work in the long run – it means that you can give more time to the artists that you really like and push that more, and hopefully they will do more stuff with you. Last year I did exhibitions for one month. This year the shows are only three weeks. That's because I've promised too many people shows, and the second part of this year I do one month again for my favourite artists. (G4)

One interviewee mentioned how they had been reducing the length of shows in order to maximize the number of artists involved with the gallery. This particular gallery works with a core group of thirty artists:

> There's very good work out there, but we just don't have the space for it. We used to have ten exhibitions a year. We're now running thirteen to fourteen. We're doing two-and-a-half weeks change-over, or two-and-a-half weeks exhibitions, and some exhibitions are three-and-a-half weeks. So we have a quicker turnaround now so we can fit in more, so it's definitely busier in here. (G3)

The imbalance between galleries' capacity to represent new artists and the number of artists seeking commercial representation produces a situation of scarcity in which galleries are free to choose the type of art they want to promote. This is clear from the following comment:

> Artists make constant applications to all the galleries. There are a lot of artists, so what we do [is] we allow them to submit applications twice a year. We usually get about sixty or seventy applications and I see maybe three studios from each of those. So we accept applications, but we don't look for them, or solicit them. Very occasionally an exhibition results. I do approach artists at various times whose work I feel absolutely fits with something that the gallery is working on. (G1)

Galleries seem to have the upper hand as they can clearly select what art they want to represent, as is the case with this gallery director, who can choose from a large number of offers. Initially, a scarcity of gallery space seems to lead to a form of autonomy or freedom for gallery directors to select the best possible works available to them. However, galleries are particularly interested, not only in promoting a certain aesthetic, but also in creating a type of relationship with artists; an amicable and lasting relationship that can be sustained in the long run.

The galleries aim to work with a few artists 'effectively'. This type of relationship demands an investment of time by gallery owners and directors. This is how one interviewee makes this point:

> If I take an artist to work with me it's for a solo show, and that is a very large investment emotionally and financially, and we tend to build up a longer-time relationship with that artist from day one. And as you do that over a period of ten years, obviously your portfolio fills up. We can only work effectively with a certain limited number of artists, so as a gallery evolves the opportunity for artists to enter does narrow down. (G1)

This gallery works very closely with eight artists: 'we discuss every single element of what they do and their future plans'. This is not to say that galleries are not willing to take on emerging young artists, but for them this type of relationship is not always ideal:

> Years ago we used to have a policy of trying to nurture new artists and every year we had a new artist exhibition, a particular group show of maybe three to four artists each year . . . But, to be honest with you, we found a lot of the young artists didn't have the commitment to stay with the gallery and they'd go off and show somewhere else, or whatever, so we're showing probably less or making less of a big fuss of new-coming artists. If we like the work we'll show it, but we won't make such an emphasis on the fact that it's an emerging artist, because usually they don't stay in one place for very long. (G3)

It must be pointed out that even though the Dublin sub-field is relatively young, the majority of galleries have had enough time to build up a reputation for themselves and the artists they represent (most of whom are in mid-career or already well established). Time is on their side because they work with a core group of artists whose reputations they have been promoting over these years. This position in the sub-field gives them the 'luxury' of deciding whether or not they wish to promote emerging artists. In other words, it gives them the freedom to negotiate what type of relationships will prove, in the long run, worth maintaining. Another well-established gallery, for example, has chosen to promote emerging artists:

> We have a lot of fairly well-established artists associated with the gallery, but we certainly don't need any more, and also when taking on an artist we have the top of it fairly well covered. So, with the money that's out there for established artists, we have enough artists to supply

> the works to these people. If we are taking on someone we would really like to take someone at the lowest price and then just build it up over a period of time. (G7)

It can also be argued that galleries must start by building up relationships with emerging or young artists. This is how a director describes the early days of his gallery:

> [There] was a demand for space – most of the artists that I showed, they couldn't get shows anywhere else. There were two types, the younger artists who couldn't get a leg in, or the old, disenfranchised artists who for whatever reason couldn't get shows in galleries. So it was a bit of an oddball, but it was an appeal. It was supposed to last a few months, and it ended up lasting five years in that particular place. (G4)

This suggests that well-established galleries enjoy greater autonomy or freedom to choose which artists to work with than galleries that have been in the business for a relatively short space of time. The mention of a group of 'disenfranchised' artists points to the fact that new galleries must start with artists who are not well known, and have less autonomy than their better-established rivals to negotiate whether or not they want to work with emerging artists. Time, then, is a crucial factor in increasing the sub-field's autonomy. It gives galleries the opportunity to keep increasing the symbolic capital of the artists they represent. In turn, representing well-known artists can result in more artists wanting to work with that particular gallery. One conclusion to be drawn from this is that galleries exist in a hierarchy, one in which those at the top are able to reject, and even 'disenfranchise', artists.

If we look at the position of a gallery which has been in the sub-field for even a relatively short time, we can see the difference time makes in developing this business. Referring to how the gallery has changed over the years, its director says:

> The emphasis is on quality, as opposed to quantity. Quality comes into the person, as in the person you can deal with, and also then the work as well. Otherwise, eventually there's a difference of opinion, and that's the end of it. That's difficult, and I've found that very difficult in the last few years, when you come to a point when you realize that your reasons for giving shows in the past were trying to help someone out or different kinds of reasons, but in the long run that doesn't work. What works is getting on well with the person, being able to talk straight to the person, and also liking the work. (G4)

We can see here the early stages of a struggle to negotiate an optimum relationship with certain artists where the emphasis is on 'quality'. Gallery directors need time to identify which particular relationships can work in the long run. Similar reasons for choosing an artist are recorded by the manager of a leading gallery who described the important ingredients for a successful relationship as: being able 'to establish whether this is a personality that we can work with'; the quality of the work; and the commitment of both parties to building up a long relationship. But why is it important to work with the same artist for a number of years? Or, in what ways are autonomy and time related? The answer is that reputations are not created overnight; rather, they are built over a number of years. As the same interviewee says:

> There are artists that we represent, such as Fionnuala Ní Chiosáin. Now, in Ireland, to some extent, she's well known, but that's because she's been represented by our gallery for over six years. And Elizabeth Magill is someone who is incredibly talented, but again we work with her, we've been working with her for years, and we've been working on her international reputation, and it's all coming together now. And suddenly these people say that we only represent well-known artists. That's not true. In actual fact, we have been working with them for years, and because of the work that's been going on in the gallery their reputation has changed. And, you know, this will be the work that we will continue to do. But, you know, you can't just appear and have this strong reputation; it takes a little bit of time. (G6)

Another gallery director refers to time as an asset. It allows a gallery the possibility of promoting its artists in the long run, as well as giving it 'a good pedigree':

> I think because we have been around for so long that quite a few people get to know us, and they get to know the sort of work we handle, and we have, like, a fairly good pedigree. Most of our artists have actually become quite well known and gone up in price . . . so our pedigree is there and speaks for ourselves. We don't have to push too much now. (G7)

This is a good example of autonomy: this gallery does not have to strive to conquer the market; its reputation and position in the subfield speaks for itself. Yet there are also drawbacks at this point. The same gallery director mentions the difficulties they have when trying to sell works by emerging artists:

> You take a young artist and you think it's very exciting yourself, and it takes a very, very long time for people to come here and buy them rather than the others. Everybody likes the icon; nobody likes the unknown, really. (G7)

In some cases, having well-established artists associated with a gallery does not necessarily help it promote the reputation of its emerging artists. This is how the same gallery director sees the conflict:

> Why come here and buy an X when you can have a Y. Y may just have been a very nice work on paper, but it's a very, very similar or lower price to a slightly bigger X. Admittedly it was a small Y and a fairly large X, but when you come and you see it for yourself, it may be a small diamond or a large piece of something else, and you may go for the small diamond. (G7)

Another gallery provides us with a contrasting example of this time-related autonomy; for them, working with established artists gave them the luxury of developing emerging artists. As one interviewee explains:

> We're kind of known for encouraging young emerging artists, and we're very lucky to have a stable of established artists, which gives us the luxury to be able to dovetail on their reputations . . . and so far we are very successful. (G2)

In this way, the risk involved is minimized, since one bad show, although not good for the gallery's finances, is not going to have a huge effect on the gallery's reputation in the field.

As was said earlier, for Bourdieu a field's autonomy is linked to its capacity to generate scarcity. Initially, the sub-field of commercial galleries seems to enjoy a certain degree of autonomy by generating two types of scarcity: accepting only a small number of galleries into the association, and representing a small number of artists, lower than the amount of artists seeking representation. This analysis has shown that insisting on relationships that promote artists in 'the long run' also increases a gallery's autonomy since it increases scarcity for artists – that is, only a few can benefit from this kind of relationship. Given that relationships in 'the long run' need to be cultivated over a number of years, time is a crucial factor in this type of practice. Those galleries long established in the sub-field are more likely to be involved in this form of relationship than those in business for a relatively short time. Time also gives galleries the luxury of working with well-established artists, hence taking on new artists is a minor risk because they do not rely exclusively on them to keep their businesses afloat. To continue with this analysis, I explore next other forms of scarcity in the sub-field by focusing on two types of practice: the promotion of Irish art abroad, and the sale of artworks.

INTERNATIONAL RENOWN: PROMOTING IRISH ARTISTS ABROAD

The main task of commercial galleries is to promote their artists. This involves a set of common practices, such as showing their artists work in solo or group exhibitions, which are always accompanied by the publication of a catalogue. The form of catalogues varies according to the gallery's budget, and whether they are for well-established artists or emerging talents. Galleries will produce a three-fold catalogue for the latter and an elaborate catalogue for the former. Gallery shows include organizing openings, though most of my interviewees said that openings are not a major selling event; rather, sales are made in the few days beforehand. One gallery director refers to them as 'a very quiet affair. On average, the little bit of selling is done before the opening; now you just have the artist and some artist's friends, a few sort of regulars, but very, very few'. All these practices – publishing catalogues, organizing exhibitions and openings – are forms of investment designed to give artists a public profile, that is, symbolic capital. In addition, all galleries advertize in newspapers and magazines in Ireland. The supplement to *The Irish Times* (The Ticket) and the *Gallery Guide* published by the ICAGA are some of the main ones; others include *Circa* magazine and the *Irish Arts Review.* In general, galleries have a very small advertizing budget, so this is not their main promotional tool.

The form of advertizing varies according to the way directors promote their galleries. Of the seven interviews, six respondents said they had promoted their galleries internationally at different stages, and another gallery director planned to give her gallery an international role by exhibiting abroad. Three galleries advertize in international magazines; one of the reasons mentioned was 'to build our international client base more aggressively'. Five galleries have set up their own websites to promote themselves internationally. Apart from these forms of publicity, a very important practice in the creation of an international reputation is galleries' participation in international art fairs. The international art world operates as a source of symbolic capital for artists and galleries respectively. Most importantly for the present argument, it reveals the existence of another type of scarcity in the sub-field: international renown. The sub-field, as presented here, is positioned within the boundaries of Dublin's art world. This is the crucial source of national reputations, but galleries seeking international renown for their artists need to operate in an international art world. Taking part in international art fairs allows Dublin galleries the possibility of obtaining a position in the international field of commercial galleries. By the same token, exhibiting foreign artists in Dublin creates an international reputation for the galleries involved. These are then two practices that help counteract the scarcity of international symbolic capital in the Dublin art world.

All the galleries in the sub-field have participated, or have an interest in taking part, at international art fairs. Two galleries in particular are very active. In 2000, one took part in art fairs in Europe and the United States – London (UK), Basel (Switzerland), Chicago (US) and the Armory Show in New York (US). Another gallery has participated in art fairs in Cologne (Germany), Basel (Switzerland), and Chicago (US). Two other galleries, although less active, have also taken part in art fairs in the US and Europe respectively. An interviewee refers to the importance this has for Irish galleries:

> There are so many places that are coming to the fore, countries that are opening new museums, and there is a huge international art contacts that really needs to be discovered, you know. Especially when you're in Ireland, you need to work twice as hard. (G6)

Participating in art fairs involves a huge expenditure. An interviewee referred to a cost of over €30,000, which means that in order to break even they need to sell from €60,000 to €75,000 worth of works. Not surprisingly, gallery directors choose their art fairs carefully. One in particular mentions that, before embarking on such a project, he travels to art fairs 'as much as possible to assess which ones are the ones that would suit me best, or would be best showing in, and they were always with a view to showing in one in Europe, one in the US, and one in London'. International fairs are a luxury not all galleries can afford. One, for example, needed a private loan to finance its participation in an art fair in London. Expenses can be ameliorated when, as in this case, three galleries shared the cost of transporting artworks.

Besides their financial expense, art fairs are described as 'hugely risky' because they may not produce the results expected – sales or contacts – a risk which increases if we consider that the possibilities of establishing contacts is built up only after repeated visits. As one interviewee says:

> Even now not many art galleries do that, or Irish galleries do that, because it's a very expensive thing to do. It's hugely risky, especially when you're doing it for the first time. Now that the gallery is established to a certain extent, people would come back to us in the art fairs, but it takes a lot of building up and that's a high risk factor. And, you know, there were years when there was a lot of trying out, when you kind of go to the art fair, it doesn't really seem to work, it's not the result that you thought would be, or maybe a huge loss. (G6)

But there are other factors influencing galleries' participation in art fairs, despite the investment of time and money they require. One interviewee mentions the positive effect Ireland's favourable economic climate and the growing interest in Irish culture now has. This quote highlights the fact that the sub-field of commercial galleries is influenced by developments in a wider cultural field, which have an effect on its practices:

> There has been a lot of interest in Irish culture internationally, so when you go to these art fairs, people didn't even know where Ireland was [but] now there's a better interest. So when you go away you get a lot more feedback from people who have a general interest in Ireland, and they are quite interested to see what kind of artists we have. I suppose another thing would be that, with the economic climate at the moment, not that we can afford to, but you're more likely to take the risk. It's a very risky thing to go and do . . . It's just the times that we're living in at the moment are just a little bit easier. Ten years ago, the galleries could hardly even afford the rents here in Ireland. (G3)

Despite the fact that financial risks can be minimized by developments outside the sub-field, participation in art fairs continues to be a difficult affair. So why is it important for Irish galleries to take part in these international events? Is the sale of artworks worth the investment? According to two interviewees, the benefits lie in the possibility of Dublin galleries finding representation for their artists by galleries abroad. One gallery director refers to this:

> This is really the . . . fruit of repeated visits to art fairs, when galleries get to know the artists I work with – apart from any sales I might have needed to have at the fairs. I'm also looking for contacts with other galleries who would pick up on some of my artists. I don't pick; they pick me. Or I hope they pick me, and that's happened for a number of my artists, like Alice Maher, Clare Langan [these] are artists of mine who so far have been picked out and are represented by galleries abroad. (G5)

The ultimate aim of art fairs is not to sell art, but to promote Irish-based artists abroad:

> When we go out there we do quite well. I mean, each year we have broken even, I suppose, which is good. The gallery breaks even, but we make money for our artists. We also have introduced a couple of artists to international galleries through the art fairs; that's when we meet other galleries . . . It's very good not only for making clients or international contacts, but it's good for meeting other galleries and getting new international galleries for our artists. It's not just for selling, it's for promotion, for promoting artists. And a lot of artists may be very well known here and have sell-out exhibitions, but they've got to go further afield, and there's no point just staying in Ireland. (G3)

Another practice galleries have drawn from the international art world is to exhibit art from abroad in Dublin's galleries – even when these art spaces can scarcely contain local artists. The exploration of this paradox, however, can provide us with further insights into the scarcity of symbolic capital within the sub-field's national boundaries. Showing international artists in Dublin, or 'importing' art from abroad, usually – though not necessarily – with an amount of symbolic capital attached to it, has proved to be a successful gambit for some now prestigious galleries in the field. It helps galleries increase their symbolic capital, giving them prestige as agents of cultural consecration, which in turn increases the prestige of their artists. As an interviewee comments on his gallery's work with international artists:

> It's something that we would consider very important to do, and actually I think that's what has put the gallery in the position that it's in . . . I would say that the shows that we have had have always succeeded on one level or another, even if they haven't been financially successful. Very often they have helped to increase the reputation of the gallery, to strengthen it, both in Ireland and abroad, and that helps to strengthen the position of our artists, because of the reputation of the gallery. (G6)

One gallery which brought international artists to Dublin did so with the added risk of exhibiting relative unknowns. As the gallery director explains:

> The idea of showing international art with young or non-Irish artists was partly to show people outside that I was serious and committed and interested in showing very good, the best of contemporary art. That I was interested in the very best that was available, [in bringing] art as best as that was possible in an Irish context . . . If I spend the first five or ten years showing unknown artists brought from home, it's not going to create the same kind of waves or interest or send out the same kind of signals. So I just went for a kind of fast-track approach really. (G5)

Another gallery brings around 10 per cent of its exhibitions from abroad. Here the emphasis is on building up an international taste among its local clients, one based on the work of well-known foreign artists:

> So it's just bringing in international work to our Irish clients as well. I mean, we don't want to just keep feeding them with Irish work only, we want to show them that there's more out there as well. And a lot of the foreign exhibitions that we would have, they could be artists who people have never heard of here, but they are in every single museum collection in the world . . . So we just try to broaden people's horizons, I suppose, and for our clients as well. (G3)

This discussion on international renown has illustrated another side of the scarcity issue. The sub-field of commercial galleries creates scarcity because it can only produce national reputations for the artists involved. In order to give their artists reputations outside Ireland, galleries need to take part in the wider international art world. Participating in international art fairs and exhibiting foreign art are practices that give both galleries and artists international renown. They can offer high amounts of symbolic capital to artists and galleries. Financial investment and a high degree of risk characterize these practices, but international prestige is another step towards autonomy for galleries. It gives a few high levels of symbolic capital, as is does for the artists whose work they represent abroad.

SELLING ARTWORKS AND PUBLIC COLLECTIONS

The sale of artworks helps sustain the sub-field because it provides galleries with a financial return for their businesses. I said earlier that commercial galleries occupy the middle ground between the autonomous and heteronomous poles of the field of cultural production as theorized by Bourdieu. They are not driven solely by the search for financial profit, but also by the attainment of symbolic capital for their artists. The aim in what follows is to focus on the sale of artworks as a practice that also produces symbolic capital. Bourdieu highlights this issue when he argues that in the FRP economic profit is normally disavowed. What prevails, instead, is a 'profit of disinterestedness', in a field driven by the search for symbolic capital. But this raises the question: how can we regard the practice of selling art as a disavowal of economic profit? All galleries usually benefit from a 50 per cent commission on their sales, a heavy reliance on financial gain.

Commercial galleries sell to individuals, small and large businesses, corporations, and private collectors such as the AIB, the Bank of Ireland, KMPG, Anderson Consulting, as well as the Arts Council. All galleries mentioned that sales had increased as a result of the country's economic prosperity, but two interviewees were adamant that Ireland's new wealth did not automatically lead to more people buying art:

> In Ireland people with money buy a fast car, a better dress. Buying art is something that is quite specific and quite possibly even an elite pursuit or interest, and is something that you really have to educate yourself in before you start to do it properly or do it and enjoy it . . . That's a small market and it has increased, but not commensurate with the boom. (G5)

For the interviewee below, it is the quality of art that has created an interest among some people. His statement links in with what has just been said: art appreciation takes time, and those individuals with more money 'who don't buy art are not going to buy art':

> The gallery has got better, the location is better, and there are more people coming in. And there is more interest, as opposed to people having more money in their pocket. Because I find that people with more money do go on holidays and buy a new car. But as regards to more money for the arts, I find that people who don't buy art are not going to buy art if they have more money. (G4)

Another interviewee refers to the investment of time people need to make if they are to appreciate art:

> There are people who are quite knowledgeable; they know exactly what they want. They have impressive collections over many years. And then there are the new IT guys, if you will. It's not that they don't have the knowledge – they have this kind of Kevin Clainy taste, and all this minimalist stuff, which is great fun, but I think it needs more time. They just haven't got the time . . . and it's not because they aren't knowledgeable about art, they just haven't got the time. (G2)

The mention of time as an important factor in evaluating artworks brings out differences between gallery buyers themselves. There are those who have been acquainted with artworks for a long time; they possess an aesthetic disposition and know 'exactly what they want'. Conversely, the 'IT guys' may know about art, but still need the necessary time to build up the knowledge that allows them to distinguish 'good art' from all the rest on offer. But the most prestigious buyers are not affluent clients or even knowledgeable collectors, but the purchasers of museum collections. As one interviewee put it, 'that's the ultimate goal'. Two other gallery directors noted the importance of selling to museum collections:

> Of course, selling art: that's how we function. We have to, and it's, of course, it's an important part of this, especially to museum collections, because it's great for us to be able to say we're selling to such and such a museum collection. Having said that, it's also very important for the art to be out there, for the people to see the work. (G6)

> It's very important for my artists to be in [museum] collections, however big or small the work they buy is. (G5)

Further evidence of this is found in artists' resumés, which some galleries produce on their website. These typically include a description of their art practice and the type of media they work in; solo and group exhibitions; participation at international events; and, importantly, all the collections displaying works by the artist concerned. However, the capability of museums to legitimate artworks by including them in their collections raises an interesting issue, because a museum such as IMMA, established in 1991, is able to endow the work of artists with symbolic capital even though it has not been running for a very long time (see chapter 4). An interviewee made this argument in relation to IMMA and its role in promoting Irish art:

> It's very nice to have a big brother or a big sister, feeling that there is a museum where your artists may one day end up. And, when you're

> travelling, it's a kind of common platform for many other international museums and galleries, who may be less aware of the smaller galleries, of the private galleries, but who should be aware of the museum. So it kind of clarifies a presence for contemporary art in the city, and I think the absence of a major museum of contemporary art would be unthinkable at this point. (G1)

But how does IMMA create prestige for itself? The making of IMMA's collection is the topic of chapter 4; for now, suffice to say that this is a question that deserves exploration.

And yet the symbolic capital obtained by artists who sell their works to museum collections presents a paradox, too, because the commercial galleries in this study have sold very few works to museums in Ireland. One long-established gallery has sold all of seven works to IMMA, while the Hugh Lane Gallery, 'when it was active, bought in twenty years two or three pieces'. When asked as to the reasons for not buying more artworks from galleries, an interviewee said: 'I don't actually know why they don't buy. It could be a personality thing . . . I think obviously directors have a particular type of taste, and maybe we don't fit into their taste'. (G7)

Another interviewee made the same point, arguing that museum purchases are related to the type of art galleries sell:

> A lot of our artists here would be quite representational and traditional. It's not very sexy work, so they're going to look towards artists who have a greater international dimension, or artists who are very much in the news or getting a lot of publicity. So they'll buy our senior artists, but our work isn't really what they are looking for, and that's just the museum's policy. (G3)

So galleries receive the highest amount of symbolic capital for artists who sell works to museum collections, but museums seek to purchase particular types of artists, such as those with an international reputation, who might not be represented by the commercial galleries. This does not seem to be a clear-cut rule of the sub-field – another gallery has not sold any paintings to any museums apart from IMMA, but despite its short time in the sub-field, has developed a good working relationship with the museum and sold it four paintings. This suggests that museum directors may be interested in collecting art by emerging artists, also, which is the kind of work a new gallery is able to promote. This is how an interviewee refers to IMMA's former director:

Declan bought four paintings from me by three different artists. But the confidence is really good because he is interested. He comes in once or twice a year, and he invites you up to their place, and he kind of makes a big deal about you, which is nice because no one else does. I mean, the Douglas Hyde Gallery don't, the RHA don't, the Hugh Lane doesn't. I'm not even in their invitation list . . . But the museum, they make a big deal. They let you know what's on, they are nice and friendly, they introduce you to people, and say how good you are and how well you're doing, which is nice to hear, and that's why I love going to the museum. (G4)

But there is a common thread running through these views. The sale of artworks to Irish public collections is a practice generating scarcity in the sub-field of commercial galleries, because galleries are not able to sell high amounts of works to such collections. So, while offering the maximum amount of symbolic capital to artists, it also maintains the sub-field's scarcity. Another side to this issue is when there are certain works which can only be of interest to certain museum collections. This is the case with a gallery that sold a film installation to IMMA:

The number of sales I have made to Irish museums has been very small. They've made some key purchases . . . I would not have sold that to any other client. I haven't since to anyone else, it's really only museums, and it was back then the only museum that would buy that kind of work. (G5)

Moreover, despite the galleries' efforts to invite public galleries and museum directors to their openings, as well as contacting them whenever they have works that may suit their collections, none of the interviewees reported an enthusiastic response. This opens up a further issue, wherein the scarcity of purchases has led to the lack of a representative public collection of Irish art. I will deal more specifically with this in chapter 4, but it is important at this stage to point out the struggle of a commercial gallery which intended to fill a 'gap' in the FIA, but found that it could not:

Over all the years we are asked quite often where can people see what's been happening in Irish art over a period of time, and there's just nowhere to send people. And it's just an awful gap if you've been working here for so long, and at this stage I'd like it to be something that we could help. And I know we could. We started our own little group, about five people altogether. In a very short period of time we

> realised between the five of us we could actually piece together Irish-related art over fifty or sixty years. We could piece together quite well, still with a few gaps that we hoped to fill. (G7)

The group in question consisted of this gallery director, two collectors, one artist and one art historian. The project has yet to materialize.

The scarcity of purchases by Irish public institutions brings me to the end of this analysis of the sub-field of commercial galleries. The overall aim was to evaluate the practice of making symbolic capital. I started from the premise that the assessment of aesthetic value is the result, not of an individual's aesthetic preferences (e.g. gallery directors' tastes), but of the articulation of a range of practices in the sub-field. I have followed Bourdieu's argument on how the agents' capacity to produce aesthetic value is related to the amount of autonomy enjoyed by the field, focusing on the notion of 'scarcity', which he suggests as the measure of a field's autonomy. Scarcity operated in a number of practices: the building up of a relationship between artist and gallery that will work in 'the long run', participating at international art fairs, exhibiting foreign art in Dublin, and selling artworks to Irish public collections. Most importantly, scarcity is not only created within the sub-field of commercial galleries, but also originates through the sub-field's position in a wider art world. The international art world and the sub-field of public galleries, here seen as Irish public collections, exemplify the kind of relationships in which the sub-field is involved. This suggests that a field's autonomy is not only directly related to the practices taking place within the field itself, but is made possible by the strategic operations of commercial galleries both at a national and an international level.

THE SUB-FIELD OF PUBLIC GALLERIES

The rest of this chapter continues the assessment of autonomy in the FIA by looking at the sub-field of public galleries, which includes four institutions: the Royal Hibernian Academy (1823), the Douglas Hyde Gallery (1978), the HLMGMA (1908), and the IMMA (1991). The public galleries sub-field is characterized by its reliance on external sources of funding from public institutions such as the Arts Council, Dublin Corporation or the Department of Arts and Culture. They seek additional income from private sponsors or individuals willing to contribute to the galleries' finances. The main task of public galleries is the collection and exhibition of art, though only the HLMGMA and IMMA collect actively. They create symbolic capital for the artworks they collect and/or show, and in turn obtain recognition from the public. The more visitors they have, the more successful their shows are held to be. In this case the sub-field would be closer to the heteronomous pole of the FRP as described by Bourdieu, because their role is to produce 'cultural goods' for the public. However, the sub-field also relies on other forms of symbolic capital, such as reviews by art critics, who contribute by evaluating the galleries' various practices.

As has been said, the main determinant of a field's autonomy is its capacity to generate symbolic scarcity, as opposed to economic scarcity. A common thread running through these four institutions is that they all deal with contemporary art. They are autonomous because they have the power to choose what specific aesthetic they want to represent (or collect) and how they want to use or exhibit them. In this sub-field, however, scarcity acquires a new form: it is shaped by the overlap in the representation of a similar type of art by the different institutions involved.

INSTITUTIONAL OVERLAP

Art critic Brian Fallon has tackled the issue of an 'overlap' amongst Dublin's various public cultural institutions. In an article in *The Irish Times,* he referred to 'an overlapping of aims and interests' between public art galleries and museums, resulting in the public galleries' inability 'to make the most of the resources at their disposal'.[15] He adds that they 'function in a way virtually unrelated to one another. That is not the same as outright rivalry, but there is no cohesion evident, no obvious attempt to define reciprocal roles'.[16] This lack of cohesion manifests itself in the existence of various galleries acting as venues for temporary exhibitions of contemporary art; as a result, a number of galleries, says Fallon, are exhibiting works by the same artist, as in the case of Sean Scully's work, which has been shown at the DHG, IMMA and the HLMGMA. Arguably, an exhibition of this artist's work will not have the same impact when the public is able to see it at four different venues. Moreover, the public galleries must compete for the right to exhibit such an artist's work; in effect, the ability to produce symbolic capital is in itself a source of struggle.

Art critic Aidan Dunne has exposed another side to the debate. In an article in *The Irish Times* entitled 'Wanted: Good Home for Art'[17] he discussed the lack of public gallery space in Dublin, an issue which arose when two internationally renowned Irish artists, Sean Scully and Hughie O'Donoghue, donated works to the Irish state. The question was, where should they be housed? Dunne suggested the Crimea Banqueting Hall as an obvious choice, adding that it should then 'come under the auspices of an existing institution', with IMMA as the 'logical candidate', or possibly the HLMGMA. In the end, this donation came to nothing due to a 'lack of political will'.[18] The HLMGMA, however, managed to secure a substantial number of Scully's paintings to be exhibited in the gallery's new extension.[19]

The problem seems twofold: one of setting up distinct roles and functions between the various institutions; and adding new ones, such as the compilation of a representative collection of twentieth-century Irish art. However, the peculiar situation of the public galleries sub-field helps shed new light on the issue of scarcity discussed in this chapter. In the sub-field of commercial galleries, scarcity was either created by the limited amount of artists galleries were able to represent, or by the sub-field's relation to other fields – the international art world, Irish collecting institutions etc. The sub-field of public galleries reveals a rather different picture. Scarcity is generated in terms of aesthetic, because there are too many galleries dealing with the same type of art. Even though there are many more artists than public galleries in Dublin, public institutions often struggle to exhibit or collect the same Irish artists. From this point of view, aesthetic scarcity prevails in the sub-field. The remainder of this chapter will flesh out various aspects of this competition in aesthetic in all the sub-field's public galleries.[20]

EXHIBITING ART: THE DOUGLAS HYDE GALLERY AND THE IRISH MUSEUM OF MODERN ART

One common practice all public art institutions share is their role in providing venues for the temporary exhibition of contemporary art. But, when venues exhibit the same artist, this form of practice can lead to a 'competition in art displays', such as when the HLMGMA and IMMA both exhibited artworks by Francis Bacon in 2000. This competition was aggravated when the authenticity of the drawings exhibited at IMMA was disputed. An article in the *Sunday Times* noted that there was a division amongst experts on the matter, and as a result IMMA was not allowed to use Bacon's name and could only exhibit them as 'works attributed to the artist'.[21] The HLMGMA, meanwhile, put up an exhibition of some of Bacon's key works, a move debated by the press at the time, which questioned whether it was the role of a national institution to show works 'attributed' to Bacon, while a municipal gallery hosted an exhibition of some of his best originals.

This example illustrates a deep conflict over the remits of the various institutions in the sub-field. The relationship between the DHG and IMMA highlights another aspect of this conflict. As I noted earlier, since its establishment in 1959 the College Gallery – forerunner of the DHG – aimed to foster an interest in the visual arts by building up a comprehensive collection of pictures. The provision in 1967 of an exhibition space, the Exhibition Hall, facilitated the organization of exhibitions of work by Pablo Picasso, Andy Warhol, the pop art of major American and British artists, and retrospectives of Irish artists such as Paul Henry and Norah McGuinness (Dawson, 1987: 39–40). Importantly, the role of both the College Gallery's collection and the Exhibition Hall has been seen as filling the lack elsewhere of 'a significant collection of International Modernist art' (Walsh, 1991: 21). Arguably, this role was more appropriate to a collecting institution such as a national museum of modern art, which at the time was still absent from the FIA. However, the opening of IMMA in 1991 put an end to this situation, and obliged the DHG to reconfigure its role, until then regarded as the provider of the major contemporary arts venue in Ireland (Walsh, 1991: 21).

At the time of its foundation, IMMA did not have a huge art collection, a circumstance which may have influenced the emphasis it subsequently gave to temporary exhibitions. This policy was detrimental to the DHG, because IMMA was now taking up 'the prime position on the stage that the Douglas Hyde has hitherto dominated' (Hutchinson, 1991: 21). The DHG's new director, however, was optimistic, when he wrote:

> But this is as liberating as it is challenging. The Hyde can now make the most of its assets – an enviable position in the centre of the city, ample space, and a university context – to carve out a new niche for itself. The gallery can adopt a more focused exhibition policy, take more risks, and still be an intrinsic part of the fabric of the art scene. Given the right shows and a high level of intellectual debate in its

> publications, there is no reason why the Douglas Hyde should not increase its constituency and simultaneously continue to contribute to general artistic discourse. (Hutchinson, 1991: 21)

As it sought to redefine its role, the DHG aimed initially to increase its symbolic capital by 'making the most' of its geographical position in Dublin; an important point when we consider that IMMA is located in Kilmainham, about two miles from the city centre. To continue increasing its symbolic capital, the DHG was to introduce a new exhibition policy also, which meant redesigning the type of aesthetic it supported. But a new aesthetic proved not to be enough.

Three years later, the DHG's director reassessed the gallery's position vis-à-vis IMMA, and said:

> [We're] no longer the senior contemporary art gallery in the country. IMMA, given its current focus, has taken over that role. This means, for instance, that a famous international artist like Anselm Kiefer, who showed at the Douglas Hyde in 1990, would probably choose to exhibit at IMMA rather than here, were he invited to do so. A national institution, by definition, has real status. (Smith, 1994: 80)

But the disadvantaged position, or displacement in the FIA, suffered by the DHG led to a period of struggle and competition between both institutions. As Hutchinson said, if he felt the work of an artist was particularly suitable to the gallery's exhibition programme, 'I would try to convince him or her that the Douglas Hyde was the right place in which to show' (ibid: 80). Scarcity in the attainment of symbolic capital led to a struggle over the legitimation of the same aesthetic, in a race where the DHG felt it needed to maintain its symbolic capital in the FIA.

Almost ten years after IMMA's opening, the DHG's director continued to see too much of an overlap in roles. 'Our institution would like to see more of a differentiation of roles', since 'all of us, to a greater or lesser extent, are going for the same things'. As to the consequences of this situation, he adds:

> I don't think it has eased our path at all . . . there's more competition between institutions than there was. This is partly because everybody is a little more professional than they were ten or fifteen years ago.[22]

He saw improvement in the FIA overall, because 'there is more activity going on and IMMA is, of course, a major player in that activity, and without IMMA the whole scene would be devoid of a major voice'. However, there is also the need to redefine the roles of museums in the sub-field. 'It would be good, I think, in broad terms, to be able to look at a contemporary artist and then go to a museum and see the sources from which he or she is taking ideas'.[23] In this view, the museum's task would be to portray how certain artists become classics or icons, how a canon of values is formed.

This situation can be resolved by redefining the roles of each institution. In this scenario, IMMA is a museum, as opposed to a gallery space for the exhibition of contemporary art. It is difficult to predict whether this is a viable solution, given that IMMA has both roles. Maybe Fallon's proposal is what the FIA needs: 'Greater co-operation between the public art institutions and some over-all monitoring of their activities, without any sacrifice of their independence'.[24] Fallon is arguing for a reinvention of the overall structure of the sub-field, but this can be difficult to achieve. As I noted, a field's autonomy lies in its capacity to generate scarcity. Scarcity is generated in two ways: when different institutions try to fulfil a similar role in the sub-field, and when they want to exhibit a similar type of aesthetic. It is less likely, for example, that such a struggle would take place between the National Gallery of Ireland, which collects and exhibits, mainly, Old Masters, and the DHG exhibitions programme. This argument leads to a different conclusion to Bourdieu's, which sees scarcity directly related to autonomy. That is, the more scarcity a field is able to generate, the more autonomy enjoyed by that particular field. While the public institutions involved create scarcity in the field, as in the case of commercial galleries, the important point, and what differentiates this form of scarcity from that in the sub-field of commercial galleries, lies in the effects it has in the sub-field. Namely, it reduces the autonomy of some agents such as the DHG, which now has to struggle against the 'real status' of a national museum.

MODERN ART COLLECTING: THE HUGH LANE MUNICIPAL GALLERY OF MODERN ART AND THE IRISH MUSEUM OF MODERN ART

Although chapter 4 focuses on the practices involved in the making of a collection for IMMA, it is fitting at this point to discuss some aspects of the competition between the museum and the HLMGMA. One key issue is that, due to limited funding, collecting institutions such as the HLMGMA and IMMA rely heavily on donations to fund their collections. This point becomes apparent if we consider their respective acquisition budgets, which position the HLMGMA in a very disadvantaged position in realtion to the IMMA. From 1998 to 2000 the HLMGMA had an annual budget of €38,000. In 2001 its budget was €34,400, in 2002 €46,400, €56,000 in 2001, €46,000 in 2002, €35,000 in 2003 and 2004 and €20,000 in 2005.[25] In 1991 IMMA had a budget of €114,000, in 1993, 1994 and 1995 €127,000, in 1997 and 1998 €190,000, in 1999 €259,000, in 2000 €317,000, €380,000 in 2001, €512,000 in 2002, €463,000 in 2003, €464,000 in 2004 and €600,000 in 2005.[26] These acquisition budgets are low if compared with the prices paid for the work of some of the most well known contemporary Irish artists; for example, in 2001, Louis le Brocquy's *Travelling Woman with Newspaper* (1947) reached a record for the artist when it was sold in Sotheby's London for €1,741,722. At a smaller scale, more recently, in 2005, Tony O'Malley's work fetched a record for the artist when his *Haria, Lanzarote* (1988) sold for €63,000 in a Dublin auction.

To help ameliorate this disadvantaged economic situation, tax relief incentives were introduced to encourage donors resident in the Republic of Ireland to give their 'heritage items' to national collections. Section 1003 of the Taxes Consolidation Act 1997 provides for 'a non-refundable tax credit of 100 per cent against the value of the item to be donated'. The current maximum approved expenditure per year is €952,000, and a minimum of €95,000.[27] The tax act, however, applies only to items donated to the National Archives, the National Gallery, the National Library, the National Museum, the Irish Museum of Modern Art, and the Irish Architectural Archive. The HLMGMA does not qualify on the grounds that it is not a national institution. This situation gives IMMA an advantage in the sub-field of public galleries, helping it attract those individuals or groups who want to donate their works as part of the tax relief incentive. In so doing, it facilitates the attainment of symbolic capital in the form of works for the museum's collection.

And IMMA has successfully secured important donations for its collection through the tax relief act. Amongst some of these are: the Ferguson collection, a collection from the Bank of Ireland, a body of work by artist Brian Maguire, and Irish works from the Foley collection. Conversely, the director of the HLMGMA has pointed to the detrimental effect the exclusion of the gallery from the tax act has had on their collection: 'with that incentive we would be able to add to our collection of early twentieth-century Irish art; people would buy for us because they like this collection'.[28] The present legislation creates competition between IMMA and the HLMGMA, and here IMMA seems to be the winner. However, it is possible to interpret the museum's seemingly favourable position as a mixed blessing. As a senior curator for the collection at IMMA explains,[29] once the yearly limit for donations has been reached, collectors may decide to hold their donations until the following year, or they may not donate at all. This was not the case before the tax relief was put in place. This seems to suggest that the tax incentive, which puts donors in a more financially advantageous position than they were, also means that national institutions such as IMMA now have to work harder to obtain donations that would have been given to them in the first place.

Let me now link this discussion to the scarcity issue. I mentioned earlier that in the case of the DHG and IMMA scarcity prevailed for two reasons: firstly, because they exhibited a similar type of aesthetic; and, secondly, because they both wanted to play a leading role as exhibiting venues for contemporary art. In the present example, both the HLMGMA and IMMA aim to collect a similar type of art: contemporary Irish art. Even if the HLMGMA were to be included in the tax act, we would still have conflict between these two institutions, on the grounds that they collect a similar aesthetic. It would be more favourable for donors, however, who would be able to choose which institution they want to donate or loan their artworks to. With regard to the sub-field's autonomy, aesthetic scarcity in the practice of public collecting leads to struggles between agents, as we have seen. Most importantly, the existence of both aesthetic and financial scarcity in the practice of collecting reduces, rather than increases, the autonomy of the institutions involved, and this needs to be ameliorated in two ways: in the redefinition of the types of art to be collected and exhibited by each institution, and through the intervention of external forces, such as the drawing up of new legislation.

REINVENTING THE ROYAL HIBERNIAN ACADEMY

As I said earlier, the main priority of public institutions is to create symbolic capital for the artists they represent. This is also the case for the RHA, which is, as we have seen in chapter 2, an artist-run institution and the longest in the FIA. The aims of the academy are 'to encourage, advance and promote the practice of the visual arts in Ireland and the Irish public's experience of visual art' (Fallon, 2000: 11–12). My interest in what follows is to flesh out how this aim takes shape through what I call a redefinition in the production of symbolic capital by the RHA, a change that keeps a balance between two poles: tradition and innovation. Let us first review the RHA's traditional practices: membership, educational approach, and the academy's annual exhibition.

The academy is limited by charter to thirty full members and ten associate members. When a vacancy occurs, the members elect one of the ten associates to fill it. At present, the academy is seeking to expand its membership, but this process is curtailed by the restrictive conditions set out in the academy's charter of 1823, which can only be changed by an act of the Oireachtas (the houses of parliament) (Mulcahy, 2002: 42). The idea now is to expand the number of academicians by instituting a new class of senior member called senior ranking academician. This would enable the academy to bring in another ten people (ibid: 44).

At present, the academy offers an education programme, which includes lunchtime tours and evening talks. In chapter 2, I mentioned the importance of the RHA's schools in the training of artists, particularly around the end of the nineteenth century. The schools were closed in 1939 (Fallon, 2000: 13), but the possibility of re-opening them remains open to discussion. While this project has not materialized, it is relevant to mention the type of teaching the academy's schools would attempt to provide if it did. An underlying belief of the academy is the 'centrality of drawing to the practise of art' (ibid: 11) and the academy's schools would attempt to maintain a 'fundamental training in the traditions'. Arthur Gibney, President of the RHA, outlined his views on the training of future artists, and how they differ from the teaching students receive on the technique of drawing at the National College of Art and Design:

> They should [study drawing] but we don't think they do. There is so much pressure on students today to pick up all the experimental aspects – video, photography – that we feel that there's a dearth of fundamental training in the traditions. We're not interested in producing academic painters. We're interested in producing painters who have a view of tradition. I mean, we feel that the whole ideal of Academies originally was a synthesis of the arts and the study of the

> technique. Sort of a classicism and classical values, rather than the reproduction of classical formalism. And what we want to look at really is a school that teaches very high values – visual values. The visual is going out of art at the moment. It's a very traditional ideal. (Mulcahy, 2002: 47)

Gibney's support of traditional skills and perspectives stand in contrast to some of the authors mentioned earlier, in particular, Danto's arguments on how artworks 'can look like anything at all' (1997: 16).

A further aspect characterizing the academy as a traditional institution is its annual exhibition. The RHA follows its inheritance, a tradition of organizing an annual exhibition of work by academicians, which was first put in place in 1826 (Turpin, 1991: 198). It invites an open submission by other artists also, and receives an average of 2,000 entries. The exhibition displays some 400 paintings and as many sculptures, and has a turnover of around €6 million – the RHA takes a 25 per cent commission on sales (Mulcahy, 2002:45). An innovation in the annual exhibition is the inclusion of film and photography:

> [We] do value traditional relationships and disciplines and we are anxious that they should not be overlooked. We don't see ourselves at the cutting edge of experimental or installation art. It's not our constituency. But we have opened up to film as an art form, and photography. (Mulcahy, 2002: 47)

Alongside the more traditional aspects I have presented stands the RHA's eagerness to be innovative. This point becomes clear in the academy's exhibition programme, which is not run by academicians, but by the academy's director. It involves two types of exhibitions. The Ashford Gallery provides an exhibition space for artists – both academicians and emerging – and is usually designated for people who would find it very hard to get an exhibition at any of Dublin's commercial galleries because they have no previous selling records. Exhibitions at the Ashford Gallery change every three weeks, and the gallery's commission is 40 per cent (Mulcahy, 2002: 44). The Gallagher Gallery fulfils a different purpose, showing more established artists. A novelty here is the introduction of retrospectives of senior academicians' work, which create a sense of the RHA's history. These have included Melanie le Brocquy (1999), Camille Souter (2001) and Charles Brady (2002). The gallery also shows works by mid-career artists such as Grace Weir (2000) or Siobhán Hapaska (2001), both of whom represented Ireland at the Venice Biennale in 2001. Underlying this exhibition programme is the reinvention of the type of aesthetic represented by the academy. As the academy's director explains:

> It's very important that as an artist-run institution we are seen to have a fan loyalty to all forms of art, because I don't believe in form anymore as a designation for different types of art, I think all forms are valid now . . . What I am very interested in is this idea that with Asian work you're using very contemporary media to treat very traditional subjects . . . and that's an important element to get in here into the country, and also into the academy, because the academy is said to be a traditional institution, so you have to find a way to deal with those traditional topics.[30]

The position of the RHA in the FIA can be described as trying to find a balance between two roles – keeping the RHA's structure as a traditional institution with a board of academicians, which continues to hold an annual exhibition; while reinventing the RHA by playing the role of both commercial gallery and leading exhibition venue, bringing to the public work by Irish and international artists.

CONCLUSION

This chapter has provided an empirical platform for the analysis of the practice of collecting, which is the subject of chapters 4 and 5. The practices examined in this chapter do not take place in a vacuum. They are not simply the result of the tasks carried out by commercial or public galleries. The promotion of an artist's career either by selling and/or exhibiting, or collecting his/her work needs various forms of support, e.g. economic capital is necessary to run commercial and public galleries; similarly, commercial galleries draw symbolic capital from the international art world. Yet the attainment of these support mechanisms positions participants in the sub-fields in asymmetrical power relationships. The analysis of IMMA's collecting practices will shed new light on some of the existing relationships between fields.

CHAPTER 4

The Making of a Collection for the Irish Museum of Modern Art

POSTMODERN INTERPRETATION AND COLLECTING PRACTICES

THIS CHAPTER EXPLORES Bauman's notion of postmodern interpretation with a study of collecting practices at the Irish Museum of Modern Art, covering the first decade of the museum's existence, from 1991 to 2001. As discussed in chapter 1, postmodern interpretation can take two forms, legislation and translation. Postmodern legislation differs from Bauman's notion of modern legislating practices, which was analysed in chapter 2. It is situated in a world of postmodern communities, and its main function is to validate these communities, setting up their rules and criteria of criticism, as well as spelling out who the participants in a given community are. Postmodern translation facilitates communication between communities, so that statements made within the system of knowledge of one can also be understood in the other. The main theoretical question this chapter seeks to answer is whether those engaged in the practice of making IMMA's art collection articulate a postmodern legislation, or whether postmodern translation prevails. This involves asking: what is involved in the task of legislating validating communities, and how does translation between communities occur?

But drawing on Bauman's notion of postmodern interpretation poses an analytical problem, because postmodern intellectual practices occur in and between what Bauman calls postmodern communities, whereas the analytical framework used in this book follows Bourdieu's model of intellectual practices in cultural fields. The location of intellectual practices in communities and fields, according to who is theorizing them, raises the need to forge a new analytical category, reconciling the properties of both fields and communities. This means being able to designate, firstly, what type of intellectual practices occur initially in these communities/fields, who the agents are on and off communities/ fields; and, to identify, secondly, what empirical reality is being represented with the notion of community/field. The practices discussed in this chapter are those directly involved in the process of making a collection for IMMA. They were carried out by a wide range of individuals – IMMA's director at the time of this research, Declan McGonagle, as well as curators and board members – and aimed to produce symbolic capital for artworks included in the museum's collection. Symbolic capital refers to prestige and recognition, but what is explored here are the characteristics which make artworks suitable candidates to increase their symbolic capital by becoming part of a public collection. As seen in chapter 3, the practices of commercial and public galleries help create reputations for the artists they collect, exhibit, and/or represent, but some of these practices play an important role also in increasing the prestige of the businesses or institutions involved. In this sense, the production of symbolic capital is a two-way process: the more well-known the artists being exhibited, collected and/or represented are, the more symbolic capital they create for those supporting their work. This chapter continues this line of analysis and explores the role of IMMA's collecting practices in the production of symbolic capital by asking the following questions: how does IMMA produce and increase the symbolic capital of its collected artworks? And how is IMMA able to provide symbolic capital for itself; does it rely on the help of other institutions to do so?

IMMA is an institution involved in the collection and display of modern art. This role makes it part of the FMAC (chapter 2), together with the HLMGMA, as well as being a participant in the sub-field of public galleries (chapter 3). The analytical category community/field, however, encompasses another way of representing IMMA's position: it can be interpreted as a sub-field in the FMAC located within the FIA. The main reason for designating IMMA as a sub-field, as will be seen in this chapter, is that IMMA has been given a distinctive individual identity, which differentiates it from any other collecting and exhibiting institutions in the FIA, including the HLMGMA. But does this mean that all institutions are sub-fields? I would argue against the idea that all art museums can be theorized as sub-fields. A sub-field is brought about through the definition of its boundaries – in other words, by defining its general approach to collecting and exhibiting art, its engagement with the society of which it is part, and its relationship with the public. As shown in chapter 3, the lack of an Irish museum of modern art was made manifest before IMMA's foundation, but the precise nature of its function is something that has been shaped by those in charge of running the museum from day to day. Thus a component of this study of collecting practices is to identify the practices involved in giving IMMA its purpose. This entails focusing on the production of the sub-field's boundaries, the type of knowledge or worldview that gives IMMA its own distinctive position. Setting up the boundaries of postmodern communities is a concern in Bauman's theory of intellectual practices; the difficulty, he says, is 'how to draw the boundaries of such community as may serve as the territory of legislative [postmodern] practices' (1987: 5). I argue that Bourdieu's concept of symbolic power is pertinent to the study of a sub-field's boundaries. He defines this power as 'the legitimate vision of the social world and its divisions. It does not exist *per se* in the ideas expressed by agents, but in the belief of the legitimacy of the words' (Bourdieu, 1977: 117). Setting up and legitimating the boundaries of a community can be translated into the making of symbolic power for, in this case, a sub-field. That is, at stake is the validation of a community, from its aim and purpose, to the ways in which it seeks to implement its role.

AN OVERVIEW OF IMMA'S COLLECTION

Before starting to analyze IMMA's collecting practices, it is pertinent to provide an overview of some of the works included in the museum's collection at the time of this research. In 2001, it included over 4,000 artworks, mainly by twentieth-century Irish and non-Irish artists, of which approximately 330 were purchases made by the acquisitions sub-committee.[1] The collection has been developed by purchase, loans and donations, as well as by the commissioning of new works.[2] IMMA inherited from the Royal Hospital Kilmainham (RHK) the Madden Arnholz print collection, donated in 1987, spanning the history of European print-making up to the end of the nineteenth century.[3] But the backbone of the collection was the donation by collector Gordon Lambert of more than 300 pieces, particularly Irish works dating from the early 1960s onwards. This donation was made to commemorate IMMA's opening, although Lambert continued to be a benefactor to the museum until his death in 2005. In 1990 the O'Malley collection of 150 works by major artists like Jack Butler Yeats, Louis le Brocquy and Paul Henry was offered on permanent loan.[4] Part of the Lafrenz collection was offered on an eight-year loan in 1992,[5] and three years later IMMA secured a ten-year loan of works by print-maker Mary Farl Powers.[6] In 1996 the Weltkunst collection of contemporary British art was loaned for ten years. It includes sculptors' drawings by leading British artists from the early 1980s to the present day, such as Richard Deacon, Anthony Gormley and Damien Hirst.[7] In 1997 Vincent and Noeleen Ferguson donated thirty-five works by Irish artists or artists closely associated with Ireland, a small collection which represents most of the dominant strands in Irish painting. The donation includes paintings by Brian Maguire, Elizabeth Magill and Michael Mulcahy.[8] In 1998 IMMA accepted on a two-year loan the Musgrave Kinley Outsider Art Collection. Set up by the late Victor Musgrave and curated since 1984 by Monika Kinley, the collection comprises over 750 works by artists outside the traditional mainstream world of art. In 1999 the loan was extended for another six years;[9] the loan was extended indefinitely in 2001.[10] In 2000 there were three donations and loans. The Jefferson Smurfit Group plc donated 150 prints, mainly by Latin-American artists, from the collection Smurfit: Cartón y Papel de México Collection. A long-term loan of fifty works was made by Maire and Maurice Foley, who have also funded the purchase of other works for the museum's collection.[11] That same year, IMMA received a long-term loan by George and Maura McClelland of 400 artworks from the 1970s, '80s and '90s. The collection is particularly strong in mid-twentieth-century Irish painters and sculptors, and Northern Irish artists in particular.[12]

MAIN PLAYERS BEHIND THE MAKING OF IMMA'S COLLECTION

The main participants involved in making IMMA's collection are the museum's director, its non-executive board, and the museum's senior curators. The first board was set up in February 1990 when the Taoiseach (prime minister)[13] appointed a chairperson to run the board for IMMA's first five years. Usually boards consist of twelve to fifteen members appointed by the Minister for Arts, Heritage, Culture and the Gaeltacht (changed in 2002 to Minister for Arts, Sport and Tourism), and include politicians, businessmen, architects, art collectors and critics, as well as artists. There is a close relationship between political power and the management of cultural institutions, since board members are political appointments. The museum's first board had to appoint a director, a task given to a temporary sub-committee. Boards are divided into various sub-committees: acquisitions, finance, buildings and operations, human resources, and education and community. Decisions regarding the collection need the approval of the board, and are first made by the acquisitions sub-committee, whose task is 'to identify and recommend acquisitions by purchase, donation or long-term loan'.[14] With an average of four to five members, the sub-committee meets once a month or every six weeks; unless an urgent decision needs to be made, in which case a new meeting is arranged. IMMA's director, who acts as chief executive and manager of the museum, also participates in sub-committees. The senior curators of IMMA's programming departments – collection, temporary exhibitions and education and community – play a significant role in the process of collecting by attending and bringing their own proposals to the acquisitions sub-committee.[15] In practice, all board members have the opportunity to attend any of these sub-committees, but there is always a core membership designed by the chairperson, which together with the chairperson and the director have a vote in acquisitions. Senior curators do not have a vote.

The following analysis draws on data obtained in twelve open-ended interviews carried out between 2000 and 2001, and included the three senior curators of IMMA's programming departments, as well as those board members who agreed to be interviewed. While a particular attempt was made to interview board members who participated in the various acquisitions sub-committees, interviews also include members who were not part of this sub-committee, but who had their own views on IMMA's collection. The sample obtained is representative of the workings of acquisitions because it includes members from different boards, but is limited in that, even though all board members were contacted, not all agreed to be interviewed. The first board ran until 1994, and was followed by a second board from 1994 to 1999, and a third board, which started in February/March 2000. At the time of the interviews IMMA's third board had just been appointed. This board differed from previous ones in that only two members were re-appointed – a greater number had kept their position in previous boards. The most relevant interviews in terms of exemplifying the practices of collecting are those with members of the first and second boards because the acquisitions sub-committee of the third board had only been active for a short space of time.[16]

Given that public access is not granted to meetings of the board or those of the acquisitions sub-committee, this research is based on the statements obtained in interviews with board members. This information is complemented by various other sources such as newspaper articles, museum catalogues and press releases. Most of the interviews referred to here were with members of the first and second boards, which spanned IMMA's first ten years in operation. This means that their practices took place in the context of an emerging institution, thus what is presented is the practice of making a new collection. It is possible that if the present analysis had been based on data collected from later boards, the results or relationship between legislating and translating practices would have differed consistently.

At the time of the interviews, IMMA's director was about to leave the institution as a result of a disagreement at board level concerning the renewal of his five-year contract. Although this chapter will not be dealing with the public debate behind this episode, it meant that the director was not available to be interviewed for this research. To offset this, I have relied on alternative sources, such as previous interviews given by the director and newspaper articles more generally. In view of this delicate situation, and despite the fact that the interviews did not deal with the conflict between board and director, the identity of board members has been kept anonymous; numbers have been added to the material quoted to make clear when they belong to the same interviewee. The names of IMMA's staff members included in this research have been made public with their consent.

THE IMPORTANCE OF BEING AN IRISH MUSEUM OF MODERN ART

On 5 October 1987, Taoiseach Charles Haughey announced the establishment of a gallery of modern art in the Royal Hospital Kilmainham (RHK). A former retirement home for the British army built in 1686, the RHK is situated about two miles from Dublin's city centre. The announcement marked the end of a long struggle to designate a function for the RHK. Its origin goes back to August 1978 when the Department of the Taoiseach issued a press release announcing the Taoiseach's approval of a plan to proceed with the restoration of the building.[17] The idea was to utilize it as a conference centre for Ireland's Presidency of the European Council of Ministers in 1984.[18] Beyond that, the building was to be given a public use and 'should be available to as wide a sector of the public as possible'.[19] A committee was set up to report on its possible uses, but even after its 25 million restoration in 1987, the future of the RHK, widely regarded as Ireland's finest seventeenth-century building, was still not secure.[20] The proposal to use it as a conference centre was dismissed when Dublin Castle was found to be a more appropriate location.

The announcement that the RHK would become the long-awaited institution of modern art created controversy from the beginning. Indeed, every single aspect – its location, funding, function and collection – stirred public opinion. It meant a proposal to have the gallery in Stack A, an 1820s building in Dublin's docklands, was turned down. Renovating Stack A would have required major financial expenditure by the government, while the RHK seemed a better choice because it needed only minor alternations to be converted into a museum. It also pre-empted the possibility of housing part of the National Museum in the RHK. On 17 November 1989, the Taoiseach announced that Ireland's gallery of modern art would be opened in 1991 as part of Dublin's City of Culture programme.

IMMA was opened on 25 May 1991. To commemorate the occasion, Taoiseach Charles Haughey gave a speech which can be understood as an attempt to settle some of the controversies surrounding the museum. He referred to the country's vitality and creativity in the visual arts, a movement which had started in the nineteenth century, continued after independence, and was still in place. The museum, 'a cultural priority of high order', was to give Irish art its proper place, both in its national context and internationally:

> Outside the creativity of the individual artists themselves, I am convinced that nothing could have a more profound effect on the general level of artistic achievement in our country than the establishment of this Museum. By means of it, Irish art will not only take its place internationally but will also go one step nearer to taking the place it should undoubtedly have in the life of Ireland itself.[21]

The rest of the speech responded to some of the criticisms launched against the museum. It emphasized that the RHK was the right location for the museum because it situated Ireland in line with other European countries, like Italy, France and Spain, where historic buildings had been turned into art museums. The museum was not to be a neutral white space for the exhibition of art because in a historic building 'art is not robbed of its place in the historical continuum in which we all live'.[22] Moreover, IMMA was to give Irish art the prestige it deserved by placing it alongside foreign works and thus making it known worldwide. This opening speech is an example of how IMMA was being constituted as a sub-field, with its own distinct identity. As will be seen later in this chapter, some of the issues raised by Haughey acquired a new significance as they were incorporated into IMMA's worldview, particularly the idea of an historic building as a setting for the display of art.

REINVENTING THE ROYAL HOSPITAL KILMAINHAM: A WORLDVIEW FOR IMMA

IMMA's appellation immediately calls attention to its boundaries vis-à-vis other institutions. As we saw in chapter 3, the foundation of a national museum caused the restructuring of the FIA, particularly in relation to the position of the DHG. But in order to maintain its primary position as the only national institution for the collection and exhibition of modern art, IMMA relies on a series of intellectual practices that reproduce this status. Two practices in particular have served this purpose: the creation of IMMA's worldview, or *raison d'être;* and the development of a policy for its collection.

The term worldview is not originally IMMA's, but it is used here to bring together public statements about the museum's role and function made by its director, mainly in a number of press interviews. However, McGonagle also made clear that his views on the museum needed the general consensus of the board: 'All the board wrote that. We talked about what it would be, how it would work, what general remit we needed'.[23] The board had an instrumental role in transforming the director's philosophy into a publicly known worldview for IMMA, yet the ideas I present here are distinctly his. In an interview he offered in *Artscribe* in summer 1990 he referred to the opposition between process and product, use and ownership, and the need for art to address its context. These concerns, as we will see, are also present in IMMA's worldview. But the need to redefine the notion of museums as 'treasure houses of art' is a constant theme in the director's thinking. As McGonagle points out, 'I would hope that every word in the title [Irish Museum of Modern Art] would take on a completely new meaning in the future'.[24] The 'treasure house' type museum which emerged in nineteenth-century Europe was concerned with fixing values through the collection, classification and display of objects. For McGonagle, this model was redundant; rather, 'the function of museums at the end of the twentieth century has to be to test and unfix values'.[25] This view was also echoed in another interview only a few days before IMMA's opening, when he addressed the need to rethink previous definitions of museums, art and buildings:

> One of our tasks in the long term will be to redefine what a museum can be, first of all here in Dublin and in Ireland, but then in Europe and the future. There are lots of definitions around about art, about museums, about buildings. We have to keep what's of value but reject what's redundant.[26]

The idea of rethinking definitions of art and of museums based on testing and unfixing values, is characteristic of a postmodern critique of modern art as seen in chapter 1. In modernity, modern art was something that could be deciphered, understood, analyzed by aestheticians and art critics, whereas IMMA articulates a distinctively postmodern stance, which goes against any attempt to fix any definitions of art and of museums. For now, two questions come to the fore: how is the distinction between the museum as a treasure house and a new museological model achieved? And what does it seek to reject or keep? An answer to these questions can be found in IMMA's initial exhibition catalogue, *Inheritance and Transformation*, which carried a foreword by McGonagle. He referred to the inheritance of a 'modernist, hierarchical, centralist world' in which Ireland was beyond the Pale; this modernist world had been transformed into a 'problematic, millennial world' and in this new context 'the Pale cannot exist'.[27] The reference to a change from a hierarchical to a problematic world is linked here to Ireland's status as a British colony, when it was 'beyond the Pale'. In the new post-colonial situation, the hierarchies which prevailed during modernity are to be transcended, problematized, and part of this task is to define IMMA's function in Irish society:

> In Ireland, at the end of the twentieth century the Museum of Modern Art must acquit its public responsibilities by making a conscious contribution to the process of transformation of our social and cultural inheritance which is already under way. The task will involve redefining existing language and creating new structures which will serve this inclusive rather than exclusive approach. To engage with this reservoir of meaning is to engage with artists and non-artists as equal participants in an ongoing cultural process, not as producer and consumer.[28]

This comment raises a number of interesting points, which can help structure the main arguments behind IMMA's worldview. Firstly, the notion that museums can contribute to a process of transformation of existing social and cultural values. Secondly, in order to be part of this transformation, museums need to develop new agendas in two ways: by redefining an existing language and creating new structures. One example of redefining an existing language is the promotion of an alternative way of thinking about art, which is one of IMMA's founding principles. For McGonagle, a new notion of aesthetic is part of a wider need to keep up with a changing world:

> We're at a moment when all economic, social, political and cultural structures, which had seemed very secure, are being turned upside down. I don't think any word as crucial as art can retain the meaning that we thought it had.[29]

In this context, the museum's specific task must be to renegotiate existing forms of knowledge about art and its value, and the art world more generally. Namely, definitions of 'artist and non-artist, and of the categorizations which had traditionally ascribed value to art, artists and cultural institutions in society'.[30] In an interview, the director explained how the museum was to take on this task of redefining art:

> What we have to do is to understand that art in particular is contested rather than consensual. Our job is to exhibit that contest. Sometimes we do that within exhibitions, with the le Brocquy show, for instance. It was a clear contest with his earlier work and his later work. Sometimes we do it between exhibitions, like with the le Brocquy, the Beverly Semmes and the Event Horizon. And sometimes we do it between individual works, like the collection show, different approaches to a theme. The idea is that we always have four or five shows running; a multiple experience rather than a singular experience; a contested experience rather than a consensual experience.[31]

Chapter 5 discusses some of the complexities involved in the idea of art as a contested area by exploring the visual arrangement of various exhibitions of IMMA's collection. For the moment, it is fitting to reflect further on the notion of a shift from art as consensus to art as a source of contest. The related argument, that IMMA's task was to create a multiple, contested experience for viewers, was facilitated by the museum's location in an historic building. In fact, the benefit of locating contemporary art in such a place was another argument in how IMMA sought to redefine the experience of looking at art:

> At the end of the twentieth century, the new agenda, far from finding a white cube somewhere, is to locate art in a place that is highly charged politically and socially in ways that everyone can understand. The clean white box came from an attitude that disconnects art from life. That's not what we want here.[32]

But the agenda of locating art in a classical architectural context was not merely a way of defying a 'white box' space or exhibition design. It went further than a mere attempt to redefine ways of seeing or experiencing art; according to McGonagle, IMMA's location in a seventeenth-century building, a former retirement home for British soldiers, is what made it such a crucial player in the transformation of social structures:

> [The RHK] places us in a European context. You can't walk in here and not think of other European references. What we've to do is not pretend that we're living without a past but to acknowledge it and explore it and use it in some way in the transformation process that's at work in society. That's the task.[33]

McGonagle's views shed new light on a point made earlier on; in order for museums to be part of a transformation of existing values they needed to develop new structures. The RHK seemed to provide this opportunity. It was a key reference in situating Ireland as part of a wider European context because the building is suggestive of similar architectural contexts on the continent – McGonagle was probably thinking about the Hôtel des Invalides in Paris. It also brought to out how the function of a museum was to explore the past, and how through this exploration IMMA was participating in a wider transformation process. But the idea of engaging with and exploring the given past has further consequences. It positions IMMA as a key institution involved in helping redefine Ireland's colonial history, of which the RHK, a former hospital for British soldiers, is part. The proposal for a new museological agenda is in this way linked to a conceptualization of a millennial, post-colonial world.

The role given to Irish art in helping to blur concepts such as core and periphery, and to address questions of identity, facilitates an understanding of McGonagle's thinking as to how IMMA was to deliver its aims. As he explained in an interview:

> What does it mean to be Irish, for example? This debate has been going on in theatre and literature far longer than in the visual arts. I think that being able to engage with that debate and being able to

> contribute to it could put us culturally in the centre rather than on the margins. What in the '70s used to make Ireland marginal, that is, the unsettled nature of the identity issue, when everything seemed settled in Europe, all of that has changed, so the very thing that used to make us marginal can now make us central. (Castle, 1991)

The implication here is that Irish art can re-position Ireland, from the periphery of Europe to its centre, by engaging in a critical debate over issues such as national identity. In this way, Irish art is seen as a redeeming force; it not only addresses its local context, it also helps transcend it. However, the idea that Irish art can bring Ireland to a cultural centre undermines an earlier argument IMMA's director made on the need to redefine artistic values and definitions. Here the hierarchy between centre and margin is being kept, although Ireland can claim to have moved its position in this hierarchy. A related argument, running through the distinction between the local and international contexts, is how the museum should engage with these two constituencies:

> I regard the museum as a conversation. We should be in conversation with everyone. No one should be left out, locally, nationally, internationally. You have to be international and local at the same time. I believe it is possible for anyone to negotiate the meaning of contemporary art, if given the opportunity. And it's up to us to provide that access to local people.[34]

IMMA's three programming departments – education and community, exhibitions and collection – all work together to put into effect IMMA's worldview, and its emphasis on being both a local and an international museum.

The education and community department (E&CD) is built around the perception of art as part of its constituency, and of IMMA as an inclusive museum. The link between art and its community or context is clearly stated by McGonagle: 'What I'd like to move away from is the idea of the quality of art being determined separate from a wider constituency'.[35] The museum's task here is to address its local constituency of Kilmainham, and Dublin. He explains how:

> In all of its aspects, IMMA will emphasize the connection that exists between the artist and the art institution, the society and community within which they both work . . . we will address the particular locality of Kilmainham and Inchicore and extend that address to other parts of the city of Dublin and indeed other parts of Ireland. (McGonagle, 1991: 62)

The education and community programme, organized by the E&CD, exemplifies at its best IMMA's role as an inclusive museum. It is part of McGonagle's attempt to redefine the role of cultural institutions, particularly the notion that the audience for contemporary art lives in the wealthy areas of Dublin, not in Kilmainham. A museum's task is to renegotiate this hierarchy between art audiences by expanding, as opposed to limiting, public participation in the visual arts. In fact, this is a second premise shaping the E&CD. Senior curator for the department, Helen O'Donoghue explains its remit:

> Our brief in the Education and Community Department from the outset has been to be inclusive rather than exclusive and the programme aims to establish new ways of creating a forum where artists and public(s) can meet and where meaningful exchange and reciprocal learning can take place . . . The Museum aims to develop opportunities for the public to participate in cultural activity, to encourage personal expression through creative opportunities and to develop confidence when encountering contemporary art.[36]

The international remit of IMMA finds its expression in all three programming departments, but its most obvious expression lies in the activities of the exhibition department (ED). Temporary exhibitions are designed to establish IMMA as a museum with an international orientation. The department brings together international and national artists, and collaborates with international museums in the exhibition-making process, e.g. through loans of particular artworks. Writing on the museum's first ten years, the senior curator of the ED says of its programme:

> The policy of the Exhibition Programme is to make exhibitions of twentieth century and contemporary art by emerging and established contemporary artists as well as by historically important twentieth-century figures. Since its inauguration the Museum has consciously positioned itself and all its programmes in an international context, and, after ten years of consistently innovative, entertaining and thought-provoking programming, has established itself as an international Museum with a proven reputation, whilst at the same time developing effective working relationships with national and local constituencies.[37]

The organization of temporary exhibitions is seen as giving IMMA an international reputation, while the museum is also able to operate at the level of the local, developing relationships with its surrounding community and the country at large. IMMA's collecting policy will be addressed in detail later in this chapter, but it is important to point out now how the collection department (CD) reflects the museum's worldview of being local and international at the same time. As the senior curator of the CD, Catherine Marshall, explains:

> We don't want this place to be just about Irish art; we want it to be completely international . . . So we are saying that it is the Irish Museum of Modern Art just because it is sited in Ireland and because the way this place develops is shaped by Irish minds and Irish history and an Irish context, but the art collection is not bound by Irishness at all. (Marshall, interview, 2001)

The intellectual arguments presented here constitute a system of knowledge, which delineates the boundaries of IMMA as a sub-field. The making of these boundaries is a practice which creates symbolic power for IMMA, giving it its distinct role and identity. This discussion has focused on this knowledge-making practice, highlighting the type of role and function IMMA is meant to fulfil. Starting from the premise that the museum poses a challenge to the treasure-house model, its worldview is based on the possibility of creating new structures and ways of thinking about the role of museums in the twenty-first century. A crucial issue here is how IMMA is defined as bringing in a new kind of museum, which can contribute to the transformation of social and cultural values. Other related arguments in its worldview are its aim of redefining existing ways of thinking about art and the experience of viewing it: by proposing art as a contested concept, exhibiting it in an historic building, and giving it a key role in repositioning Ireland from the 'periphery' of Europe to its 'centre'. Finally, IMMA is presented as an inclusive museum, one which encourages the surrounding community to take part in the visual arts, while also establishing relationships at a national and international level. The museum's three programming departments are charged with developing these various forms of engagement.

The making of IMMA's worldview exemplifies the workings of postmodern legislation, which seeks to legitimate the boundaries being set up for IMMA as a sub-field of the FIA. The validation of IMMA's sub-field is dependent only on the criteria developed within the sub-field itself; it does not need to have its worldview endorsed by other agents, such as commercial or public galleries, in the FIA. This is not to say that IMMA does not need to be accountable, for example, in terms of museum visitors, to the Irish government, from which it receives its funding, as will be discussed later on in this chapter.

The discussion so far has shown how IMMA's three programming departments follow and put into practice the museum's worldview. In so doing, they are endorsing and legitimating the boundaries of the sub-field. Defining a museological agenda for IMMA, a particular aesthetic for this new model, and exploring the role of museums as agents of transformation are ways of setting up what Bauman (1987:5) calls 'procedural rules' for a given sub-field. These rules, or knowledge framework, give IMMA a particular standpoint in debates over, for example, what counts as value in art.

A POLICY FOR AN ART COLLECTION

Although IMMA's director had referred to his ideas for a collection in various press interviews,[38] they were also presented to the public in the first catalogue for the museum's collection published in 1998.[39] In its foreword, he refers to the collection's development since the museum's opening in 1991. By now, the museum owned 583 artworks, including donations. The Contemporary Irish Art Society and the Friends of the National Collections (see chapter 3) were amongst those who donated works to the museum. Loans, both short and long term, have added to the collection. Most important in this discussion is the formulation of a policy for collecting: 'the Museum only purchases current work by living artists, which includes those artists who work collaboratively, and encourages loans and donations of works going back to the nineteen-forties'. The difference in emphasis between purchasing contemporary works while also accepting loans and donations of more historical works is strategic, because the museum's budget only allows the purchase of contemporary works; historical works tend to be more expensive. The museum's policy of collecting works by living artists is presented, in fact, as one aspect of the new way of thinking about museums:

> In Museum practice generally it is no longer taken as a given that collecting institutions can provide a complete permanent consensual representation of anything. As a new institution the Irish Museum of Modern Art is in a strong position to be part of this new thinking and to represent the present by collecting works more or less as they are made. The centre of gravity of the Collection therefore is in the present and, if maintained, this process will ensure that the Museum's Collection will become historical over time and be representative of its own period.[40]

The use and definition of the collection is linked to the museum's worldview; as is stated in the catalogue, IMMA's collection is 'directly related to the strategic identity of this Museum'.[41] An example of this is the juxtaposition of exhibitions of the collection with exhibitions in other programmes – education and community, for example – to challenge the existence of a 'single chronology of art in the second half of the twentieth century'. The collection has a key role in this process; as McGonagle says, it is instrumental in negotiating value in art:

> It is not necessary, therefore, for the Museum to own any one specific chronology of the past in order to show it. The problem with a singular reading of the past is that it can turn artworks into specimens which, like butterflies, have to be killed in order to be classified. Art making is dynamic. Its meaning has to be negotiated each time it is experienced and the Museum aims, in building its Collection in the present, to sustain rather than suffocate that dynamic and that process of negotiation for the public. The alternative would be to accept pre-determined art historical and institutional boundaries where the task would be to fill up a given matrix rather than renegotiate the matrix itself.[42]

The policy defining the collection echoes the museum's worldview, in particular its aim of redefining an existing language of aesthetics. If exhibitions were a means of providing a multiple and contested experience for viewers, the collection has a similar purpose: to help renegotiate a museological agenda in which museums open up the meaning of artworks to their audiences:

> The making of this Collection and indeed this Museum is based on the idea that artists, the Museum and the viewer are in history and not merely observing it. Since the targets therefore are moving rather than fixed this Collection can never be complete. In that sense the Collection will always be in the making.[43]

So far, collecting is seen as a reflection of the museum's overall worldview. However, in order to explore further the intellectual practices involved in developing a policy for collecting, it is appropriate to look next at IMMA's conceptualization of the term 'modern art'.

The definition of what counts as 'modern art' is the key to IMMA's criteria for collecting, and has partly developed as a response to what has been referred to in chapter 3 as an 'institutional overlap' in the FIA, an overlap which occurs when two institutions collect and display the same type of art. IMMA's director was quite explicit about how the museum's collection is directly related 'to the other public collecting institutions in Ireland with which this Museum shares aspects of art activity in the twentieth century'.[44] The HLMGMA is a case in point, as both institutions are part of the FMAC. The overlap in the type of art they collect is precisely the reason why IMMA's policy has been designed to draw a line in relation to the type of 'modern art' it includes. Marshall explains the situation: 'it was appropriate for us to have some kind of starting point because otherwise there is too much duplication going on between the other national collecting institutions and ourselves' (Marshall, interview, 2001).

IMMA's collecting policy is related also to other sets of practices taking place in the FIA and the international art world. The definition of 'modern art' included in the policy is based on some of the events in the history of the FIA, and on developments in a wider international art world. Marshall clarifies this link:

> [1940] it's really the year in which modernism took off in Ireland . . . in which the White Stag group were established in Ireland. They were a very avant-garde, international group. They came here to get away from the war in the rest of Europe. It's also around the time, 1943 to be more precise, when the first Irish Exhibition of Living Art was held . . . the first really modernist forum in Ireland. The third reason for picking that period, the 1940s, is that it was a period of great change internationally and international modernism really took off around then with the New York school. Artists from Europe flew into New York to get away from the political climate, so it was as good a point as any; good internationally and good nationally, so we pitched at that. (Marshall, interview, 2001)

The term 'modern art' follows developments outside IMMA's sub-field. IMMA collects from the 1940s because this was an exciting period in Irish art and a time of change at an international level. IMMA's collecting policy is also concerned to create a link between Irish and international art. Marshall explains how:

> The vast majority of works in the collection are Irish because it's what we know best . . . But I think it's equally important that we temper that with good international works so that the Irish artists that we buy are not being put into a ghetto of some Irish collection that is only known to be Irish. It says something really significant about Irish artists like Kathy Prendergast or Dorothy Cross if their work is shown alongside Damian Hirst or Gilbert and George or the Kabokovs . . . We don't think they are inferior to those international artists, and

> equally it means that when international curators and critics and visitors come to visit the museum . . . they also see Irish art of quality on an equal footing and they go away talking about it. (Marshall, interview, 2001)

This policy can be seen as a way of setting up an international standard for Irish art; that is, a practice meant to increase the symbolic capital of Irish art in the juxtaposition of displays of Irish and international works from the collection. Chapter 3 gave a similar example of some commercial art galleries bringing art from abroad as a means of giving symbolic capital to their businesses. The difference is that IMMA's desire is to incorporate works of international renown from outside Ireland in order to accentuate the high standard of Irish art.

The discussion of IMMA's policy has introduced two different aspects of policy-making. Firstly, how it follows the principles shaping IMMA's worldview; in this sense, it can be argued that the making of this policy articulates a postmodern legislation, developed in a way that gives the museum a role in the type of art that should be collected. A particular example is the view that collecting does not intend to fix value in art – that is, owning 'any one specific chronology of the past in order to show it'. Collecting, as seen here, is a practice which follows the museum's basic principles: the negotiation of aesthetic value each time audiences experience art in the museum. Secondly, IMMA's collecting policy has an international element. The museum's definition of 'modern art' follows developments in the FIA and internationally, while there is an emphasis on collecting international art as a foil for Irish works. The important point here, and what differentiates IMMA's worldview from its collecting policy, is that this second aspect of policy-making illustrates another type of skill in postmodern interpretation: translation between fields. Translation is a practice whereby events outside IMMA's sub-field are incorporated into one particular practice of the sub-field, the making of its collecting policy, particularly the description of 'modern art' which it employs. This example helps shed new light on Bauman's notion of postmodern translation. For him translating is an expertise geared towards avoiding the distortion of meaning between communities. Each community has a distinct knowledge system, and thus it requires the intellectual skill of translation to make knowledge comprehensive to individuals in different communities. But the type of translation at work here supports the practice of postmodern legislation, exemplified in the creation of a collecting policy. Postmodern translation is the practice involved in providing IMMA's professionals with the necessary knowledge, or concepts from surrounding fields, e.g. 'modern art', to make a distinctive policy for IMMA's collection. The rest of this chapter explores how these frameworks are put to work in the practice of collecting, as well as assessing how far it can be argued that collecting is a form of legislation and/or translation.

THE MAKING OF IMMA'S COLLECTION: ACQUISITIONS

The museum's collection is mainly the responsibility of the collection department (CD), which is in charge of its exhibition programme and the proper storage of all the artworks. But collecting is a concerted effort, and it involves the efforts of IMMA's two other departments, the exhibition department (ED) and the education and community department (E&CD), as well as the activities of the acquisitions sub-committee.

Collecting and the Exhibition Department

The ED is in charge of organizing a calendar of temporary exhibitions for the museum. Some of its exhibitions have brought to Dublin artists, both Irish and non-Irish, with international reputations, such as Pablo Picasso, Ilya and Emilia Kabokov, Juan Muñoz, Antony Gormley, Gilbert and George, Louis le Brocquy, Kiki Smith and Sean Scully. But the ED also brings works by young international artists, and in so doing it expands their reputation. A case in point is video artist and photographer Gillian Wearing, whose work was exhibited at IMMA in 1997, the year she was awarded the Turner Prize (the £20,000 sterling prize is the British art world's most important award).[45]

The ED has been successful at organizing awards for artists through initiatives such as the Glen Dimplex Artists Award and the Nissan Arts Project. The Glen Dimplex Award was launched in 1994 with a prize worth some €20,000. The award is open to Irish artists for work exhibited at home or abroad in the previous year, and to non-Irish artists who have exhibited in Ireland.[46] Its purpose is to place Irish art in an international context, and raise the profile of contemporary art and contemporary Irish artists. Irish art critic Aidan Dunne has defined it as the 'successor to the GPA Emerging Artists Award', a scheme in place during the 1980s (see chapter 3);[47]

this connection indicates the important role the ED can play in producing symbolic capital for artists in the FIA. The Nissan Arts Project, sponsored by Nissan Ireland, started in 1997 and continued in 1998 and 2000 when its budget topped €125,000.[48]

The organization of exhibitions and the provision of awards are ways of assigning symbolic capital to artists and the artworks exhibited. In turn, exhibiting works by renowned international artists like Picasso increases the symbolic capital of IMMA's sub-field, seen in its ability to secure exhibitions of works by prestigious artists. Through its exhibition programme, the ED has built a network of contacts with artists, and is thus able to encourage them to sell, donate or loan works to the museum's collection. The museum also buys from the exhibition programme:

> There's a very strong relationship between the international exhibition programme, or, if it's Irish, and acquisitions, because you know it builds up a memory as well, and it means if you've got a good work you know it's a good opportunity to buy pieces. Artists . . . it's like they go away feeling fantastic every single time, and that's absolutely true. So a lot of times they want to donate work and they certainly want to discount work because they want to be in our collection, as much as I want them in our collection. And then it's very nice because it's a continuum and it's a way of getting international artists' work into the collection. (MacParland, interview, 2001)

Through its ED the collection has received works from well-known artists such as Juan Muñoz's *Conversation Piece for Dublin* in 1994, (see image 3, chapter 5), which had been on loan to the museum since the artist's exhibition at IMMA that year. Purchases of works from previous exhibitions offer the advantage of bringing high amounts of symbolic capital to IMMA's collection because they are acquired at a stage when they have already been legitimated by the institution, and usually by other public museums or exhibition venues where they have also been exhibited. This type of purchase provides a twofold transaction of symbolic capital. On the one hand, it increases the collection's prestige by obtaining works which already possess an important amount of recognition, both nationally and internationally. On the other hand, artists obtain symbolic capital from IMMA by having their works included in a national collection. This path to acquisitions seems to be a quite straightforward process. MacParland describes how the acquisitions sub-committee deals with these types of purchases:

> Usually the discussions in acquisitions are about the lack of money, and you are paying for something large over three years. And if we have had an exhibition here and it's been a success and we want to buy work from it, there's little point in having an argument about it because by then it's, like, it has been accepted usually, and then it's all a question of value for money. (MacParland, interview, 2001)

This comment highlights the role of temporary exhibitions in IMMA's sub-field: the artworks exhibited have already been part of a museum exhibition, and thus there is no need to argue about their artistic value; only their financial value needs to be debated. The ED acts as a mediator, bringing artworks from the FIA or the international art world into IMMA's sub-field; in so doing, it engages in postmodern translation. In this sub-field, works increase their symbolic capital simply by being exhibited in a national museum. The ED facilitates the process of translation; it helps shift artworks from being exhibition material to becoming part of the museum's collection, in a process involving various steps: bringing artworks into the sub-field, exhibiting them at IMMA and thus increasing their symbolic capital, and finally, the presentation of some of the exhibited works to the acquisitions sub-committee for approval as part of IMMA's collection.

Collecting and the Education and Community Department

The E&CD was the first department to be set up, with the appointment of its current senior curator in January 1991, a few months before the museum's opening in May that year. The department offers a series of programmes – school, community, family and artists work programmes – as well as guided tours and seminars, to encourage the public to explore artworks and artists' way of working. Its school programme offers schoolgoers guided tours, discussions and visits to the artists' studios in IMMA's grounds. The department's community programme engages with the local community of Kilmainham, providing groups such as women from the Family Resource Centre, St Michael's Estate in Inchicore, the opportunity to create their own art at workshops. A number of exhibitions have emerged from this programme: Unspoken Truths, 1992 (a cross-city project exploring women's lives); Once is Too Much, 1998 (a collaborative arts project with women and artists exploring the issue of violence in society); and . . . And Start to Wear Purple (a retrospective exhibition of older people's engagement with the museum since 1991). The appointment of a community development worker to IMMA's board (1995-2000) demonstrated the government's support for the museum's inclusive policy.[49]

The link between the E&CD and collecting emerged from conversations between the department's senior curator and the director as to the possibility of purchasing works from within the E&CD programmes. This proposal was made to the museum's board, which endorsed it, and since 1994 work created through E&CD programmes could be considered for acquisitions. However, Helen O'Donoghue, the department's senior curator, points out some of the problems they found:

> I had someone who was going to buy it. My problem was there were three young men who made it, but really [it] was one, but he just disappeared – in that I think he's gotten involved in crime or something. So I couldn't track the boy down. We still have the chair in the museum, but I couldn't track him down and I would have needed his permission to make an acquisition and go through with that, so that has been put on hold . . . Because of the complications around making an acquisition, I must say that there are probably things that if somebody said to me, why did you not consider that, [it] would be for other reasons, as opposed to it being a good piece of art or not. (O'Donoghue, interview, 2001)

Despite these obstacles, the department has succeeded in having a piece of work acquired for the museum's collection, a video made for the Unspoken Truths project, which involved women from the Family Resource Centre, St Michael's Estate, Inchicore, working with artists from all programmes at the museum over a period of five years (1991–1996). The museum acquired the video installation, *Open Season* for just over €5,000.[50] One influence in the purchase was McGonagle's personal interest in the work. A board member explains:

> Declan McGonagle was really interested in one of the video pieces. It's up on the museum at the moment. It's the one – there's a curtain, it's a hospital bed and it's about violence against women. But he really liked it because those rooms were hospital rooms. He really liked that piece and he wanted to buy that and everybody else around at that time wanted to buy it as well. They bought it for £4,000, but it broke history, and it wasn't because I was in the museum, they bought it because the art was good. (8)

There are a number of factors which make *Open Season* a desirable work to include in the collection. Apart from being representative of the museum's activities, and the fact that McGonagle had an interest in it, *Open Season* was included in the Once is Too Much exhibition. I mentioned earlier how the ED created symbolic capital for the artists and works exhibited; the present example is no exception. The following extract is from the director's contribution to the exhibition leaflet accompanying the exhibition:

> Once is Too Much is a manifestation of empowerment. It speaks generally about the capability of those who are disempowered through economic, social, cultural or violent marginalisation, to empower themselves. It is already clear that culture can be the servant of that process, indeed, I would argue that culture, what we make and what we do to say who we are, is *the* key mechanism for self-validation. However, it is also clear that inherited institutional hierarchies have not always assisted this process, that they too often have seen themselves as defending rather than sharing culture, as if culture was merely an antidote to reality rather than a means of renegotiating it ... This is not simply a matter of novel institutional convention, but a concerted attempt by this museum to provide sustained access to the emancipating power of culture, in this case the visual arts, and to fix these values in the realm of the real for the future.[51]

This long quote offers an example of the importance of exhibition-making in the production of symbolic capital. It situates the artworks displayed within particular knowledge frameworks. In Once is Too Much this process happens in at least three ways. Firstly, in the designation of art from the community as a manifestation of empowerment; secondly, in the proposal that culture is a mechanism for self-validation, and a means for renegotiating reality; and thirdly, in positioning IMMA as a participant in this renegotiation, e.g. by posing the idea that the visual arts are an example of the emancipating power of culture. Although there is room to discuss the validity of these ideas, they are useful in themselves as an example of the production of symbolic capital within IMMA's sub-field, in this case, through the practice of exhibition-making. Initially, the E&CD seems to suggest a similar type of intellectual practice at work as in the case of the ED. We see how practices within IMMA's sub-field give symbolic capital to certain works, and how in so doing they acquire legitimacy as being suitable for the museum's collection. This is a form of translation involving the creation of a relationship between the community and IMMA's sub-field. However, the ED exhibits works, which already possess an amount of symbolic capital, whereas here the task of creating symbolic capital for art from the community originates within IMMA's sub-field. This suggests at least two arguments. First, that there are various forms of translation between fields. The E&CD plays a key role in the creation of symbolic capital for community art, whereas the ED tends to increase the symbolic capital of artworks already in possession of some degree of recognition. Second, how one agent within a given field, in this case IMMA's director, who was responsible for the legislation of the sub-field's boundaries, can carry out another form of practice. His participation in the publication for the Once is Too Much exhibition points up his role as translator, clarifying the symbolic capital that community art has for a museum like IMMA.

The discussion of the role of the ED and the E&CD in collecting has shown various instances of postmodern interpretation as translation within a sub-field, and between a sub-field and other surrounding fields. This is a useful distinction to start evaluating the practice of general acquisitions, or those which do not originate from the activities of these two departments; they are put to the museum's board by IMMA's acquisitions sub-committee at its members' suggestion. All purchases must fulfil a criterion of value, as the collection's senior curator, Catherine Marshall, points out: 'The bottom line is we buy things that we think are good art'. The following discussion identifies the requirements that need to be in place for an artwork to qualify as 'good art', and their role in fulfilling IMMA's worldview.

IMMA's worldview

One factor influencing acquisitions is their ability to meet the guidelines set out in IMMA's worldview and collecting policy. 'Good art', in principle, stands for its capacity to follow at least some of IMMA's principles:

> They are good because they raise questions, they don't offer comfort as much as they challenge, but they contain some kind of promise within them that they are worth that challenge . . . All the works that we buy work on a number of different levels . . . We've tended to buy things that will yield up a lot more than one reading or one meaning, or will be useful over a wide variety of cultural contexts. (Marshall, interview, 2001)

The view of artworks 'yielding more than one reading' and 'offering challenge' echoes ideas presented earlier in this chapter, in particular the definition of art as contested, as opposed to consensual, and being able to create multiple viewing experiences. Collecting is thus a selection process governed by the criteria set out in IMMA's worldview. The following comment by Marshall develops this point:

> A collection like ours, we'd like to feel that has been built up over a period of years, and will go on to be built up in the same way. And we buy things after we carefully consider them over and over and over again. We don't buy on a whim. We try to have that extra investment of, is it really going to serve our collection? Is it really going to serve the public, this place? The national programme? How will it fit within the sort of general philosophy and policies that we have? So, all of those things, I would like to think, are part of an organic whole, so it's definitely not about flash buying in order to impress somebody. (Marshall, interview, 2001)

IMMA's collection is built up with expertise and dedication, following a particular worldview set up for the museum. This suggests that collecting is a practice, which creates symbolic capital for the art-works acquired, by drawing on the boundaries established for the museum's worldview and its collecting policy. An added consideration in acquisitions is the purchase of works that can be used and fulfil various requirements within IMMA's sub-field. Buying works which can be handled in the national programme, for example, means that considerations such as size and fragility need to be taken into account:

> We like to show things in constant rotation, we like to show things in the national programme. So I like to think that the work that we buy is capable of being handled from time to time, taken in and out and shown in rotating displays and so on. Very, very precious material would be damaged if it is moved around on a constant basis, so I think that's a consideration, but it's not an overriding one.[52] (Marshall, interview, 2001)

But apart from fulfilling IMMA's worldview, there are other concerns informing the selection of works for the collection, and these highlight the relationship between IMMA's sub-field and other fields. As a leading institution in the FIA, IMMA has a responsibility for collecting examples of Irish art that have received special recognition at an international level; such as the case of Kathy Prendergast, an Irish artist whose work won a prize in the Venice Biennale. A board member refers to the need for these kinds of purchases:

> The fact that Kathy Prendergast had won one of the major prizes in the Venice Biennale meant that we had to buy it. You know, there was no question; we have to acquire that because if you don't do that it means that nothing outside can affect what we do. This was a major honour given to an Irish artist and, yes, of course, we acquired it. (5)

Collecting thus articulates two forms of translation. In the case of selecting works which follow IMMA's worldview and fulfil other requirements of the sub-field itself, translation occurs within IMMA's sub-field. In the last example, collecting operates as a translation between fields. Events in the international art world, such as the Venice Biennale, prompt the need for IMMA to add to its collection the works which have acquired this distinction.

Negotiating financial resources

To prepare for its opening in 1991, IMMA was given an initial budget for acquisitions of just over €300,000,[53] and that same year it was allocated a budget of €114,000.[54] Each year, IMMA receives a sum of money for acquisitions from the Department of Arts, Heritage, Culture and the Gaeltacht, and the museum can use up to 40 per cent of that amount for expenses such as paying for the storage and conservation of works.[55] But purchases for the collection need to be assessed in terms of the financial resources available. Chapter 3 pointed out that financial autonomy was a characteristic of the sub-field of public galleries, in the sense that they were allocated public funds to finance their activities. However, interviews with board and staff members reveal a lack of financial means in IMMA's sub-field. To supply this scarcity, the various departments have sought external sources of funding for their programmes – the ED has managed to establish relationships with sponsors such as Glen Dimplex and Nissan, for example, to create awards and exhibitions. Collecting is another practice which is under-funded. The comments below are very clear on this point:

> The issue of us having a bigger acquisition budget to buy more and better art, all the time it's actually a big question. Our acquisition budget is tiny compared to European or international collections. (Marshall, interview, 2001)

> We've made some good purchases, but we're only dipping . . . the money is so small, so insignificant in purchasing terms today. (1)

> We were not financially supported to the extent that the other museums of that calibre around Europe and the world are. So I think the acquisitions budget is a joke, in all honesty. You wouldn't even buy one decent work for what the acquisitions budget is. (2)

The difficulty for the acquisitions sub-committee is how to continue acquiring works for the collection with such a low budget. One way of dealing with this obstacle is to arrange deals with commercial galleries to pay for works in instalments. A board member makes this point:

> It tends to be more Irish artists who tend to be certainly cheaper than the international ones, but we also have a policy then of spreading – if it's something enormous, like £100,000, spread it over two or three years. And the international artists and galleries are very good about that; they'll do that. We pay it on the long term; we can split it up and spend £20,000 this year and the following year. (6)

The sub-committee, then, is not entirely restricted to acquiring certain works only because they are more affordable than others, though they may have to rely on help from agents outside IMMA's sub-field, such as commercial galleries. Another task for the acquisitions sub-committee is for its members to agree on the art that needs to be bought. This is related to a combination of things:

> We were a small group on the acquisitions committee. Some board members, and the director, obviously, and curatorial staff as well. And they brought, well any of us could make recommendations, and we discussed the recommendations and we sort of tried to watch the funding. It was trouble free, hassle free, except that money was always a problem. We never had enough money. And, I mean, there were no horrible arguments, or people pushing their idea. There were a couple of things bought in my time that I wouldn't personally have purchased, but there was general agreement at the table that they wanted it, and so it was fine. (1)

Apart from the everyday management of finances, the personal taste of board members is a key factor in the purchase of works. The expression 'I wouldn't personally have purchased' is suggestive of the need, sometimes, to agree with the majority. MacParland makes a similar point when she says:

> There's a lot of debate on that committee, but it's pretty good, it works pretty well. It's pretty fair . . . There are compromises, and there are things that I would not choose, that I would not bring forward. But at

> the same time, for the money, and if somebody is very enthusiastic, and three board members agree, you know, we don't usually have a fight, but it's a compromise then. (MacParland, interview, 2001)

Acquisitions involve a process of negotiation and agreement amongst the members of this sub-committee. There are at least two types of negotiations at work: financial resources and personal tastes. The issue of personal taste was raised in chapter 3 with regard to the aesthetic dispositions of commercial gallery directors, when it was found to be a crucial factor in the creation of symbolic capital for Irish art because gallery directors represent and promote the art they like. Acquisitions present a situation in which the individual aesthetic dispositions of sub-committee members play a secondary role, for at least two reasons. Firstly, because there needs to be an agreement amongst members, so concessions need to be made. Secondly, aesthetic dispositions are only one factor amongst others, such as the need to work with a small budget or the requirement to acquire works which fit into IMMA's worldview. This argument provides a further insight into the nature of collecting. It helps redefine the idea of translating within one sub-field. It is a practice that needs to negotiate between individual taste and other factors, both within and outside the given field; and those factors have an effect on the type of art purchases. This point will acquire wider relevance in the last part of this analysis of acquisitions, which discusses the use and transference of capital by those individuals involved in collecting.

Putting capitals into practice

The possession of adequate forms of capital is a key asset for those in charge of acquisitions. Two types of capital, cultural and social, play a role in the accumulation of symbolic capital for IMMA's collection. Cultural capital, seen here as knowledge or expertise about the national and international art world, is an important factor because it determines the contribution a board member can make to the process of acquisitions. IMMA's three senior curators have a better knowledge of what is being exhibited than other members, and are thus key players in bringing proposals to the sub-committee. One board member points out that:

> A lot of what we bought were objects that were brought to us by the curators. You know, they'd be out there looking at the exhibitions. We would, too, but, you know, they'd be seeing more than we saw. They'd bring their material. They'd know the gaps and so on. (1)

The cultural capital of board members is equally important to the practice of acquisitions. For example, an artist and board member refers to the importance of having links with the artistic community, and understanding its perception of the museum. This interviewee was able to contribute to the acquisitions committee by voicing the expectations artists had from the museum (4). In other instances, board members brought legal or financial expertise to the selection process. Another sub-committee member offers a more detailed account of how one's own cultural capital can be put to the service of IMMA's acquisition process:

> I was determined that the sub-committee of the board dealing with acquisitions should acquire Irish art . . . in a sense, my own interest was in that area. It acquired more than Irish art, but I was specifically watching that aspect . . . I would have been instrumental. If my period on the board comes down to anything, it's probably those two acquisitions [Kathy Prendergast and Shane Cullen] . . . they were things that I personally sought. It was within a policy that I had, which the board shared – there was always an open door in all those issues. (5)

Acquisitions occur through a combination of cultural capital, knowledge of contemporary art, and an individual's aim to purchase Irish works for the collection. This quote also sheds light on a point raised earlier. It shows that aesthetic dispositions acquire a crucial role when they are used strategically; that is, in combination with the possession of a particular cultural capital and individual determination.

Another board member saw it as his responsibility to increase his cultural capital. Visiting art exhibitions and artists' studios was a way of keeping up to date with the work of contemporary artists, which IMMA might be interested in buying. An interesting point is how he made use of his social capital to promote the museum:

> Part of our responsibility was to go to see artists' work, so that was part of what I had to do. So that was very practical and I did, and then also in terms of my own contribution to it, because I was representing the biggest arts programme in the country, I used to keep the interest of the museum very much close to my heart. So if I knew there was something coming up, I'd make sure there was an interview. So, from that point, they were the practical things that I was able to do. But, certainly, keeping up to date with exhibitions and going to visit artists, that was all part of my brief. (2)

This quote illustrates how collecting can articulate a flow of two forms of capital: social capital is transformed into symbolic capital.

Social capital, in terms of contacts and position in the art world, was deployed by this board member to promote the museum, while IMMA increased its symbolic capital through his promotional work.

This flow or exchange of capital can take other forms. Two interviewees mention how being on IMMA's board is seen as a sign of distinction:

> If you're writing, as I do, for journals, and they want a mini biography, it's quite nice to be able to say you're on the board of the IMMA. People think she's got a bit of clout. It doesn't mean you've got clout at all, actually, but it's picked up in that way. (1)
>
> Being on the board is also seen as increasing one's cultural capital, or knowledge about the art world. (2)

On other occasions, some board members felt a certain conflict between their position on IMMA's board and the acquisitions sub-committee, and their activities outside the museum. One board member, in particular, decided not to take part in the sub-committee because it could clash with his private interest in art collecting:

> There were plenty of people there with their own opinions about what the museum should spend their money on. I also felt, to some extent, I was a collector myself and there might have been times when I might have been competing or could have been in a competitive situation, and the museum wasn't short of people with the talent and the ability to make their own selection, so I just didn't bother going for that reason. (3)

Overall, the use of cultural and social capital, that is, knowledge of art and contacts in the art world, was a helpful resource in counteracting the paltry acquisitions' budget. One interviewee refers to the museum's reliance on 'sympathetic' friends. As he explains with regard to acquisitions:

> It was all done on favours and friends and people who were sympathetic. That was the way it was done. And, again, that was where the board members' knowledge of the world of art, the chief's executive's knowledge of people and socializing with them and writing to and about and for them, was all very useful. (2)

In this area the director played a key role, using his network of contacts to help secure acquisitions for the collection:

> The acquisitions budget was absolutely minimum, thus it required a very significant PR exercise with many of the major collectors and major museums around the world. Again, this is where McGonagle was very successful. He had the stature, he was known, and also he knew the international art world as a contributor to many magazines, as a highly respected writer and critic. He knew his way around, as did a number of the board members . . . It was so important for us to be able to show and get loans and come to positive agreements with some of the top artists in the world. So we were able to get favourable terms where we were able to purchase – some of them would contribute pieces of their work because they liked the surrounding, the approach being taken. (2)

This last discussion on the use of social capital illustrates a further aspect of collecting as a form of translation; having contacts with other museums, and having collectors help secure purchases and loans for IMMA's collection. Translation occurs when capital is used and brought to IMMA's sub-field. In turn, board members gain prestige, knowledge and, in some cases, decide to promote the museum from their position outside IMMA's sub-field. The last two examples, in particular, provide information about how interpreters can carry out the two roles Bauman outlined: translating and legislating. The director's role is a case in point. Earlier on in this chapter it was shown how his worldview for IMMA and his collecting policy articulated a form of postmodern legislation, and were a means of giving symbolic power to IMMA's sub-field, setting up its boundaries. Moreover, he was able to translate between IMMA's sub-field, using his knowledge and contacts as an internationally respected writer and critic, to secure acquisitions and loans for the collection.

LOANS AND DONATIONS

The last part of this chapter deals with the process of selecting loans and donations for IMMA's collection. It differs from acquisitions because it does not require a financial transaction; however, it involves a transaction of a different kind, because having a loan or donation accepted not only increases the symbolic capital of the works in question, but also that of their donors or lenders, e.g. private or corporate collectors. The following discussion of the process behind the acceptance and rejection of loans and donations is structured along the same lines as the previous analysis of general acquisitions, and focuses on IMMA's worldview, negotiating financial resources, and putting capitals into practice.

IMMA's worldview

The museum is quite free to select donations which suit the collection. Marshall comments on their ability to control which loans and donations they select:

> I wouldn't actually have a major problem about the way the collection is developing at the moment because, the first thing we should say here is, we only accept loans or donations of artwork that we want to have in our collection . . . We are very free about the way we select from donations and loans on offer to us. We've been quite ruthless about that, and I'm happy to say that good collectors are also in favour of that policy. Even the kindest and most generous of people to us have offered us work from time to time that we haven't taken, and they have understood that. It hasn't been an issue. (Marshall, interview, 2001)

The fact that collectors are willing to acquiesce to the museum's view is telling of IMMA's leeway in this form of collecting. But there are specific criteria, such as the museum's collecting policy, which dictate what is accepted or rejected. One board member refers to the rejection of donations as follows:

> Supposing you were going to be given a magnificent Paul Henry; that is hard to fit into the philosophy of the IMMA, very easy to fit into another entity like, say, the Municipal Gallery or National Gallery . . . It would have been easy to say, thank you, we'll accept it. The person gets the tax write-off, but the artist had no place in the going forward of the museum. The artist was dead, it was an Irish artist, had no real relevance to any intellectual route forward for the museum, so in those instances we had to say no. (2)

The expression 'is hard to fit into the philosophy' highlights how loans and donations must follow some of the principles of the museum's worldview and policy. Irish artist Paul Henry (1878–1958) was producing work from the beginning of the twentieth century, so some of his early work would not fit into IMMA's collecting policy, which starts from the 1940s.

Another consideration in selecting works for the collection is their suitability for display. The ability to include the works in exhibitions was a major concern in the choice of loans and donations for this board member:

> I am all for donations, but I think the donations have to be monitored. [You] don't take anything that comes. You have to be very selective, so that what's coming in is good and it's adding to the collection, and it's not just, oh yes, we'll take anything . . . As a whole, we had to know that we could use it, display was uppermost, and something that was only to just be given and put in storage: no good. (1)

The public's demand is another criterion at work. Indicators such as comments on the museum's visitors book, or evidence of visitors numbers at retrospectives by Irish artists, for example Mainie Jellett and Patrick Swift, has encouraged the museum to accept loans of historic works. Marshall refers to the public's preference for historical works: '[you] can never actually completely satisfy public demand for more and more historical works in the collection because that's what the public know about'. The acceptance of loans and donations is a practice that requires balancing the demands from outside IMMA's sub-field, the public's preferences, with the requirements from within the sub-field, e.g. opportunities for display. The Musgrave Kinley Outsider Art Collection, (see chapter 5 for a discussion of its display) helps clarify the process of accepting a loan. The collection comprises examples of outsider art, a term used to designate 'the work of artists with little or no formal artistic training, in particular, socially marginal individuals who, for various reasons and without prior instruction, begin to paint, sculpt or draw' (Bowler, 1997: 11). One of the reasons which led to the acceptance of the collection was its relevance to the museum's collecting policy:

> We accepted a loan of an outsider collection because . . . the programmers and the previous board believed that it was absolutely appropriate to this museum, with its policy about questioning who is an artist, what is an artist, who should be in an art collection, who should be in a public collection, and so on. We very much believe that is up to us to raise those discussions, and how better to do it than by bringing a collection of outsider art. (Marshall, interview, 2001)

The acceptance of the loan complies with the museum's worldview,[56] particularly the idea of redefining existing ways of thinking about value in art and the definition of an artist. Yet this loan differs from other loans and donations, which are usually a means to accumulate symbolic capital for the artworks, the collectors, and of course the artists. This last factor does not apply in this example, because the acceptance of this loan was not driven by the prestige gained in having outsiders' works displayed in a national museum. The collector of the outsider collection makes this point:

> Prestige doesn't really come into it, because outsiders were never out for prestige. It's just that we wanted to show these wonderful works to people who don't know anything about art, and to people who know something about art, because it's very interesting in relation to what people consider art, and what people consider works produced by professional artists. (Kinley, interview, 2001)

The collector's main interest is not in the creation of symbolic capital for her collection, but to bring it to a public institution where it can be used to raise questions about value in art, e.g. whether non-professional artists are also capable of producing good art. In fact, the reason why this collector, Monika Kinley, decided to loan the collection to IMMA was very much because of the musuem director's views on value in art: he 'would appreciate that the best of outsider art is just as important as mainstream art'. Her comment exemplifies the way in which IMMA is perceived as being able to produce symbolic capital for outsider art – here is a museum where there are no distinctions made between outsiders and non-outsiders – mainstream artists – as both are exhibited together, following the same display principles. As Kinley adds, the idea is to do away with the need to follow any such distinctions: 'I've tried to collect the best of it, as far as we could afford it. We do consider it as good as what is shown in the museum . . . hopefully, one day they won't make the distinctions'. Marshall notes the importance of display practices where IMMA's policy is to exhibit outsider and mainstream works together:

> My secondary aim is to integrate it into exhibitions of our more mainstream collection so that all the time we are saying that this is quality art – I mean, reinforcing that. This is quality art, irrespective of where it comes from, but I was hoping that in the process of doing that, it also raises questions for the public about who is an artist, what is an artwork . . . We think the work these artists are doing is art whether it is inside the gallery or it is not. We are saying that, whether they were educated or not, it is still artwork, and bringing them in here we hope will help keep these questions open for people. You know, keep them questioning what is going on rather than defining what it is. (Marshall, interview, 2001)

The acceptance of loans and donations articulates two forms of translation. Firstly, translation is a way of ensuring that loans and donations comply with the museum's policy; while, secondly, collecting is a practice which contributes to the making of symbolic capital for outsider art. In the discussion of artworks created within the E&CD programme, it was mentioned that IMMA's sub-field plays a key task in the production of symbolic capital for artworks from this collection. This entailed a translation whereby art from the community was created and given symbolic capital within IMMA's sub-field, through its exhibition at IMMA, and, in one case, its inclusion in the museum's collection. The present case illustrates a similar type of practice. Artworks from a private collection are brought to IMMA's sub-field, and in the process, translation occurs in two ways: by giving symbolic capital, prestige, to the collection, and by emphasising its artistic quality. The work of outsider artists is already endowed with symbolic capital as part of a private collection, but its symbolic capital increases in IMMA when the museum sanctions its display as 'good quality' art.

Negotiating financial resources

Loans and donations are also important because they supply historic works for the collection, which IMMA cannot afford to purchase. As one board member explains, the government is not going to provide enough funding to buy these types of works, so the only way of having them in the collection is through donations:

> The cash value of the donations we've got must run into millions, so I would actually think that collectors like to see their collections ending up in public institutions . . . The idea of museums buying treasure-pieces or wonderful paintings is really not on because the amount of money involved is too great. Whereas collectors want to see a happy home for their collections, which they have spent a lifetime of enthusiasm building, and therefore that's the natural way to put together the collections of treasure-pieces – donations rather than purchases. (3)

This comment reflects a point made earlier about the advantages of lending privately owned artworks to a public, national collection. It also highlights the fact that IMMA benefits from donations because they provide historic works for its collection. Another issue is the possibility of accepting donations which are acquisition-led; that is, chosen by the museum. Marshall explains this:

> It's also fair to say that [a] number of recent donations have been donations where we wanted to buy a particular work or a body of work, and we went to generous people who are well disposed towards contemporary art and said to them, could you buy it for us? Because we haven't got the money to do it, and then we acquired it as a donation from that person. But it was acquisition-led, purchase-led, if you like, and there have been a few major donations to us that went down that road. (Marshall, interview, 2001)

But apart from these benefits, loans and donations bring a responsibility which does not occur in acquisitions. As mentioned in chapter 3, the Irish government instituted a tax-relief scheme to promote donations and loans to public institutions, and the availability of such incentives means that the museum must exercise some control, to distinguish between those collectors seeking prestige for their collections, and those making a genuine contribution to the museum. A board member expresses this concern as follows:

> If some piece has been part of a long-term collection in the museum, or exhibited there, it adds a certain cachet to it. And I think that's where we need to be careful in the museum's role in dealing with collectors, because often they could be just trying to enhance the value of their collection . . . If that's what their motivation is, rather than actually contributing something to the gallery, I think we need to be careful about it . . . I know the tax laws, and we're going to get a brief on it, because if you give work to a gallery, not even permanently, then you can get tax relief and then you can claim the works back after so many years. I don't think that's very healthy for the growth of a collection. (7)

This comment gives a further insight into the criteria governing the acceptance of loans and donations: the need to control the shape of the collection. Apart from the ethics of this type of practice, for example ensuring that collectors genuinely want to give their works to IMMA, the museum must secure the possession of loans of works for a sustained period of time. While this practice may be advantageous for private collectors, it also requires the exercise of a great deal of control from the acquisitions sub-committee. The need to control the acceptance of donations is raised by another board member, whose aim is to maintain a balance between acquisitions, on the one hand, and accepting loans and donations, on the other:

> There are major gifts coming and, you know, that was a kind of pressure on the museum, not buying; but I felt that the museum has got to keep controlling the shape of it, not just receiving from others. (5)

Too much emphasis on accepting loans and donations may be detrimental to the shape of the collection. The issue is to be able to build a collection upon purchases, rather than merely accepting donations. As one of IMMA's senior curators explains:

> I would say that almost everything we own has a quality; is good quality. We haven't accepted any rubbish or bad donations. I would have my favourites, but it's gone from strength to strength, and it's huge. But I suppose when we initiate purchases rather than accept donations, we should be really saying, well, what is it that we really want? What do we focus on in the next three years? (MacParland, interview, 2001)

This comment suggests that the museum is reliant on donations, rather than being acquisitions driven – as was said earlier, the collection consists of over 4,000 artworks of which only about 330 were purchases. The practice of accepting 'almost all donations' has been the subject of criticism by a board member:

> There were some very important artists but they were only represented by one or two fairly minor works. Now, these works were generally donated to the museum, and I still have a problem with the form of those donations. I feel that the museum accepted almost all donations, and thus accepted works that were less than great. (4)

There is a lack of agreement amongst those interviewed as to the amount of loans and donations suitable for the collection. Translating, in this case, entails the control of the type of art entering IMMA's collection. The last example in this discussion will reveal a similar concern with the issue of control.

Putting capitals into practice

In the analysis of acquisitions, it was pointed out that the possession of cultural and social capital by members of the acquisitions subcommittee was a key asset in securing new works for the collection. In loans and donations, there is a need to control the requirements lenders and donors sometimes demand – they may insist on conditions for the display of their artworks, for example. Marshall clarifies the museum's policy in these situations:

> What has been an issue with lenders and donors, and specially with donors, is they will give an artwork provided we say we hang it permanently somewhere, or we will call a gallery after the person who

> donated it. We have always refused to go down either of those roads. (Marshall, interview, 2001)

Both collecting and display are practices which give symbolic capital to artworks, and the individuals involved in the making of IMMA's collection see it as their task to control its allocation. The refusal to meet demands from donors and lenders is also endorsed by a board member who says:

> Someone could not say, I will give you this painting but I want it hanging six months of the year on show in the museum. We absolutely refused that outright. We said no, it has to be within the context of a show that has been put on, and a show will not be put on just to facilitate one painting or sculpture . . . On the acquisitions sub-committee we used to have a lot of people saying, we will give you this, and then, of course, there was the attraction of a tax write-off . . . So we had a lot of those presented to us, and in the main we said, thank you, but no. (2)

Although the museum has no set exhibition policy, the display of works given on loan or donation follows certain guidelines (see chapter 5). They are usually given an initial showing to mark their arrival at IMMA:

> We try to call attention to that new donation, and to the process through which the donation came about, because we want other people to get excited about that process as well. And also to honour it and celebrate this important new body of work in the collection, and then thereafter we integrate it fully into the collection, and we use it as if it's always belonged there. Rarely, then, we go back to a big show with that collector's name on it. (Marshall, interview, 2001)

The provision of exhibition space is a way of allocating recognition to loans and donations. An example of this practice is the dedication, in June 1999, of part of the museum's exhibition space to honour art collector and donor Gordon Lambert.[57] The act of naming a gallery after a collector is not only a way of increasing Lambert's renown, it also increases IMMA's symbolic capital by demonstrating the relationship between the museum and such a distinguished collector. IMMA wanted to commemorate Lambert's contribution to Irish art generally, although he never asked for such an honour. This was something the museum's board was aware of:

> Gordon never asked for that. It was something that the museum did in 1999 as a gesture of gratitude, because he had been such a generous, giving donor, who never actually laid down any conditions on us at all. I think the board was very mindful of the fact that he was getting older, and that he had done so much for Irish art, and indeed for modern art in Ireland over the last fifty years; that it was appropriate to make a special gesture in his favour. (Marshall, interview, 2001)

This last discussion on the use of capital shows that IMMA has the upper hand in the distribution of symbolic capital through the practice of exhibitions. I said earlier that translation entails a control of loans and donations with regard to the type of aesthetic they represent. Translating can also control the exchange of symbolic capital. For lenders and donors, this exchange occurs when their works are accepted for the collection and exhibited in the museum. But, for IMMA, the task is to ensure that this exchange of capital is based on a real disinterestedness on the part of those involved in it.

CONCLUSION

I would like to end this chapter by opening up some questions which will be dealt with in the conclusion. (So far, only chapter 2 has looked at the possibility of change in fields, but the exploration into collecting practices presented here offers some insights into how IMMA can be said to participate in a form of cultural change). One principle in IMMA's worldview is the idea that museums can participate in the transformation of social and cultural values. It could be argued that collecting contributes to this process, through the selection of works which can help raise or challenge existing views on art value. The acceptance of the Musgrave Kinley Outsider Art Collection is a clear example of how collecting can help the museum promote its ideas on questioning the nature of aesthetic. However, the questioning of value in art cannot occur without visitors or audiences, who play a vital role in this process. In fact, IMMA's involvement in the process of transformation seems to be more as a mediator between artists and the public. In order to have a clearer picture of how the museum puts its worldview into practice, we need to look at exhibition-making; an analysis of exhibitions can further our insights into collecting, since this is another process which assigns symbolic capital to the museum's collection.

CHAPTER 5

Displaying the Collection

EXHIBITIONS AND EXHIBITION FIELD

THIS CHAPTER EXPLORES three exhibitions of IMMA's collection in order to continue with the analysis of postmodern interpretation in chapter 4. Exhibitions of IMMA's collection are an integral aspect of collecting because collected objects do not have meaning *per se* but only as part of an exhibition which shapes their meaning (Hooper-Greenhill, 2000). The ideas and values held by museum professionals in charge of exhibition design, together with the placement of objects within frameworks of intelligibility or interpretation, create symbolic capital for the artworks on display; that is, specific ways of thinking about and experiencing art. A key argument in this chapter is that exhibition-making is a practice characteristic of postmodern translation, a view which raises a number of questions. What does postmodern translation consist of with regard to exhibition-making? What is the relationship between IMMA's worldview and IMMA's exhibitions? And how do IMMA's exhibition practices fit into existing debates about exhibition design?

This chapter conceptualizes exhibitions of IMMA's collection as part of an Exhibition Field (EF) where postmodern intellectual practices create meaning for artworks. As seen in chapters 2, 3 and 4, intellectual practices are articulated within fields. The EF includes those set of practices involved in exhibition design. It is important, however, to distinguish between exhibitions of public art collections and other types of art exhibitions, such as displays of paintings in commercial galleries or in auction houses. These address an audience of prospective buyers, whereas exhibitions of public collections are not intended to generate revenue from the sale of their works. Rather, a characteristic of exhibitions of public collections is how they are informed by the values or worldview laid out by each particular institution. For example, the HLMGMA does not display its collection in exactly the same way as IMMA, mainly because it does not participate, at least not to the same extent, in IMMA's concern with the negotiation of meaning in art. And yet, despite variation in exhibition design, there is still a core of techniques which have their origins within the EF, and which are shared by staff at museums and galleries. The history of their development needs to be spelled out next, because they still inform contemporary display practices, including those at IMMA's exhibitions.

PUBLIC MUSEUMS AND THE GENESIS OF AN EXHIBITION FIELD

The foundation of the first public museums in eighteenth-century Western Europe brought with it alternative ways of thinking about collecting and exhibition design. Prior to the French Revolution, for example, collections had been displayed in privately owned spaces, like palaces, castles or houses, accessible by invitation only, and following a method of exposition which emphasized resemblances between things (Hooper-Greenhill, 1989: 64). The foundation of public museums, and the use of their collections, was linked to broader changes in the nature of knowledge. The French Revolution, in particular, 'created the conditions of emergence for a new "truth", a new rationality, out of which came a new functionality for a new institution, the public museum'. Hooper-Greenhill refers (ibid: 63) to the appearance of a 'new field of use' to explain how the collecting practices of kings, the aristocracy and the church were 'rearranged in other contexts as statements that proclaimed at once the tyranny of the old and the democracy of the new'. This Renaissance episteme began to weaken in the face of a new attempt to establish a more scientific approach to the classification of things. The nineteenth century was characterized by a tendency towards specialization and fragmentation in knowledge, and was indicative of a shift to a classical episteme (ibid: 66). Although its manifestations varied depending on which countries and institutions were affected, in general terms it meant a progressive turn towards classifying collections as part of a series, rather than in terms of resemblance. Public museums reflected this change by dividing their collections into more specialized areas; the British Museum set up branches devoted to natural history, science, antiquities etc (Lorente, 1998: 24). Another development was the creation of museums and galleries for the works of living artists, which were separated from historical works (Hooper-

Greenhill, 1989: 70). The MGMA is an example of this specialized approach to classifying collections.

The French Revolution led to the reappropriation of royal and aristocratic collections, as well as those belonging to the church. The Louvre was transferred from royal hands to the new state and transformed into a public museum. This move was followed in other European countries, where royal collections were also converted into museums: the Viennese Royal Collection opened to the public in the 1770s, the Dresden Gallery in 1743, the same year the Uffizi collection in Florence was donated to the state (Duncan and Wallach, 1980: 452). France paved the way for a new form of classifying and exhibiting collections, re-ordering the art-viewing experience in the process (ibid: 455). The appearance of a 'curatorial gaze', first established in France and extended across Europe (Hooper-Greenhill, 1989: 67), was a new museological practice. It transformed the way art was exhibited: royal collections were meant to dazzle and impress viewers with a display of richness and splendour (Duncan and Wallach, 1980: 455), whereas in public museums artworks were arranged as part of an art history programme:

> The paintings were divided into national schools and art-historical periods, put into simple, uniform frames, and clearly labelled. A guide to the museum directed the visitor's tour of the collection. A walk through the gallery was an organized walk through the history of art. In other words, the royal collection was organized into a new iconographic programme . . . In the museum, the work of art now represented a moment of art history. It exemplified a particular category within the new system of art-historical classification. (Duncan and Wallach, 1980: 455–6)

Artworks represented a 'moment of art history'; they served to illustrate the discipline of art history, and as a result 'whatever meaning a work of art owed to its original context was lost' (ibid: 456). Art history was a history of national and individual genius, and works needed to be stripped of any references to their original functions and renamed, with labels drawing attention to the artist, his dates and nationality (ibid: 463).[1] Added to this, in the nineteenth century public art museums were committed to the education, enlightenment and improvement of their public by giving them lessons in art history (Duncan, 1995: 16). Today most art museums have changed this emphasis and are more overtly concerned with inducing an aesthetic experience in their audiences, an intense absorption, or identification between viewer and the work on display. The first official doctrine of the aesthetic museum was Gilman's *Museum Ideals of Purpose and Method*, published in 1918 by the Boston Museum of Fine Arts (ibid: 16). Despite minor changes in exhibition design, this type of museum continues to isolate objects for visual contemplation and suppresses 'as irrelevant other meanings the objects might have' (Duncan, 1995: 17). Artworks are detached from any social and political implications, even though these are part of their original context of production. Examples of this trend are the National Gallery in Washington DC, the Tate Gallery in London, and the Museum of Contemporary Art in Barcelona. Closer to the topic of this chapter, we look at this doctrine's application to exhibitions of modern art.

The most authoritative history of modern art came to be represented at the Museum of Modern Art in New York (MoMA) (ibid: 103). Under the influence of museum director Alfred Barr (1929–43), MoMA incorporated 'aesthetic installations' into its exhibitions (Grunenberg, 1994; Staniszewski, 1998), a practice that became the norm for twentieth-century modern museum practices (Staniszewski, 1998: 66). MoMA's collection became the authoritative history of modern art, not only because its collection had some of the most well-known exponents of modern artistic practice, but also because it was presented in a way which transformed the public's perception of art and art history (Duncan, 1995: 103). The history of modern art was presented as an unfolding succession of styles or movements; and as Duncan notes, 'few other museums can offer . . . so many chapel-like rooms exclusively devoted to *the* major art-historical figures' (ibid: 105–6). The museum is still organized as a 'ritual space'; its various rooms celebrate individual achievement and the progress of modern art, with displays of works by artists such as Pablo Picasso and Jackson Pollock as crucial examples of artistic excellence (ibid: 108).[2] Hanging pictures in chronological sequence depending on style and period, with identity labels giving title, date and name of lender, are some of the techniques used for that purpose. The use of didactic labels in displays was a novelty introduced by Barr:

> [They] were compositions in which wall labels explicitly linked the works of art historically and conceptually, making visible the unity and coherence of the show. Barr's labels enhanced the sense of the exhibition as an entity unto itself. (Staniszewski, 1998: 64)

In addition to this arrangement, Barr's approach was to present works in a way which highlighted their aesthetic dimension (Grunenberg,

1994: 204). This gave prominence to the works of art over architectural and site-specific associations: placing paintings on neutral-coloured or white walls, positioning them at just below eye level, and keeping them well spaced. Even labels served to reinforce 'the aesthetic validity of an exhibited work' (Staniszewski, 1998: 66).

The spaces described by Grunenberg and Staniszewski are not restricted to MoMA; they are typical of a more generalized form of exhibition design and gallery space, what O'Doherty calls 'the white cube'. White cube is a metaphor for a space disconnected from the outside world: 'windows are usually sealed off. Walls are painted white. The ceiling becomes the source of light' (O'Doherty, 1999 [1976]: 15). In his collection of essays, *Inside the White Cube*, he launches a critique against the view that any gallery space is implicitly neutral. Like Duncan, he acknowledges the relationship between gallery design and the projection of a particular view of art history: 'the history of modern art can be correlated with changes in that space and in the way we see it'. For O'Doherty, the 'white cube' is the ideal context for the 'aestheticization of art'. '[The] ideal gallery,' O'Doherty insists, 'subtracts from the artwork all cues that interfere with the fact that it is "art". The work is isolated from everything that would detract from its own evaluation of itself' (ibid: 14).

Despite the prevalence of the 'aestheticization of art' model in exhibition design, alternative exhibition techniques have posed a challenge to Barr's methods.[3] After the end of the First World War, what Kachur terms the 'ideological exhibition space' started to flourish in Europe and the US, and lasted until the beginning of the Second World War. From around the 1920s, neutral presentation was abandoned in favour of a more 'subjective format' (Kachur, 2001: 6) as international avant-gardes such as Dadaism, Surrealism or Russian Constructivism established new parameters for exhibition design. Surrealist and Dadaist artists took up installation design techniques (Staniszewski, 1998: 4), as they were 'fascinated with the possibility of creating public exhibition spaces, and saw installation design as one of many new arenas of mass communication that would transform modern life'.[4] This trend is exemplified in Dadaist displays, where exhibition spaces are made resonant to the type of artwork exhibited, for example echoing 'political protest artworks'. Constructivist installations also experimented with the exhibition space, with its colouring, for example (Staniszewski, ibid: 6–7).

But the most persuasive challenge was posed by Surrealist artists from 1938 on, when they started to impose their artistic style on their displays. A paradigmatic example of 'ideological space' was the 1938 Surrealist exhibition *Exposition Internationale du Surréalisme* in Paris, whose overall space was aimed at discomforting the viewers. They were faced with a corridor lined by sixteen mannequins on one side, which had been dressed by a particular artist/writer. This use of space produced a specific relationship between the viewer and the exhibition; as Kachur (2001: 37) puts it: 'An unexpected, more corporeal interaction thus replaced the usual encounter with pictures on a wall. Instead of the eye taking refuge in a pictorial space, the spectator's body was confronted by a series of kinaesthetic equals, life-sized personages'. Such unexpected encounters continued in Marcel Duchamp's installation, 1,200 Coal Sacks, consisting of 1,200 empty coal-bags hanging from the ceiling. Although the sacks were filled with newspapers, their intended effect was to 'discomfort the viewers', who were made to feel uncomfortable at the possibility of a sack falling on their heads.[5] Another design technique was to exhibit paintings in a space where it was difficult to see them, thus challenging the idea that paintings have to be seen fully in order to be appreciated. Again, this lack of visibility sought to reverse the expectations of the 'aestheticization of art' model, where artworks were properly lit. A description of the Surrealist Gallery at the Art of this Century exhibition in New York in 1942 refers to some of the gallery's effects:

> [A] stage set for a sensorially augmented aesthetic experience that affected the viewer's sight, hearing, and touch. Each work had its own spotlight, which went off every two or three seconds; the lighting was engineered so that half of the paintings were lit half of the time. Every two minutes a recording of the roar of a train was sounded. Paintings, mounted on wall hinges, enabled the visitor to tilt them to his or her desired viewing angle. (Staniszewski, 1998: 22)

At work here is a shift of focus, moving away from the object towards enhancing, or giving priority to the environment created for the appreciation of art. But the international avant-gardes' challenge to existing ways of exhibition design went further than a simple change in the style of displays. Hetherington argues that the artistic practices of, for example, Marcel Duchamp's readymades, e.g. the making of a urinal, and its subsequent placement in a museum, challenged modern ideas about the positioning of the viewing subject:

> [The] Dadaist project is fundamentally about restoring heterogeneity to the object world by challenging bourgeois conceptions of art and

> art's taming within the disciplined exhibitionary spaces of the gallery and the museum and their associated positioning of the viewing subject. (Hetherington, 1999: 68)

A similar concern with the presentation of works also informs Serota's book, *Experience or Interpretation: The Dilemma of Museums of Modern Art* (1996). His discussion of the history of exhibition techniques follows the same line of argument made so far, although it gives a more precise definition of exhibition practices. He differentiates between a 'curatorial *interpretation* on the works' (1996: 8), which has informed curatorial practices since the mid-nineteenth century, and a contemporary role where the curator is 'a maker of *mise-en-scène*' (ibid: 10). Curatorial interpretation refers to the display of artworks by national school, and can be found, for example, in the Louvre. It also applies, as in MoMA, to the organization of works by movement, so that works by different artists are combined to 'give selective readings, both of art and of the history of art' (ibid: 8–9). According to Serota, this curatorial role has been superseded by that of curators as makers of *mise-en-scène*, or settings for the contemplation of artworks. In the aesthetic museum, viewers can take a more active role in appreciating and understanding artworks, because its exhibitions offer 'an absolute concentration of focus on the work of single artists', thus forcing viewers to develop their own reading of the work 'rather than relying on a curatorial interpretation of history' (ibid: 10). Serota adds:

> The evident limitation both of the labyrinth and of the flexible space [at MoMA] was one factor which encouraged a new form of display in the late 1980s. The Pollock display at the Museum of Modern Art is but one example of a much wider trend which within ten years has established a new, now even dominant convention for the presentation of twentieth-century and contemporary art. It is a convention which gives absolute weight to the work of individual artists, which favours presentation over analysis and which undermines the traditional priority given to the curator as the person who exercises discriminating judgment over selection and display in the museum. (Serota, 1996: 15)

However, in saying that modern presentation undermines the former priority of curators, Serota seems to be doing away with the principle of presentation itself. While there may have been a change in the conventions for the display of artworks, the judgement and intervention of curators still underlines the practice of creating *mise-en-scène*. The specific form this takes is an issue that will be addressed in the analysis of IMMA's exhibitions. Moreover, there is a need to question the pervasiveness of the aesthetic model as a form of curatorial practice – in MoMA both aesthetic and educational approaches to art co-existed. The example of Surrealists exhibitions has even suggested that exhibition techniques are sources of competition in the creation of forms of art appreciation. The questions we need to ask here are: how far does exhibition-making at IMMA illustrate the arguments made so far as regards a shift in curatorial strategies? And how is exhibiting, as a translation practice related to IMMA's worldview, an example of postmodern legislation?

CURATORIAL PRACTICES AT IMMA

So far this chapter has referred to the development of an EF, looking in particular at the changes in exhibition design and the conventions of displaying the display of modern art collections, with particular reference to MoMA. To complement these ideas, and begin the analysis of IMMA's exhibitions, I focus next on the views of IMMA's curators. They do not constitute an exhibition policy *per se* as IMMA does not have an exhibition policy outlining a set of specific guidelines for the display of works in the museum. Rather, the material included here is drawn from interviews with the two curators in charge of exhibiting IMMA's collection. The issue is to explore the relationship between exhibiting practices and the museum's worldview. Is IMMA's worldview relevant to the practices of the museum's curators? Or is curating a practice that sets up a new worldview for exhibitions, to the extent of going against the ideas formulated in the museum's worldview? And, finally, how closely do IMMA's curating practices relate to Serota's distinction between curatorial interpretation and the making of *mise-en-scène*?

IMMA's collection is exhibited in temporary exhibitions and thus it can be used around different themes and topics. The idea of using the collection in changing displays is part of the museum's collecting policy, says, senior curator of the collection department (CD); this practice allows 'more multiple interpretations of the artworks' than if it were put permanently in one place. By showing the collection in different contexts nothing becomes fixed in one place, with one identity (Marshall, interview, 2001). Questioning the identity and value of artworks is one of the aims of IMMA's curators when they put together an exhibition:

> Wanting always to question value; that is a guideline for nearly everything we do, so that's postmodern. But we don't go downstairs to hang a show saying, I'm going to be postmodern today. We do go down saying we're going to put together a good exhibition that is, hopefully, challenging and questioning, and if we put one cultural icon in one place, we try to put something that challenges that icon in another place. (Marshall, interview, 2001)

The exhibition spaces at IMMA resemble the white cube referred to earlier, with white walls and high ceilings, but the museum is an historic seventeenth-century building, which ensures that the display of art is not devoid of context:

> We do show work within the building in something that approaches the white cube, we have lovely clean modernist spaces, but those modernist spaces exist within, very much within the framework of a historic building, and they are here because modern art looks good in them. So they are there to show the work the way the artists want their work to be shown, and against clean white walls, but very much integrated into a bigger whole. (Marshall, interview, 2001)

IMMA's inclusion of artists in deciding how their work is displayed goes against the principles of an aesthetic museum; exhibitions in this type of museum would isolate artwork from its context of production, including any particular meaning given to it by the artist who made it. The following comment by Marguerite O'Molloy, assistant curator, CD, explains how, because collecting is informed by the principle of buying works which seek to redefine identity, exhibitions become a way of bringing this debate to the public:

> I think that the arguments are, in a way, addressed already. The decisions for the works that are going into the show have been made, and they are picking up on the idea of art as redefining identity . . . The work has already been purchased by the museum, so that's when the debate on redefining identity is addressed really, I think. So if you're displaying the work, again you're not really doing that job twice . . . I am not saying it's done already. I mean, if you are trying to address how a work is displayed or received or read, then you're going to be presenting it in a certain way, but you're still dealing with a work that has been chosen by the museum because it engages in the redefinition of identity. (O'Molloy, interview, 2002)

A common practice in exhibition design is to work with artists and consult them about any requirements for the exhibition of their work. This is seen as part of the museum's policy:

> IMMA is really excited about working with living artists, so that carries with it a responsibility to always try to show their work in a way that the artist is comfortable with. We would always consult artists before we install their work for the first time; we bring the artist here to show us how to install it, if it is problematic in any way, or to work out even what rooms in the building are suitable for their work, and so on. And that's an absolute part of our policy . . . I think the artist made the work with a particular set of ideas in his or her head and we would, of course, want to tap into those. (Marshall, interview, 2001)

The museum's decision to involve the artist in the presentation of his or her work does not seem to constrain the role of curators in the design of exhibitions. This becomes a collaboration between curators and artists to ensure artworks are presented in the best possible way; the way a work is exhibited, whether it is put on a pedestal or on the floor, contributes to its meaning:

> If somebody makes a picture and they decide that there isn't supposed to be a frame, you don't put a frame on it. You know, these are modes of display and presentation of the work, which are bound up with the meaning of the work as well, so to change that or to see that it's limiting, well, no, it's not limiting at all. (O'Molloy, interview, 2002)

A priority for curators is to put together exhibitions which offer a comfortable space for the appreciation of the artworks on display; by their lighting, positioning, and of course allowing space for the public's contemplation:

> You're trying to organize that the exhibition shows the work to its best advantage; so that the room is well lit; that the pieces hang correctly; that it's positioned well; that aesthetically it looks good; that if there are any requirements for a video that the video is working – you know, basic kind of requirements . . . For me, an exhibition should look good; the bottom line is it's a visual thing – it should look great. It should be exciting and should be well lit. It should be well positioned; works should be given enough space to breath. (O'Molloy, interview, 2002)

The phrase 'to its best advantage' must be understood in context, a context linked to the museum's principles. Arguably, in a museum like the Louvre, where the convention is to group artworks by period and school, displaying works to their best advantage would involve a different use of the exhibition space. Here, the opinions presented so far suggest that exhibition-making at IMMA is a form of postmodern translation in that it puts into practice the museum's worldview, with its emphasis on challenging value in art and providing multiple interpretations for artworks.

Works from the collection are also shown with text panels offering an explanation of the exhibition's *raison d'être*, as well as texts referring to individual works. This form of display differs from the shows organized by the exhibition department (ED) which use only 'very minimal modernist labels'. The lack of a proper budget for exhibitions of the museum's collection is only partly responsible for this use of texts; the aim is to avoid resembling a 'white cube' by providing viewers with a context for the interpretation of artworks:

> That's usually because their [the exhibition department's] shows are very much more focused; the ancillary information that you might need is usually in the form of books and catalogues, and they would have much more reading material on offer. The collection department doesn't have a budget to bring out nice books every time – doesn't have any budget for that. We're lucky if we get a little exhibition guide. But from the first day that I came to work here, and I think that might have to do with my background as a teacher and lecturer in history of art, I said that from the beginning we would offer extended captions. And that is a postmodernist idea, I think, not a modernist one. It's completely against the white cube aesthetic. (Marshall, interview, 2001)

The size of the artworks is another element which influences the way they are presented. The arrangement of works needs to consider their size, what works are suitable to be positioned together, and whether they look well visually. The spatial arrangement of works, and the location of a museum or gallery – whether it is a historic or new building – support the creating of different meanings. But once these requirements are taken into account, curators are able to create particular interpretations of the artworks, depending on how and where they are exhibited. This is facilitated by using artworks offering multiple meanings, as in the case of the Irish Art Now exhibition, whose works toured to different venues in the US, with different results:

> It's very interesting, because basically you have the same works in five different venues and you see a completely different reading of some works depending on what they are placed beside, or what sort of building they are in, the history of that building. There are all sorts of ways that these works can change, even though this is an exhibition doing a very specific thing. It's presenting a particular reading of Irish art in the '90s, poetic and political . . . You can't pin down the work, saying, you know, this work is only saying this one thing. The works

> have multiple meanings; the displays would reflect that, so each individual in the four different venues would add their own take. (O'Molloy, interview, 2002)

While artworks can take on various meanings due to their physical characteristics, or the ways in which they are presented, curating practices can also fix or close off meanings, or open up new interpretations of the works on display:

> You can either be opening up new readings or closing them off . . . You are either opening it up to the possibility for a new meaning, or new reading, or you're not; or you're saying this is it, and it's defined. Sometimes you can find that a very straightforward or conventional, or traditional way of presenting work can be restrictive, in saying that it's laid in stone, this is what this work means. But if you can manage to create a more open exhibition then you have more possibilities for the work being accessed by a greater number of people. (O'Molloy, interview, 2002)

This comment is a useful way to focus on the sorts of models invoked in the views above. IMMA's curating practices resemble the two models of curation suggested by Serota: curatorial interpretation and the making of *mise-en-scène*. Curatorial interpretation occurs when curators are able to have a more involved role in exhibition design, and create meanings for the artworks with the use of text panels and extended captions. On the other hand, IMMA's exhibitions are also acting as *mise-en-scène*, facilitating a context for the public to engage in the interpretation of art, by creating spaces which are well lit and have enough space to move around. These initial suggestions need to be explored further through an analysis of the actual exhibitions. The rest of this chapter is devoted to analyzing three exhibitions of IMMA's collection: Irish Art Now: From the Poetic to the Political (2001–02), Art Unsolved (1998), and Art Without Precedent (2000). It discusses the main points raised so far in order to reflect, more generally, on the intellectual practices involved in exhibition-making.[6]

EXHIBITIONS: INITIAL QUESTIONS

The museum exhibition space consists of the RHK's building, the National Galleries built onto the gardens surrounding IMMA to increase the amount of exhibition space available, as well as the gardens and courtyard. The main building is divided into east and west wings and has two floors. The ground floor holds the east wing galleries and the Gordon Lambert Galleries in the west wing. The landing next to the reception area offers some exhibition space, which is used by both temporary exhibitions and exhibitions of the

IMAGE 1. Entrance to the Irish Museum of Modern Art. East Gate. Photo: author.

IMAGE 2. Entrance to the Irish Museum of Modern Art. East Arch. Photo: Irish Museum of Modern Art.

IMAGE 3. Irish Museum of Modern Art courtyard. Juan Muñoz, **Conversation Piece for Dublin**, 1994, Resin, sand, and cloth. Photo: Irish Museum of Modern Art.

IMAGE 4. Reception Area. Irish Museum of Modern Art. Photo: Irish Museum of Modern Art.

collection. Exhibitions of the collection are usually located in the west wing on the first floor, although at times they can also occupy the east wing. The courtyard and gardens are used to exhibit the collection's outdoor works.

So far this chapter has argued that exhibition-making is a form of translation within IMMA's sub-field, putting into practice the museum's worldview by using existing exhibition techniques, part of the exhibition field. This point has been raised in our interviews with curators; now we explore whether this form of translation, or delivering IMMA's world-view, also occurs in the actual exhibitions of works from the collection. How is translation put to work in the exhibition, setting through the selection and positioning of artworks, and the use of texts and labels? What types of texts, labels and captions are used in the exhibitions? Are they educational, situating the works displayed within a period of art history, or do they merely enhance the aesthetic qualities of the artworks? Our focus in explaining these exhibition designs continues the discussion of translation with regard to Serota's models of curatorial practices.

IRISH ART NOW: FROM THE POETIC TO THE POLITICAL

Irish Art Now was the first travelling exhibition of IMMA's collection, put together as a touring exhibition to the US. Independent Curators International (ICI) initiated the project, and IMMA's director curated the show: he selected the artworks, and wrote an essay for the catalogue[7] which presented the themes the exhibition sought to address.[8] Initially, the exhibition was to be shown in the US only, but in the process it was decided to exhibit it in Dublin to celebrate the first touring exhibition from the collection.[9] On its arrival at IMMA after its two-year tour, the exhibition had its final showing in 2001–02, and ran from November until March. Although the director was the exhibition's curator, by the time it arrived in Dublin he had already resigned from his post. The collection department took over both the spatial arrangement of the works and writing the exhibition's wall text. The following analysis focuses on the exhibition at IMMA.

The Irish Art Now exhibition includes forty artworks by thirteen artists working in different media – painting, photography, sculpture, video and installation. As the title indicates, they are all of Irish background. In this sense, the exhibition represents a wide variety of artistic practices by artists from both sides of the border. A maximum of three works per artist are included; in some cases there is only one, as with Alanna O'Kelly's video installation, *Sanctuary/Wastelands,* and Maurice O'Connell's installation *Never Mind 'Kangaroo', Just Answer the Question.* Only a small number of works per artist is included in order to portray the artistic practice of a group, as opposed to an in-depth focus on works by the individual artists. Most of the works selected are part of the museum's collection, except in those cases when it was necessary to borrow recent works by an artist. All the artists in the exhibition have a certain status in Dublin's art world; the works of at least eight are currently represented by one of Dublin's leading commercial galleries.

The exhibition includes a wall text written by the collection's senior curator, following the ideas presented by the director in the catalogue published to accompany the exhibition's US tour. It also mentions the curator's name and her position in the museum – senior curator and head of collections – as a way of legitimating the contents of the interpretations it offers. Texts are important analytical tools: they link the written message with the visual arrangement of works. The text in this exhibition exemplifies a didactic approach to thinking about art. It helps viewers learn, not about the formal characteristic of the artworks, the materials used, or the process of their making, but about their context of production, explaining, in this case, how they participate in the process of change and transformation in Ireland.

The exhibition's aim is to bring 'to public scrutiny the changes that have taken place in attitudes to visual art and to art making in Ireland, during the last decade of the twentieth century'.[10] The text situates Irish art in the context of Irish society, arguing that changes in the cultural, social and political spheres of Irish life are matched by corresponding changes in the visual arts. In this way, Irish art is conceptualized as dynamic, and Irish artists as part of a group engaged in similar tasks: reflecting on the changes around them, like the population growth in cities, the feminist revolution and the development of the Irish economy, as well as dealing with contemporary issues such as the legacy of the colonial experience, or a feminist examination of religious rituals. The text also explains how the practice of these artists expresses some of the museum's ways of thinking about art:

> Ultimately the artists all share the questioning of language and communication made explicit in Maurice O'Connell's *Never Mind*

IMAGE 5. Willie Doherty. **Incident**, 1993, Cibachrome on aluminium, and **Border Incident**, 1994, Cibachrome on aluminium. Irish Art Now Exhibition. Photo: Irish Museum of Modern Art.

IMAGE 6. Alice Maher. **Staircase of Thorns**, 1997, Rose thorns and wood, and **Familiar 1**, 1994, Acrylic on canvas, flax and wood. Irish Art Now Exhibition. Photo: Irish Museum of Modern Art.

IMAGE 7. Fionnuala Ní Chiosáin, **Untitled**, 1998, Sumi ink on paper, **Untitled**, 1993, Sumi ink on paper, **Untitled**, 1998, Sumi ink on paper, and (in the background) **Modern Nature #4**, 1993–4, Acrylic and Sumi ink on paper on wood. Irish Art Now Exhibition. Photo: Irish Museum of Modern Art.

> *'Kangaroo', Just Answer the Question*. If language is indeterminate then we are all responsible for our own interpretations and our own construction of meaning; this is an uncompromisingly political position.[11]

The mention of 'we are all responsible' includes viewers, who are given an active role in the creation of meaning for the artworks on display. Qualifying this task as a political position gives a second meaning to the term 'political' in the title: not only is Irish art political, in redefining existing perceptions of its environment, but viewers are also invited to take political positions in relation to that art. The argument illustrates one of the principles of IMMA's worldview – the redefinition of ways of thinking about art. In this case, the text articulates a form of translation within IMMA's subfield by making explicit how the selection of works fits into its aesthetic outlook.

The Irish Art Now exhibition took place in the east wing of the museum, consisting of a long corridor and seven adjacent small rooms. The presentation of artworks created two types of spaces: firstly, a use of space encouraging the 'aestheticization of art', a *mise-en-scène*, allowing visitors to focus solely on the artworks; and, secondly, a more analytical approach, encouraging multiple readings and interpretations of the artworks on display.

Identity labels are used to give basic information about the works: name of the artist, title, year, materials and origin of the work, e.g. the museum's collection or a loan from the artist or a gallery. Hence their role here is not didactic, as in the case of the wall text referred above, but simply referential. As mentioned earlier, the design of exhibitions entailed a responsibility towards exhibiting the artists' works according to their specific instructions. Irish Art Now is an example of this in practice. For example, Willie Doherty (image 5) requested that his photographs be hung lower than standard practice. Other types of requirements were those of installation works, as in the case of Alice Maher's *Familiar 1,* (image 6), which needed a certain type of wall for the peg to go in, so that the flax could hang on it. Apart from fulfilling the artists' requirements, curators can also position works in ways which emphasize certain interpretations.

In the exhibition all the seven small rooms are connected, so viewers can decide whether to look at the works following the rooms' sequence, or to go from the rooms to the corridor and vice-versa. One way of starting to move through the exhibition is to walk along the corridor and start exploring the rooms attached to it. In some of the rooms, artworks are grouped by individual artist. The first room displays a single work by Maurice O'Connell, *Never Mind 'Kangaroo', Just Answer the Question.* It shows a stuffed wallaby standing on the floor next to a text with analyses of questionnaires hung on the wall. On one side of the corridor hang three ink paintings by Fionnuala Ní Chiosáin (image 7). Opposite it is an entry to room 1,[12] displaying four photographs by artist Willie Doherty. *Incident* and *Border Incident* are positioned on two consecutive walls (image 5), and two other photographs *Longing* and *Lamenting,* occupy another wall. This room provides an entrance to a dark room showing Alanna O'Kelly's installation video *Sanctuary/Wastelands*.

The next room (2) shows a different form of display; it contains works by two different artists: Ciarán Lennon, an oil entitled *Hearth*, and Billy Quinn's *Billy* (image 8). Next to the room there is a small space with a television showing Dorothy Cross' video *Storm in a Tea Cup*. This space leads to another room (3) with two works also by Cross, *Saddle* and *Kitchen Table* (image 9). Next to this room is a study space with a desk, chair and publications for the public to sit down and read. The study space is relevant for various reasons. It allows viewers to learn more about each artist from the biographical

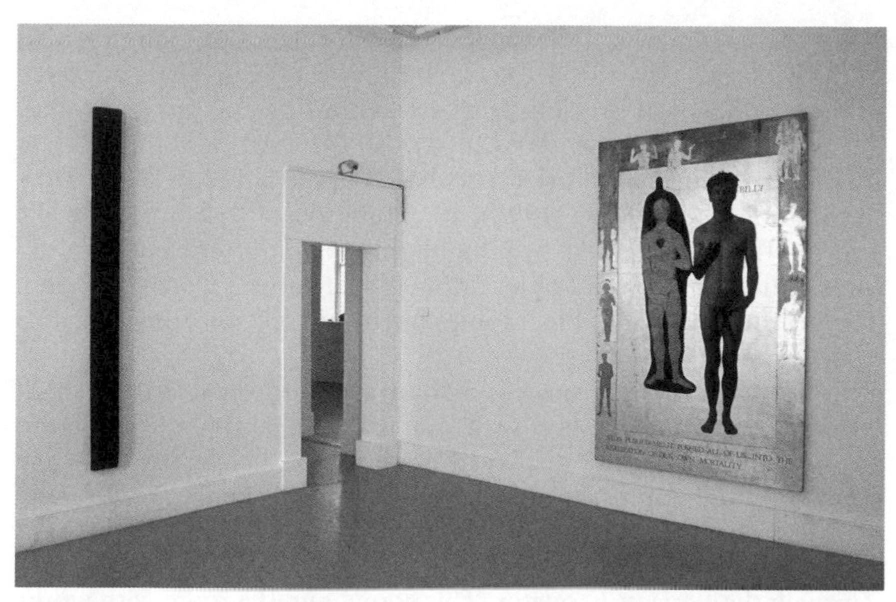

IMAGE 8. Ciarán Lennon, **Hearth**, 1990, Oil on linen, and Billy Quinn, **Billy**, 1991, Laser prints, gold and silver leaf, acrylic on wood. Irish Art Now Exhibition. Photo: Irish Museum of Modern Art.

IMAGE 9. Dorothy Cross. **Kitchen Table**, 1990, Wood, enamel, bowl, steel, glass test-tube, fossilized shark teeth, and **Saddle**, 1993, Saddle, preserved cow udder, metal stand. Irish Art Now Exhibition. Photo: Irish Museum of Modern Art.

texts; it also emphasizes the didactic ethos of the exhibition provided in the wall text. Apart from the exhibition's catalogue, there are three other catalogues of previous Irish art exhibitions: Shifting Ground, Selected Works of Irish Art (2001), at IMMA; OO44 (1994), a travelling exhibition of Irish artists based in the UK, and When Time Began to Rant and Rage (1998), an exhibition of Irish art in the UK and the US. These books help highlight the importance of Irish art outside Ireland, as well as presenting it as a subject worth studying. The desk also provides biographies of the artists, sometimes next to each of the artists' works.

Following the study space is a room (4) with six relatively small works (four hung on one wall and two on another) by Ciarán Lennon, symmetrically displayed at the same height. In the same room two televisions are positioned on white pedestals showing Caroline McCarthy's video installation, *Greetings*. A small space next to this room shows another video installation by McCarthy, *Journey Through the Longest Escalator*. This room, and the room with works by Billy Quinn and Ciarán Lennon, are the only two examples of small spaces where works by two artists are positioned together. The last three rooms again show works by individual artists: Paul

IMAGE 10. Billy Quinn, 1997. **Quinn's Da,** Laser prints, mixed media on plywood/MDF panels. Eleven panels, and Kathy Prendergast, **Stack**, 1989–91, Cloth, string, paint and wood. Irish Art Now Exhibition. Photo: Irish Museum of Modern Art.

IMAGE 11. Abigail O'Brien, **The Ophelia Room**, 1998, Three Cibachrome photographs mounted on aluminium, and **The Last Supper**, 1995, Seven Cibachrome photographs mounted on aluminium, table, chair, embroidered tablecloth. Irish Art Now Exhibition. Photo: Irish Museum of Modern Art.

IMAGE 12. Kathy Prendergast, **Prayer Gloves**, 1998, A pair of gloves knitted together in a praying-like pose. Irish Art Now Exhibition, Photo: Irish Museum of Modern Art.

Seawright (5), Alice Maher (6) and Mark Francis (7). In room 5 we see three photographs by Paul Seawright hanging individually on each of the room's walls. Room 6 contains three works by Alice Maher: a sculpture, *Staircase of Thorns,* hanging on a wall; another wall displays an installation work, *Familiar 1* (image 6); and the last work, *Coma Berenices*, a charcoal on paper, hangs on a third wall. There is a fourth work also by Maher in the small space next to the room, *Berry Dress*, shown on a glass shelf to facilitate the appreciation of the thorns underneath the dress. The last of the rooms (7) displays four paintings by Mark Francis positioned individually on each of the walls.

The displays in these rooms prioritize an arrangement by artist, with very few works included in each room. These are small spaces, with relatively low ceilings, particularly in relation to the long corridor, whose ceiling is much higher. This type of space favours an intimate encounter between viewers and the works on display. Although the windows in the rooms facing the museum's gardens can distract visitors from looking at the art, the layout of works in the spaces reinstates a sense of contemplation of the works displayed. In short, the rooms are suggestive of Serota's notion of *mise-en-scène*, as spaces which enhance the contemplation of artworks.

The long corridor, however, creates another type of viewing space. Most of the large works are located in the corridor, either hanging on the wall spaces available between the entries to the rooms or positioned directly on the floor. The demands of space may be a reason why we see works by various artists grouped together. First, on the left, is Billy Quinn's *Quinn's Da* (image 10), consisting of eleven large panels (60 x 60 inches each) of laser prints hung on the wall. Also on the left, we see another large work, Ciarán Lennon's painting *1/3/92B*, which stands 97 x 195 x 4 inches. Next to it are two photographs by Paul Seawright, *Black Spike* and *Flag,* both from his Fire Series. Image 11 shows the same side of the corridor with Abigail O'Brien's installation work, *The Last Supper*, including seven photographs, a long table, positioned on the floor, with white tablecloth and a chair. The last exhibit on this wall is O'Brien's *The Ophelia Room,* three large photographs hung on the wall. The display of works by different artists continues at the other side of the corridor. On the right, there are three ink paintings by Fionnuala Ní Chiosáin (image 7). Next are two works by Kathy Prendergast, *Love Object* (a comb and hair positioned in a glass vitrine secured to the wall) and *Prayer Gloves* (image 12) on a small shelf; close to them, in the middle of the corridor, stands her large sculpture, 108 x 104 x 28 inches, *Stack A* (image 10). Although works continue to be displayed according to artist, the use of space in the corridor offers a broader perspective of various practices in Irish art, as opposed to focusing on one artist.

The corridor provides a different viewing experience from the small rooms. This is a long, wide exhibition space with a high ceiling, and windows looking onto the museum's courtyard. In short, the intimate encounter created in the small rooms is not possible here. Viewers are encouraged more to seek relationships between the various works on display. The question is: what sort of links can be established between the artworks? Although, according to the exhibition text, all the works share an engagement in topics such as politics, gender and landscape, these connections may not be obvious to viewers, particularly to those not very knowledgeable about contemporary Irish art. This is especially the case of those artworks whose meaning may not be clear at first sight, e.g. Prendergast's *Love Object* or Maher's *Familiar 1*.

But the exhibition is intended to enable viewers to create particular links between the works. For example, at first glance Abigail O'Brien's *The Last Supper,* with photographs of women involved in a contemporary version of the religious ritual, and Kathy Prendergast's *Prayer Gloves*, are both making allusions to religious rituals. O'Brien, in particular, is clearly arguing for an alternative appreciation of a biblical scene in which women, not men, are a majority. Another possible association is that between Ciarán Lennon's *1/3/92B* and Fionnuala Ní Choisáin's work. Their abstract paintings position them as the more poetic artists in the exhibition, particularly so if we compare them to Paul Seawright's political use of photography to document the destruction in Northern Ireland, or Billy Quinn's photographs suggesting the passing of time and arrival of death (in a sequence of eleven images, the last one portrays an empty chair). Prendergast's *Stack A,* Seawright's photographs and McCarthy's video, positioned in a close space, appear to want to challenge the traditional view of Irish identity as something closely tied to the land. Similarly, O'Kelly's video and O'Doherty's photographs deal with the idea of memory and how one's idea of a landscape may not be necessarily accurate.[13]

These are only some examples, and there may be others. Overall, artworks in the rooms and corridor follow a classification by theme. Again, the ability to interpret the thematic affinities between works depends on the visitors' location within the exhibition space, and on their existing knowledge of Irish art. The distribution of works in the corridor, however, facilitates various readings. Although the use of exhibition techniques, such as the use of vitrines and shelves, does not in itself provide innovative ways of looking at art, the arrangement of works certainly does.

ART UNSOLVED

Artists in Irish Art Now are all well-known, professional art practitioners. The exhibitions from the Musgrave Kinley Outsider Art Collection provide a different perspective, as they only include artworks made by non-professional artists. Moreover, what makes outsiders different from the artists in Irish Art Now is precisely their lack of interest in publicizing their work. Another difference between outsiders and mainstream artists is that the former do not set up requirements for the visual presentation of their works. This gives curators an added responsibility because they need to devise ways to present the artworks, as opposed to ensuring that the artists' wishes are met. The display practices presented are from two solo exhibitions of the outsider art collection. The 1998 exhibition, Art Unsolved (June–October) was organized to commemorate this loan to IMMA, while Art Without Precedent in 2000 (January–May) offered a more in-depth approach to the collection with a selection of works from nine artists. The exhibition included more than 200 works by seventy artists, from a collection of more than 750 works by artists from all around the world.[14] Art Unsolved was the first public exhibition of outsider art in Ireland.

The exhibition includes two types of texts to frame the visual display: a wall text and identity tags to accompany each work. On this occasion, the wall text is co-written by the director and the collection's senior curator. The exhibition's title, Art Unsolved, is borrowed from a piece in the outsider collection by Dusan Kusmic, and is used to illustrate a general principle of all art. The wall text explains that Art Unsolved indicates that these 'artworks are ultimately unsolvable because the scientific method, the basis of consensual art history, is actually not applicable to them'. But the term 'art unsolved' has also a 'more universal application' – 'It suggests that all art is unsolvable, is unknowable, that there can be no single, permanent definition of value and meaning in art'.[15] In designating outsider art as 'unsolved' and then applying this principle to all types of art, the text calls attention to the fact that outsider art is of equal quality to any other. As seen in chapter 4, this was the aim behind the acceptance of this collection on loan: to emphasize the lack of distinctions between outsider and other works. As the senior curator of the museum's collection put it: 'the work these artists are doing is art, whether it is inside the gallery or it is not'. The text also points up the suitability of the loan in the context of the museum's worldview. Outsider artworks 'make a powerful argument for a new way of looking and thinking about art, which is open and inclusive rather than closed and exclusive'. The text continues:

> [The collection] is an appropriate loan to this Museum because of the Museum's founding principle that it must engage in the renegotiation of standing definitions of artist and non-artist, and of the categorizations which have traditionally ascribed value to art, artists and cultural institutions in society. There is currently an opportunity and, in fact, a necessity, as we face a new millennium, to create and support new, broader definitions of value in art.[16]

The exhibition is presented as an expression of the museum's worldview; outsider art helps renegotiate concepts such as artist and art value. At the same time, the text explains the difference between this art and the mainstream by referring to the unusual circumstances in which outsiders produce their work, and their indifference to the 'world of traditional art history': 'the artists who produce outsider art do not have professional qualifications'. The text describes some of the conditions in which outsiders create their art:

> Scottie Wilson ran a junk shop until one day he tried out the gold nib of a pen he had intended to melt down and became totally committed to drawing from then on. Dusan Kusmic was traumatised when a fellow inmate of a post-war refugee camp committed suicide during a mealtime. Using the bread he was unable to swallow he began to mould small objects and unleashed a flood of creative energy which was sustained throughout the remainder of his life. Although blind in one eye, Madge Gill worked at night, rarely using artificial lighting, to produce hundreds of drawings at the behest of her 'spirit guide'.[17]

There is an underlying tension in this text. Outsider art is presented as an aesthetic paradigm for seeing and thinking about all art: it is unsolvable. But the text also 'solves', or explains, outsider art by highlighting the conditions in which it was produced, the unusual circumstances in which outsiders create their work, conditions which

IMAGE 13. Various artists. Art Unsolved Exhibition, Photo: Irish Museum of Modern Art.

IMAGE 14. Three works by Dusan Kusmic (on the right side standing on a pedestal), **Untitled**, painted plaster, **Untitled**, painted plaster, **Come Ado**, painted plaster. On the left side and inside a vitrine, **Untitled**, small boots, sculpture. Art Unsolved Exhibition, Photo: Irish Museum of Modern Art.

foster this type of aesthetic creativity. The overall emphasis of the text is didactic in informing visitors about outsider art and encouraging a questioning approach to art. Apart from the wall text, there is also a study space with the collection's catalogue, Outsiders: An Art Without Precedent or Tradition (1979), and various issues of the outsider art magazine *Raw Vision*. Bearing this in mind, I refer next to the visual arrangement of works.

The exhibition was located in the east wing of the museum, the same space as the Irish Art Now exhibition. This type of space recalls, partly, a white cube: the white walls, grey floor, and lack of any ornamentation accentuate the intrinsic value of the art on display, without invoking any information on its context. But the artworks are contextualized in the exhibition; they are given an identity tag covering only basic facts such as the work's title, its maker, the year the work was made, the type of materials used and the work's source: the Musgrave Kinley Outsider Art Collection.

In this exhibition works are displayed with the use of props: vitrines, pedestals and tables with vitrines. Image 13 shows the long corridor where tables and a pedestal with vitrines are positioned to aid the appreciation of the artworks. These forms of presentation help protect fragile works, but they also create specific ways of looking at art:

> The act of placing an object in a vitrine immediately focuses attention on it and suggests that it might also be both precious and vulnerable. The vitrine reinforces the notion of the unique, untouchable and unattainable and, perhaps significantly, has its roots in the medieval church reliquary. It therefore enhances the inherent visual power of an object to catch a viewer's attention and to stimulate contemplation. The effect of placing something in a vitrine is to 'museumize' it: the glass creates not just a physical barrier but establishes an 'official distance' between object and viewer. By rendering untouchable the contained object or work of art, the more important and precious it becomes. (Putnam, 2001: 36)

Vitrines highlight the formal qualities of the works on display; they help control the exhibition space, projecting a distance between artworks. But, as Putnam indicates, they also stimulate a contemplative state in viewers – they are conducive to a prolonged gaze. Consequently, viewers are more likely to be interested in something that has been so carefully separated from the rest; presented as a self-contained entity valuable in itself. Image 14 shows the landing space. The positioning of small sculptures on pedestals with vitrines, and

IMAGE 15. Henry Darger, **Double sided Triptych**, Watercolour and pencil on paper, and Michel Nedjar, **Untitled,** (bottle), Tissue paper, earth, glass bottle. Art Unsolved Exhibition, Photo: Irish Museum of Modern Art.

IMAGE 16. Works by various artists. Art Unsolved Exhibition, Photo: Irish Museum of Modern Art.

IMAGE 17. Michel Nedjar, **Untitled,** (bottle), Tissue paper, earth, glass bottle, and works by various artists in the background. Art Unsolved Exhibition, Photo: Irish Museum of Modern Art.

IMAGE 18. Scottie Wilson, **Untitled,** Porcelain tea set. Art Unsolved Exhibition, Photo: Irish Museum of Modern Art.

bigger works on pedestals, shows a careful classification of works according to, not only fragility, but also to size. The exhibition recalls Serota's argument about the practice of creating *mise-en-scène*. Highlighting the formal qualities of the artworks is a way of aestheticizing outsider art, presenting it as valuable in its own right. But its display is also helping to deliver the museum's worldview, treating outsider art as if it were mainstream art; in IMMA they are both exhibited with the same exhibition techniques. The exhibition achieves its aim of renegotiating standing definitions of art value, as all art is presented following the same display conventions.

However, the exhibition also breaks its impulse to aestheticize outsider art by deliberately positioning the works of different artists together. This feature is prevalent in the whole exhibition space, its corridor and rooms. For example, image 15 shows one of the small rooms attached to the corridor with works by at least three different artists. The glass bottle in the vitrine is by Michel Nedjar, the double-sided triptych is by Henry Darger, and one of the drawings is by Jean-Marie Heyligen. Apart from displaying a variety of artists, the rooms show quite a number of artworks. In image 16 works by various artists are grouped together; they are symmetrically positioned, in some cases in double-line hanging. The organization of works of differing sizes in centre line alignment gives a visually balanced relationship.[18] This is a concession to viewers, at least to adults, because it places works so that the viewing height coincides with the average eye-level for adults (Dean, 1994: 57). The wall on the right side of the image includes works by at least six artists. From left to right we see works by Friedrich Schroder Sonnenstern, Richard Nie, Warren Robin, Juanita Rogers, August Walla and Michael the Cartographer.

A similar form of display prevails in image 17, with artworks by various artists, sometimes in double-line hanging. This mode of presentation evokes a lively visual aesthetic created by positioning works close together, as opposed to keeping them well spaced. It creates a sense of outsiders as being part of a cohesive group. Conversely, the display of a very small number of works, well separated, would have reinforced a sense of outsiders as individual artists. But the spatial arrangement of works is evocative of 'outsider art' in general, rather than 'outsider artist'.

This arrangement of artworks does not seem to prioritize the creation of multiple meanings, as in Irish Art Now. This is rather difficult given the amount of works (image 18), and their similar medium (they are all paintings) and size. What prevails is a space organized around the formal similarities of the works on display, as opposed to any existing thematic slants in outsiders' art. In addition, some rooms include two modes of presentation, glass vitrines and works hanging on the walls (images 17 and 18). These rooms enable two forms of looking. Some works are in vitrines, thus singling out their formal aesthetic qualities, helping to create a sense of contemplation in the viewer. Paintings are hung close together and sometimes in double line, thus projecting a vision of outsider artists as a group. The intimate encounter between art and viewers promoted by the scarcity of works in the rooms of Irish Art Now is not possible here. But most important is how the techniques of positioning and presenting works keep viewers busy looking, rather than allowing them time to look and reflect on what they see, for example emphasizing the connections between works.

ART WITHOUT PRECEDENT: NINE ARTISTS FROM THE MUSGRAVE KINLEY OUTSIDER ART COLLECTION

The artists selected for this exhibition are from a variety of countries: Austria (Oswald Tschirtner), Britain (Madge Gill, Carl Peploe and Ben Wilson), former Checkoslovakia (Anna Zemankova), France (Michel Nedjar), Italy (Carlo), and the US (Henry Darger and 'J.B.' Murry). But, most importantly, all the artists are well known as part of the established outsider art canon. The names of Henry Darger, Ben Wilson, Madge Gill, Michel Nedjar, John Murry, Oswald Tschirtner and Anna Zemankova can be found in recent books on outsider art.[19] From this point of view, the exhibition helps reinforce the reputations of outsiders who have achieved recognition, rather than exploring the works of lesser-known artists in the collection. Moreover, the biographical texts serve to create a hierarchy among the artists exhibited, since they highlight the prestige of some outsiders whose work is included in the Collection de l'Art Brut in Lausanne (Carlo, Anna Zemankova); or Henry Darger, who is presented as 'One of the most famous of all Outsider artists since his discovery in 1973'.[20]

The title Art Without Precedent gives these artists' work cohesion. All produce works following neither previous models nor examples. As the exhibition's text says: 'All share an ability to focus totally on their own inner vision uninhibited by training, received art practice or, above all, by the weight of art history'.[21] This definition of outsider art is the same as that presented in Art Unsolved. But Art Without Precedent links the exhibition to a previous event; the first landmark outsider exhibition in the UK, entitled Outsiders: An Art Without Precedent or Tradition (1979).

The text mentions the title of IMMA's first outsider art exhibition, Art Unsolved, which again is used to characterize or universalize a definition of art which transcends the boundaries between outsiders and insiders. This is a claim the exhibition aims to fulfil, as it makes 'a powerful argument for a new way of looking and thinking about art which is open and inclusive, rather than closed and exclusive'. As in Art Unsolved, outsider art is seen as providing an alternative interpretative framework for looking and thinking about art in an inclusive way. Finally, the text links this framework to the museum's worldview, the renegotiation of definitions of artist and non-artist, as well as of the categories which, traditionally, have ascribed value to art, artists and cultural institutions.

The text refers to the artists in the exhibition as representing 'most of the leading issues relating to Outsider Art'. In so doing, it supports the selection of the artists on display. It continues by describing the particularities of outsider artists' production, and elaborates on how some of them work at the margins of society; most have no professional training as artists; and few have any concern for the art market. These artists, then, are selected as representing the various traits of the notion 'outsider artist'. A biography for each of the artists on display is another source of written information provided in the exhibition space.

Biographies are important for what they say about the artists and their work, and also because they establish the artists as individual figures, even memorable characters whose lives are worth recording. The texts in the exhibition offer two types of information: didactic, personal details, and an aesthetic appreciation of the artworks. The following portrayal of Madge Gill takes a didactic stance, which informs viewers of the specific circumstances in which the artist produced her work:

> She gave birth to a stillborn daughter and in the same year lost the sight of one eye. At this time she began to draw and embroider, often working late at night with little or no light. She disclaimed ownership of her work saying that she was guided to do it by a spirit called Myninerest.[22]

IMAGE 19. Works by various artists. Art Without Precedent. Nine Artists from the Musgrave Kinley Outsider Art Collection. Photo: Irish Museum of Modern Art.

IMAGE 20. **Double sided Triptych,** Watercolour and pencil on paper, Michel Nedjar, **Untitled,** (bottle), Tissue paper, earth, glass bottle, and **Untitled,** Sculpture. Art Unsolved Exhibition, Photo: Irish Museum of Modern Art.

IMAGE 21. Carlo, Untitled, on a pedestal, and on the right, hanging on the wall, Madge Gill, **Untitled**, Ink on Canvas, **Faces**, Ink postcards, and **Untitled**, Pen and Ink. Art Without Precedent. Nine Artists from the Musgrave Kinley Outsider Art Collection. Photo: Irish Museum of Modern Art.

The aesthetic stance of biographies reveals details such as the kind of materials and skills the artists bring to their work. For example, Oswald Tschirtner's biography states:

> The minimalism of Tschirtner's pen and ink drawings is as shocking by avant garde standards as the work of the New York School in the sixties and seventies, yet he was quite unaware of art movements outside of the walls of his hospital.[23]

On another occasion, similarities are drawn between outsiders and mainstream artists, as in the case of John Murry:

> Murry's drawings and paintings, often on both sides of the paper, or like Picasso's newspaper drawings, overlaid on pages of journals and periodicals, hinge around a highly personalized and expressive form of calligraphy. The script is arranged in rhythmic groups of colours and forms and contains a spiritual message which Murry interpreted by examining it through a bottle of 'holy water'.[24]

The visual presentation of works can help assess further the balance between the didactic and aesthetic components of the exhibition, and their relation to IMMA's worldview.

IMAGE 22.Two double sided works by Carlo, both **Untitled**. Art Without Precedent. Nine Artists from the Musgrave Kinley Outsider Art Collection. Photo: Irish Museum of Modern Art.

IMAGE 23. Works by various artists. Art Without Precedent. Nine Artists from the Musgrave Kinley Outsider Art Collection. Photo: Irish Museum of Modern Art.

IMAGE 24. Ben Wilson (left), **Sungod**, Wood, and **Tree**, Wood sculpture. Art Without Precedent. Nine Artists from the Musgrave Kinley Outsider Art Collection. Photo: Irish Museum of Modern Art.

The exhibition took place in the Gordon Lambert Galleries, a space consisting of three consecutive rooms with windows overlooking IMMA's gardens. This space is smaller than the east wing, where both of the previous exhibitions took place. The even distribution of works suggests that they are all perceived as having equivalent artistic quality. The forty-one works on display are classified by artist, with more than one artist in each of the rooms. The first room as we enter the galleries (image 19) includes sculptures by Michael Nedjar, and Carl Peploe's books lay out on a table with vitrine. Another view of the same space (image 20) represents the display of a double-sided triptych by Henry Darger, and one of Nedjar's bottles turned into rag dolls. The second room (image 22) has two-side drawings by Carlo in frames and up on pedestals; hanging on the wall are Madge Gill's drawings, and, also by her, a silk embroidery displayed on a table with vitrine (image 21). Hanging on the wall are Oswald Tschirtner's drawings. The same image also offers glimpses of the third room, which holds Ben Wilson's *Sungod*, John Murry's drawings and paintings, and on the side wall between the windows are Anna Zemankova's drawings. The techniques of presentation are the same as in Art Unsolved. Some objects are in glass vitrines (image 20), other paintings are positioned in stand-up frames on pedestals (images 21 and 22), and the rest of the pictures and figures are hung on walls with an identity tag of the same kind as in the previous exhibition (images 23 and 24). These forms of presentation emphasize the uniqueness and formal qualities of the works. Glass vitrines also stimulate the contemplation of the objects because these can be apprehended from various viewpoints. Taken together with stand-up frames on pedestals, they enhance a sense of movement; they break the symmetry of the works hung on walls by allowing viewers to move through the gallery space. Conversely, paintings are hung flat against walls; this mode of presentation limits visitors' movement to the contemplation of a single perspective on the works. A more dynamic experience could be achieved, for example, by tilting paintings to a desired viewing angle. Props also serve to delimit the exhibition space; there is enough space between displays for visitors to move freely, while the symmetry of their positioning creates an ordered and controlled environment. Overall, the presentation of artworks articulates IMMA's principle of displaying outsider art as if it were any other, but most striking in this exhibition is the use of space. Compared to Art Unsolved, there are fewer objects on display, and emptier walls. A large wall has only two artworks (image 24) and paintings are hung in single-line hanging, as opposed to the double-line hanging in Art Unsolved. This is a relevant feature of the exhibition, given the relatively small size of the Gordon Lambert Galleries in comparison to the east wing in which the collection had been displayed. This is a much more intimate space, and yet the sparse displays give the impression of a much larger exhibition.

CONCLUSION

The three analyses have provided an important conclusion: the need to rethink the model of an aesthetic museum, and the making of *mise-en-scène* as the only practice prevalent in the EF in its contemporary context. Rather, it would be more appropriate to see exhibition-making as combining aspects of the aestheticization of art with a form of curatorial intervention which seeks to encourage a more didactic approach to art appreciation. Maybe the struggle between these two forms of display is what IMMA's director meant by the creation of a contest in aesthetic. But, to be more precise, what we have is the coexistence of various elements of exhibition design, which create different kinds of interpretative frameworks; two ways of creating symbolic capital for the artworks in IMMA's collection: aesthetic and didactic. In sum, collecting and exhibiting are similar practices in that they both share a commitment to delivering IMMA's worldview. It is possible to argue that postmodern translation, in collecting and exhibiting practices, supports postmodern legislation. It puts it into practice, although not without a struggle.

Conclusion

THIS BOOK HAS explored the practices involved in the making of IMMA's art collection, and contextualized the origins of modern art collecting in Ireland in the foundation of the MGMA. The analysis has been built upon Bauman's and Bourdieu's theories of intellectual practices, which have been reworked and applied to a study of art-collecting practices. In this new model, Bourdieu's concepts of intellectual practice, field and symbolic capital have been applied to the intellectual collecting practices which take place in fields, and are involved in the production of symbolic capital – seen here as prestige – and legitimacy for those artworks that become part of public collections. Bauman's distinction between modern and postmodern practices has helped structure the discussion of a possible change in intellectual collecting practices, from the example of modern legislation in the MGMA, to postmodern interpreting practices in IMMA's example.

One of the main findings in this book is that, while there is a postmodern approach to collecting and exhibiting which wants to challenge and question what counts as value in art, to focus on this one aspect and then argue that collecting is a postmodern practice would be to hide a more significant continuity between modern and postmodern collecting practices. A modern practice has not been superseded by a postmodern practice, because both share a similar legislative element in the creation of boundaries for a given field or sub-field. The foundation of the MGMA, and of IMMA has involved the definition of a new field, or production of symbolic power. The MGMA was instrumental in promoting a debate as to what a distinctive modern Irish art should be. The works in its collection were seen as a model around which a national art school would develop. In this process, the choice of Impressionist works was telling in that it set out a specific artistic style which was deemed to provide a more appropriate basis than any other. The foundation of a collection was a way of articulating a hierarchy of art, in which Impressionist works occupied the top position, one where they were seen as the main inspiration for a distinct Irish art, as against other works in a collection which also included examples of British and Dutch art. Legislation was also involved in setting up the boundaries of IMMA's sub-field, a way of giving the museum and its collection a distinctive purpose and role. In its worldview IMMA, was presented as a museum engaged in the renegotiation of all hierarchies of value in art, a participant in a postmodern discourse arguing for the deconstruction of a linear chronology in art history.

The study of IMMA's collecting practices, in particular, has helped clarify the links between legislation, the making of a field's boundaries, and collecting, which is here a form of translation, or the practice of putting the ideas constituted by legislative boundaries into practice. However, translation practices do not always follow the strict boundaries of a given field. The last two chapters have shown some instances of conflict within IMMA's sub-field. The making of its collection has followed the museum's worldview or field boundary: works were purchased which helped illustrate the renegotiation of identity in art, and loans such as the inclusion of an outsider art collection exemplified the museum's ambition to challenge the classification of art as mainstream and non-mainstream. Yet the analysis of IMMA's exhibitions of its collection has shown a tension between those practices which articulate an aesthetic approach to art, leaving it to audiences to make up their own mind about the meaning of art objects, and didactic practices in art display, which present art as something to be studied, learned about. These exhibitions are examples of conflict between the boundaries set up by legislative practices and how they are put into effect. The challenge for curators is precisely how to reconcile a didactic approach and an exclusively aesthetic one.

One of the premises of this book is that collecting does not take place in a vacuum, but is part of a context in which art is validated and assigned a reputation by the activities of those involved in the world of art. But art-collecting practices are crucial in another fundamental way; they are a means of constituting aesthetic categories, in this case 'modern art', which help distinguish and classify what modern art is, as well as its role, function and social context. The comparison between the MGMA's foundation and IMMA's first ten collecting years reveals a shift in the way intellectual collecting practices have contributed to alternative ways of thinking about the same aesthetic category. This study shows precisely the involvement of art-collecting practices in the definition of 'modern art', and how it represents knowledge about the social world. That is, there has been a change in the knowledge represented or articulated by modern art, both through its collection and display, if we compare what modern art stands for in the context of MGMA's collection and IMMA's. The making of Ireland's first modern art collection was part of a wider debate about the nature of modern art itself, and a means of renegotiating Ireland's position in modernity's hierarchy of nations. In this nation-building process, some sought to transform Dublin into an artistic capital by setting up a collection of Impressionist art which would rival London, where Impressionist works were absent from public collections. Conversely, IMMA presents its modern art collection as a means of renegotiating existing hierarchies of value. IMMA sees itself as a museum whose content and organization are set against the 'treasure house' conception of collecting, fixed on a linear model of art history and collecting only established, canonical artists. In post-colonial Ireland, and with a small purchasing budget, IMMA plays the postmodern card as a virtue and as a necessity – buying work by emerging artists, or, when it is unable to buy such work, securing loans and negotiating deals with them.

This book has presented a sociological approach to the study of art collections, arguing that an analysis of art collections needs to be situated in a context where art is produced and subsequently promoted and exhibited by art institutions. The empirical material has focused on the study of collections in Dublin and analysed some key participants in the Field of Irish Art, but all the empirical work has emphasized that practices in this field, including those of commercial and public galleries, are linked to the international art world, which has an influence on which artists are collected and exhibited in Ireland. This suggests a need for new empirical research tracing the dynamics or relationships between artistic fields in their international context, in this case between Dublin and a major art centre such as London, coupled with the deployment of theories which take into account the international dimension of these practices.

Notes

INTRODUCTION

1 The collection at the Irish Museum of Modern Art has been the subject of research (Kelly, 1999) although not from a sociological perspective.
2 The Municipal Gallery of Modern Art was renamed the Huge Lane Municipal Gallery of Modern Art in 1975 to commemorate the sixtieth anniversary of Hugh Lane's death.
3 An exception is the sociological approach developed by Witkin (1995), who centres his analysis on the content of artworks.
4 DeNora's and Hennion's work is on the sociology of music, but their approaches could also be applied to analyses of the visual arts. DeNora's (2003) study of music looks at how people use and interact with music. What music 'does' to individuals is the key issue; how it is heard and perceived, and the ways in which individuals establish its meaning.

CHAPTER 1

1 See also Price (1989) for a study of how Western academics, curators and professional art dealers were involved in the discovery and definition of Primitive Art.
2 There is a literature dealing with the practices of this profession, looking at issues such as its ethics, the definition of professionalism, or the discussion of institutional standards (Kavanagh, 1994; Dean, 1994).
3 *Irish Press,* 21 May 1991.
4 This is not the first time that Bourdieu's work has been used in sociological explorations of art value. However, neither those who apply his concepts, nor those who criticize their approach to the sociology of art (Laermans, 1992; Loesberg, 1993; Osborne, 1997; Dunn, 1998) have given enough attention to his theory of intellectual practices. Maybe this is one reason why, as Swartz (1997: 218) points out, despite the increasing interest in Bourdieu's work, his analyses of intellectuals in modern societies has gone largely unnoticed.
5 In *Homo Academicus* (1988) Bourdieu sees this opposition between 'curators of culture' and 'creators of culture', between those who reproduce existing bodies of knowledge, and those who pose a challenge to it.

CHAPTER 2

1 The impetus behind the National Gallery was the Dublin Exhibition of 1853; a large international exhibition of Irish industry. Following the model of the

London Exhibition of 1851 at Crystal Palace, it developed the concept further by devoting almost one-third of the exhibition to the display of fine arts borrowed from Prussia, France, the Netherlands and Belgium as well as from Britain and Ireland (Strickland, 1969).

2 Although the Anglo-Norman invasion of Ireland goes back to the twelfth century, Ireland only really became a British colony in the seventeenth. It was in the late eighteenth century, when the term 'Empire' was used to describe the United Kingdom's possessions, that it became possible to think of Ireland as part of the British Empire (Howe, 2000: 13). A number of studies have revealed some of the strategies whereby the Irish were represented as an 'inferior' race and a 'backward' nation. See for example Curtis (1971); Foster (1993); Douglas *et al* (1998).

3 Arts and crafts, for example, were part of the Revival; clubs and societies such as the Arts and Crafts Society of Ireland (1894), the Dublin Sketching Club, the Dublin Art Club, promoted and held exhibitions of arts and crafts, which were also taught at the schools of the Royal Dublin Society and the Dublin Metropolitan School of Art (Larmour, 1992: 50).

4 The main sources on the history of the RHA are: Strickland (1969), de Courcy (1986), Turpin (1991) and Walsh and Bouchier (1991).

5 Although founded in 1731, the Royal Dublin Society was not legally incorporated until 1750 with the granting of its royal charter. From 1740, the society subsidized Robert West's independent drawing schools, which it would take over in 1750 (Turpin, 1995: 8–9). See Crookshank (1986) for a history of the RDS.

6 Crookshank and the Knight of Glin (2002: 51) give 10 March 1766 as the first time The Society of Artists held its exhibition.

7 Another initiative to help Irish artists was the foundation of the Royal Irish Institution in 1813. Its overall aim was to encourage the fine arts, but the establishment of an academy to provide artists with a venue to exhibit their work became its main objective. The role of the Royal Irish Institution was brought to an end after helping secure the foundation of the RHA. It continued until 1840, the year when its work in the practical encouragement of Irish art was taken up by the Royal Irish Art Union (Strickland, 1969: 607–8).

8 Commercial, utilitarian ideas were an important consideration in the Dublin Society's schools from the mid-eighteenth century (Turpin, 1995: 72); in turn, the RDS did not see itself as promoting a fine art academy (ibid: 138). However, the foundation of a design school under British initiative led to a debate between the RDS and British officials. See Turpin (1995) chapter 8.

9 For an account of the Royal Irish Art Union see Black (1998).

10 The suggestion was made at the RHA's petition. An official from the Department of Science and Art, Norman MacLeod, suggested that the RDS School of Art take over the life class carried out by the RHA (Turpin, 1991: 200).

11 In 1877, with the passing of the Dublin Science and Art Institutions Act, the RDS transferred control of its schools, as well as other duties (the Natural History Museum, the Botanic Gardens, and the society's library, which would become the National Library of Ireland) to the Department of Science and Art, based at South Kensington, London. The schools were re-started under the new title Dublin Metropolitan School of Art (Turpin, 1995: 167). For further reading on the new schools see Turpin (1995) chapters 2–16.

12 For example, in 1870 the Irish Amateur Drawing Society was founded; it changed its name to the Irish Fine Art Society in 1878, becoming, in 1887, the Water Colour Society of Ireland (Barrett and Sheehy, 1996: 449).

13 A Dublin dentist, William Booth-Pearsall, set up the DSC in 1874 (Barrett and Sheehy, 1996: 449). In 1888, the DSC amalgamated with the Dublin Amateur and Artist's Society founded in 1873 – the latter had its origins in the 1872 Ladies' Sketching Club, which would admit male members and, thus, change its name the following year (Barrett and Sheehy, 1996: 449).
14 Stewart (1997) mentions a Dublin Art Club holding exhibitions between 1886 and 1892. A different initiative was the United Arts Club in Dublin, begun in 1907 by Ellie Duncan, future curator of the MGMA, which addressed all the arts and organized a number of exhibitions by artists such as John Sargent, John Lavery, George Clausen and Nathaniel Hone. See Boylan (1988) for a history of the United Arts Club.
15 Although he was originally from the United States, Whistler had also pursued his artistic career in other countries, such as Britain, Italy and France.
16 The reasons for the inclusion of these works are not revealed in the press cuttings on the exhibition; Kennedy (1991: 4) suggests that some members of the club, such as the sculptor Frederick Lawless and the painter Walter Osborne, were familiar with Whistler's work. Another reason could be his friendship with Irish nationalist John O'Leary, although Whistler himself had never visited Ireland. See Anderson (1986a).
17 *Freeman's Journal*, 29 November 1884.
18 Ibid.
19 *Dublin Daily Express*, 29 November 1884.
20 *The Irish Times*, 1 December 1884.
21 Ibid. 2 December 1884 (Anderson, 1986b: 49).
22 Ibid. 3 December 1884.
23 *Freeman's Journal*, 1 April 1899.
24 Ibid.
25 Martyn bought an autumn river scene by Monet and two Degas, advized by his cousin George Moore (O'Grady, 1996: 85; Frazier, 2000: 122).
26 *The Irish Times*, 1 April 1899.
27 *Dublin Daily Express*, 10 September 1898.
28 Ibid.
29 *The Irish Times*, 1 April 1899.
30 *Dublin Daily Express*, 1 April 1899.
31 George Russell (AE), Sarah Purser HRHA (painter), Walter Osborne RHA (painter), Walter Armstrong RHA (Director of the National Gallery of Ireland), Vice-Provost Ingram of Trinity College Dublin, politician and editor of the *Dublin Daily Express* T.P. Gill, James Brennan RHA, George Coffey (curator and keeper of Irish Antiquities in the National Museum and President of the National Literary Society (Frazier, 2000: 325)), Professor Edward Dowden, Lieutenant-Colonel George Plunkett (Director of the National Museum), Thomas William Rolleston (a leader of the Irish Literary Revival in the 1890s and sometime editor of the *Dublin University Review*), Walter Strickland (Registrar of the National Gallery), and Sir Arthur Vicars (O'Grady, 1996: 84, 156 fn. 30).
32 Original source: Murphy, W.M., *Letters from Bedford Park: A Selection from the Correspondence of John Butler Yeats, 1890–1901* (Dublin: Cuala Press, 1972).
33 *Freeman's Journal*, 21 October 1901.
34 *The Leader*, 26 October 1901.
35 *Freeman's Journal*, 21 October 1901.
36 *The Leader*, 26 October 1901.

37 Despite Purser's own success as a portraitist (see her biography by O'Grady, 1996) she was only given the title of honorary academician, HRHA, in 1890. It was not until 1923 that she was elected full academician, RHA, becoming the first woman to achieve this distinction in Ireland (O'Grady, 1996: 69, 132).

38 The initial selection of reviews was based on the albums of newspaper cuttings, part of the Hugh Lane archive, held at the National Library of Ireland. Although the albums include articles from the British press, due to the nature of this study the present sample only refers to newspapers published in Ireland. The articles quoted here have been selected according to the ideas being expressed, rather than to the ideology of the publication. However, given that the albums largely ignore the advanced-nationalist newspapers – namely, *An Claidheamh Soluis* (the official publication of the Gaelic League), and *Sinn Féin* – I have added these to make the sample as representative as possible of the differences in the press at the time. The discussion offers examples from the unionist, nationalist and advanced-nationalist press, all of which engaged in a debate about the position of Irish culture and language. The advanced-nationalist press promoted a de-Anglicised Irish–Ireland in the belief that a separate Irish culture could provide evidence of a distinct nationality and could help guarantee it politically (Glandon, 1985: vii). The nationalist press – e.g. the *Freeman's Journal* – supported the Irish Parliamentary Party in its struggle for Irish Home Rule. In 1891, the newspaper abandoned the Parnell cause to promote the anti-Parnellite faction (ibid: 2). The *Irish Daily Independent* was planned to support Parnell and counteract the *Freeman's* withdrawal from this cause. Finally, *The Irish Times*, the leading unionist newspaper, was the organ of Protestant interests in Ireland, although it provided a platform for both Catholics and Protestants among those who supported the existing political order.

39 The need for the Anglo-Irish to resolve their own identity dilemma was linked to their changing social position within Irish society. Throughout the nineteenth century, they had been progressively separated from the land, their traditional source of authority, as successive land acts led to the division of large estates into small farms run by their Catholic tenants. The Anglo-Irish had also lost political and religious supremacy. The Reform Act of 1884 gave the vote to the majority of ordinary Catholics, ensuring that, in the south and west of the country, a Protestant could no longer expect to be elected to parliament unless he supported Home Rule. In 1898 the Protestant gentry lost control of local government, when the Local Government Act created elected county, urban and rural district councils (O'Toole, 1999). Finally, the disestablishment of the Church of Ireland in 1869, forty years after the emancipation of Catholics, meant the beginning of the end in their spiritual and moral leadership of the country (Lyons, 1982: 10).

40 *Evening Herald* and *The Irish Times*, 24 October 1902.

41 Ibid.

42 *Evening Herald*, 24 October 1902.

43 *The Irish Times*, 15 January 1903.

44 *Irish Daily Independent*, 16 January 1903.

45 Ibid.

46 *The Leader*, 21 February 1903.

47 Ibid. 7 February 1903.

48 Also in 1904, Lane organized an exhibition of Irish art at the Guildhall in London. This is not discussed in this chapter, which is only concerned with events in Dublin.

49 Staats Forbes had recently died, leaving as a legacy a collection of around 4,000 pictures, including the work of John Constable, the Barbizon School, 150 works by Jean François Millet and 160 by Jean Baptiste Corot. The works from this

collection, which eventually came down to 160 in total, were to be put on sale should the projected gallery be established (O'Byrne, 2000: 61).

50 The exhibition included works by Emile Blanche, Eugene Boudin, Jean Baptiste Corot, Gustave Courbet, Charles Daubigny, Honoré Daumier, Edgar Degas, Henri Fantin-Latour, Nathaniel Hone, Augustus John, John Lavery, Antonio Mancini, Edouard Manet, Claude Monet, Adolphe Monticelli, Dermod O'Brien, Roderic O'Conor, William Orpen, Walter Osborne, Camille Pissarro, Puvis de Chavannes, Pierre Auguste Renoir, Alfred Sisley, Wilson Steer, James McNeill Whistler and John Butler Yeats (Kennedy, 1991: 9).

51 Durand-Ruel had promoted Impressionist paintings long before that school had achieved any notoriety. He had met Monet and Pissarro in 1870 when they were in London during the Franco-Prussian war. He became the single most important individual in the commercial promotion of Impressionism, representing their work as well as that of Pierre Auguste Renoir, Edgar Degas, Puvis de Chavannes and Alfred Stevens (O'Byrne, 2000: 53–4).

52 *The Irish Times*, 21 November 1904.

53 *Dublin Daily Express*, 21 November 1904.

54 *An Claidheamh Soluis*, 7 January 1905.

55 *The Irish Times*, 21 November 1904.

56 *Freeman's Journal*, 13 December 1904.

57 *An Claidheamh Soluis*, 10 December 1904.

58 Ibid.

59 *Dublin Daily Express*, 8 December 1904.

60 *The Irish Times*, 21 December 1904. Some of the prices questioned were £1,250 for Corot's *Avignon, Palais des Papes*, £600 for a Monet view of Waterloo Bridge, and £500 for Constable's *Cornfield* (O'Byrne, 2000: 64).

61 *Evening Herald*, 2 January 1905. See O'Byrne (2000: 68–74) for an account of the debate over Lane's wrong attribution of value to one Corot – *Peasants by a Lake* – supposedly a copy of a landscape, *The Fishermen's Rest at Lake Balaton,* on display in Budapest's National Museum, by Hungarian artist Geza Meszoly.

62 *The Irish Times*, 5 January 1905.

63 After the initial resolution to acquire Clonmell House had been passed, it was discovered that the Corporation had no legal power to vote any sum of money to maintain an art collection. It was only in 1911 that power was obtained from the British Parliament when a special act was passed for the purpose. However, Lane himself accepted responsibility for all expenses until 1913, when Dublin Corporation was able to take over the running of the gallery formally (Bodkin, 1956: 14–9).

64 Some of the Irish painters included were John Lavery, George Russell, John Butler Yeats, Mark Fisher, Walter Osborne, William Orpen, Normal Garstin, Frank O'Meara and Roderic O'Conor. 1908. *Illustrated Catalogue*, Municipal Gallery of Modern Art.

65 The collection included works by Charles Conder, George Frederic Watts, Wilson Steer, John Constable, Walter Sickert, Augustus John and Charles H. Shannon amongst others. Ibid.

66 The catalogue mentions portraits of Lady Gregory, Nathaniel Hone, George Russell, William Butler Yeats, Sir Horace Plunkett, T.W. Russell and Douglas Hyde amongst others, most of them executed by Irish painters John Butler Yeats, William Orpen and Sarah Purser. Ibid.

67 Lane purchased Camille Pissarro's *Printemps, Vue de Louveciennes* (1870) and Edouard Manet's *Eva Gonzales* (1870) in Paris from the art dealer Durand-Ruel during the summer of 1904, when he accompanied William Orpen on a trip to Europe (Dawson, 1993: 23).

68 *Sinn Féin,* 25 January 1908.
69 And yet, this is also debatable, as the first purchase by the French state of an Impressionist work was in 1892, when Pierre Auguste Renoir's *Young Girls at the Piano* was bought for the Luxembourg Gallery's collection (Denvir, 1993: 184). Lane might have been referring to the fact that British collections did not include examples of Impressionist works (O'Byrne, 2000: 241).
70 *An Claidheamh Soluis*, 25 January 1908.
71 Ibid.
72 Ibid.
73 *Irish Independent*, 18 January 1908.
74 Ibid. 24 January 1908.
75 *Dublin Daily Express*, 20 January 1908.
76 Ibid.
77 *The Irish Times*, 21 January 1908.
78 Ibid. 20 January 1908.
79 *Illustrated Catalogue,* Municipal Gallery of Modern Art, 1908.
80 Ibid.
81 For an analysis of the sort of nation Lane envisaged with regard to MGMA's architecture, see Sharp (2003).
82 But despite the representation of Ireland as a European artistic nation, the continuity of the project relied on municipal funds. The MGMA was a municipal gallery; it did not receive any financial help, or otherwise, from all those nations whose art it so admired, see Sharp (2003: 37).
83 For an account of the state of French Impressionism in London in the nineteenth century see Taylor (1999), chapter 5, 'Managing "Modern Foreign" Art: An Extension at the Tate Gallery'.
84 In his 1913 will, Lane left thirty-nine conditional gift pictures he had lent for exhibition to the National Gallery, to the city of London. However, his quarrels with the National Gallery's board made him change his mind, and in his 1915 codicil he left the paintings to Ireland. This incident led to a long controversy between British and Irish governments over the ownership of the pictures, and to various agreements which involved sharing some of the paintings between both institutions (O'Byrne, 2000: 228–41). The matter was not resolved until February 2006 when the National Gallery agreed to release the pictures to the now called Hugh Lane Municipal Gallery of Modern Art. *Daily Mail*, 10 February 2006.
85 An example of this trend would be the artist Mainie Jellett who, together with Evie Hone, studied under Albert Gleizes, one of the major exponents of Cubist theory and practice. See bibliography 1995, *AIB Art,* p. 146.

CHAPTER 3

1 Coulter (2003) refers to the IELA's promotion of pluralism as a strategic decision, given that the exhibition was held in the National College of Art and Design, which at the time was dominated by the RHA. Artists also sought to secure patronage and recognition from the RHA and the National Gallery of Ireland. As she says (2003: 82), the involvement of these institutions represented recognition for the IELA 'from the very heart of the establishment'.
2 For an account of the rejection of le Brocquy's *A Family* see S. Bhreathnach-Lynch, 'Louis le Brocquy's *A Family*: 'An unwholesome and satanic distortion of natural beauty'. Online article: http://www.recirca.com/articles/LeBrocquy.shtml

3 In 1959, James White took over as director of the MGMA and quickly renovated the dilapidated institution (Fallon, 1998: 264).
4 *Sunday Business Post,* 24 January 1993; IMMA press release, 'Ferguson Donation on Show at Irish Museum of Modern Art', 10 April 1997.
5 Some of the ancient sections of Rosc ranged from Celtic artefacts (1967), animal style in art across Europe (1977), and Chinese paintings from the fourteenth to the nineteenth centuries (1980).
6 *Rosc '80: The Poetry of Vision – An International Exhibition of Modern Art and Chinese Painting*, foreword by Dorothy Walker, chairman of the Rosc Selection Committee, p. 11.
7 Maurice Foley, vice-chairman and president of the GPA Group, is another figure that will be involved with IMMA, both as a donor and a board member (see chapter 4). IMMA press release, 'Loans and Donations from Maire and Maurice Foley at IMMA', 9 June 2000.
8 1992. *Contemporary Irish Art Society Exhibition*, Hugh Lane Municipal Gallery of Modern Art.
9 From its beginning in 1831, as the British administered Board of Works, the Office of Public Works has been responsible for 'the fitting out and furnishing of State buildings', and is 'required to provide art works' (Moore, 1998: 13).
10 The AIB organized exhibitions in 1985 and 1995 with a selection of works from the collection, which was accompanied by an illustrated catalogue. The OPW organizes annual exhibitions of the collection around Ireland and has published a chronology of its collection in three volumes, *Art in State Buildings* (1997, 1998, 2000). See bibliography for details.
11 Scott in 1982. *Catalogue of the 21st Anniversary Retrospective Exhibition*, College Gallery.
12 Between 1967 and 1976 over thirty exhibitions of Irish and international art – e.g. Paul Henry, Norah MacGuinness and Pablo Picasso – were organized, run by a committee comprised of staff and students (Walsh 1991: 22).
13 Calendar of Events, May to August, 2002. Irish Museum of Modern Art.
14 One gallery director has a background in art history, while one gallery manager and the director of another gallery have a background in the arts. One of the two gallery directors has been to art college. The owner of one of the galleries interviewed has no background in art history.
15 *The Irish Times*, 6 June 2001.
16 Ibid.
17 Ibid. 25 November 2000.
18 Ibid. 9 December 2004.
19 Ibid.
20 The RHA also has a permanent collection, but it is never on display, and thus it does not form part of the academy's activities (Mulcahy, 2002: 47).
21 The sketches belong to Barry Joule, a friend who met Bacon in 1978 and became thereafter his driver and confidant. *Sunday Times*, 19 March 2000.
22 Interview with John Hutchinson, director DHG, 14 November 2000.
23 Ibid.
24 *The Irish Times*, 6 June 2001.
25 Despite the fact that the HLMGMA is allocated a set budget for acquisitions, on occasions Dublin City Council, the gallery's public funding body, extends this budget to allow the purchase of specific artworks. In 1998 the gallery spent over €50,000, and €77,000 in 2001. Budget figures provided by Anne Gibney, Department of Environment and Culture, Dublin City Council, and Liz Foster, HLMGMA.

26 All the figures have been converted into euros; these calculations are only approximate, and have been updated from the time this research was carried out in 2000/01. Information provided by Catherine Marshall and Frank Brennan, IMMA.
27 'Cultural/Heritage Tax Reliefs', TSG 98/13, Department of Finance, Dublin.
28 Interview with Barbara Dawson, director HLMGMA, 26 November 2001.
29 Interview with Catherine Marshall, senior curator, 25 June 2001.
30 Interview with Patrick Murphy, director RHA, 12 April 2001.

CHAPTER 4

1 Marshall in 2001. *Celebrating a Decade,* Irish Museum of Modern Art, p. 35.
2 This list was compiled at the end of 2002 and is only intended to offer a general overview of some of the donations included in the collection, any further acquisitions, loans and donations are not included.
3 The Madden Arnholz Collection was donated to the RHK by Claire Madden in memory of her daughter Etain and her son-in-law Dr Fritz Arnholz. 1998. *Catalogue of the Collection,* Irish Museum of Modern Art.
4 American-born Helen O'Malley Roelofs acquired the collection when she lived in Ireland and Europe. She donated it to the Irish American Cultural Institute in 1979, but at the time there was no suitable venue for its display. The opening of IMMA provided an opportunity to exhibit the collection, which was loaned on behalf of Helen O'Malley to the museum as a permanent memorial to Ernie O'Malley, IRA veteran, author and art critic. The collection also includes a large body of work by American, Mexican and European artists. *Evening Herald*, 2 May 1990.
5 The works were loaned by German collector Klaus Lafrenz; they include a number of leading minimalist and conceptual artists, pieces by Michael Bauch, Hubert Kiecol and David Navros. Press release, 'Lafrenz Collection at the Irish Museum of Modern Art', 14 May 1992.
6 The loan was made by the artist's estate. Mary Farl Powers was born in America but first came to Ireland at an early age, where she became a highly influential artist and teacher in the development of print-making. Press release, 'Mary Farl Powers Loan and Major Acquisitions for IMMA', 27 March 1995.
7 The collection was created in memory of the late Adrian Ward-Jackson, an art consultant, collector and patron of the visual and performing arts. In 1994 the trustees gave the collection on loan, while they continue to acquire works for IMMA during the time of the loan. Press release, 'Weltkunst Collection of Contemporary British Art at IMMA', 11 April 1995.
8 Press release, 'Ferguson Donation on Show at the Irish Museum of Modern Art', 10 April 1997.
9 Press release, 'Art Unsolved: the Outsider Collection at the Irish Museum of Modern Art', 12 May 1998; and 'Outsider Art Collection to Remain at the Irish Museum of Modern Art until 2006', 22 October 1999.
10 Marshall in 2001. *Celebrating a Decade,* Irish Museum of Modern Art, p. 35.
11 A noted businessman and collector, Maurice Foley was a member of IMMA's first board in 1990. He was chairman of its second board from March 1997 to March 2000. Press release, 'Loans and Donations from Maire and Maurice Foley at the Irish Museum of Modern Art', 9 June 2000.
12 Former gallery owners in Belfast, the McClellands have promoted leading Irish artists such as Colin Middleton, Tony O'Malley and Dan O'Neill. Press release, 'McClelland Collection on Show at the Irish Museum of Modern Art', 4 September 2000.

13 Taoiseach Charles J. Haughey enjoyed a considerable reputation as a benefactor to the arts.
14 McGonagle in 1998. *Catalogue of the Collection*, Irish Museum of Modern Art, p. 4.
15 Other departments, apart from IMMA's three programming departments are: public relations, operations, security, finance and personnel. Interview with Catherine Marshall, 25 June 2001.
16 There is one exception; one member of the acquisitions sub-committee in the third board had been part of it since 1990.
17 Meeting of the Inter-Departmental Committee to report on possible uses of the RHK, 7 May 1980. Department for the Arts, Heritage, Gaeltacht, and the Islands.
18 Ibid.
19 Ibid. 31 January 1984.
20 Ibid. Some of the suggested uses were: exhibition of documentation pertaining to Irish writers, poets and playwrights; a postal museum of items catalogued by the General Post Office (GPO); an exhibition of Irish cartography; display of modern Irish crafts; display of paintings from the National Gallery of Ireland; the National Museum of Ireland.
21 Speech by the Taoiseach, Charles Haughey, 25 May 1991. Government Information Services, Department of the Taoiseach.
22 Ibid. Haughey had already expressed his view about the benefits of situating contemporary art in an historic building in an interview for *The Irish Times*, 31 December 1990, only a few months before IMMA's opening.
23 Interview with Declan McGonagle (Kelly, 1997).
24 *Sunday Tribune*, 19 May 1991.
25 Interview with Declan McGonagle (Kelly, 1997).
26 *Sunday Tribune*, 19 May 1991.
27 The catalogue is also the title of IMMA's first exhibition, and expresses the kind of task the museum was set up to fulfil.
28 McGonagle in 1991. *Inheritance and Transformation*, Irish Museum of Modern Art, p. 5.
29 *Sunday Tribune,* 19 May 1991.
30 Art Unsolved: Works from the Musgrave Kinley Outsider Art Collection. Wall text by Catherine Marshall.
31 Interview with Declan McGonagle (Kelly, 1997).
32 *New York Times*, 18 August 1991.
33 *Sunday Tribune,* 19 May 1991.
34 *Sunday Business Post,* 5 April 1998.
35 *Sunday Tribune*, 19 May 1991.
36 O'Donoghue in 2001. *Celebrating a Decade,* Irish Museum of Modern Art, p. 48.
37 MacParland in 2001. Ibid. p. 16.
38 See for example *Sunday Business Post,* 19 May 1991; *Sunday Tribune*, 19 May 1991 and Smith (1994).
39 Although the museum had been collecting since its opening in 1991, the appointment of a senior curator for the collection took place in 1995, and it prompted the need to define a collecting policy for IMMA.
40 McGonagle in 1998. 'A Collection in the Making', *Irish Museum of Modern Art: Catalogue of the Collection,* Irish Museum of Modern Art, pp. 4–5.
41 Ibid. p. 5.
42 Ibid.
43 Ibid.
44 Ibid.
45 *The Irish Times*, 4 December 1997.
46 Press release, 'Winner of Glen Dimplex Artists Awards 2001 Announced', 25 May 2001.

47 *The Irish Times*, 24 May 2001.
48 Press release, 'The Nissan Art Project for the Millennium Until December 2000', 27 September 2000.
49 O'Donoghue in 2001. *Celebrating a Decade,* Irish Museum of Modern Art, pp. 48–51.
50 The Unspoken Truths project was developed by the Family Resource Centre, St Michael's Estate; the Lourdes Youth and Community Services, Sean McDermott St; the artist Ailbhe Murphy and IMMA. Exhibition information, Once Is Too Much, 28 November 1997–15 February 1998.
51 Ibid.
52 The opening of the new galleries as an exhibition space allows IMMA to exhibit works, as in the case of Picasso, which require special environmental conditions.
53 *Sunday Business Post*, 19 May 1991.
54 See chapter 3 for details of IMMA's acquisitions budget.
55 This is the only figure stipulated by the Department of Arts, Heritage, Culture and the Gaeltacht. The overall funding received is divided between IMMA's various departments by the director. Marshall, interview, 2001.
56 Although the process of accepting the collection did not cause disagreement in the sub-committee, this is not to say that other board members all agreed with this policy. One interviewee, in particular, disagreed with the outsiders being part of IMMA's collection:

> That collection should be somewhere else. It could have been taken over by one of the banks or an institution that would have the resources to finance it and to take it to all parts of Ireland, but I feel that's not high art, it's not of the quality that a national collection should be – but there's a place for it. (4)

57 For an account of Lambert's role as donor see Marshall (1999).

CHAPTER 5

1 The emergence of art history as an established discipline started in the second half of the nineteenth century with the rise of higher education in Europe. It gave the discipline a 'purely formal-aesthetic conceptual foundation', while it became increasingly differentiated from a form of art analysis informed by sociological, anthropological and sociological concerns (Tanner, 2003: 8-10).
2 See Duncan (1995: 111–32) for an analysis of the gender dynamics of MoMA's ritual space.
3 Even in the MoMA there were other types of exhibition designs according to the wide range of displays in the museum, such as displays of modern design and architectural prototypes, and political propaganda. However, I have highlighted his 'aestheticization of art' design because, as we will see, it resembles in part the use of space at IMMA.
4 For further reading on novel installation designs see chapter 1, 'Framing Installation Design: The International Avant-Gardes', (Staniszewski, 1998: 3–59).
5 For a discussion of the exhibition see 'The Origin of Surrealist Exhibition Space: The 1938 Paris Exposition Internationale du Surréalisme', (Kachur, 2001: 20–103).
6 The choice of exhibitions was related to the opportunities presented at the time of this research. Irish Art Now and Art Without Precedent took place while this research was being carried out. In addition, they were selected because Irish Art Now was the first travelling exhibition of IMMA's collection, and marked the beginning of a new use of the collection. Art Without Precedent was part of the

outsider collection with which IMMA seeks to put into practice some key ideas in its worldview. Art Unsolved was chosen to contextualize further the display of outsider art in IMMA.

7 The catalogue includes three essays: one by IMMA's director, 'Renegotiating the Given'; a second essay, 'Ireland', by journalist and author Fintan O'Toole; and a last essay by Kim Levin 'Poetics, Politics and Irish Art: Thirteen Questions' see bibliography for details.

8 ICI in New York contacted IMMA's director to organize an exhibition of Irish art. Their role is to contact curators with whom they are interested in working, and invite them to be a guest curator for an exhibition they want to promote. Given that the director was also interested in promoting Irish art and the museum abroad, the co-operation between IMMA and ICI resulted in the exhibition Irish Art Now: From the Poetic to the Political, curated by the director as ICI's guest curator. ICI was in charge of organizing the venues for the US tour. The exhibition travelled to the McMullen Museum of Art in Boston, Massachussetts, the Art Gallery of Newfoundland and Labrador in St. John's Newfoundland, and the Chicago Cultural Center in Chicago, Illinois.

9 This decision was made at senior programming level, involving the director, head of exhibitions, head of collection, and head of education and community (O'Molloy, interview, 2002).

10 Wall text, Irish Art Now: From the Poetic to the Political.

11 Wall text, ibid.

12 Rooms were not actually numbered in the exhibition. I am using numbers to differentiate rooms and clarify the exhibition's layout.

13 These readings were suggested by one of the curators interviewed.

14 Press release, 'Art Unsolved: the Outsider Collection at the Irish Museum of Modern Art', 12 May 1998.

15 Wall text, Art Unsolved.

16 Wall text, ibid.

17 Wall text, ibid.

18 Another type of arrangement is 'flush alignment', in which objects are arranged so that all the top or bottom edges are aligned. As Dean notes, the 'center line/eye-level relationship is lost in this organization', which favours the distribution of works in relation to the physical space (Dean, 1994: 57), suggesting that the viewer's needs are not a priority in this form of display.

19 For example, in John Maizels' *Raw Creation* (1996), in Colin Rhodes' *Outsider Art. Spontaneous Alternatives* (2000), and in the catalogue *Private Worlds: Classic Outsider Art From Europe* (1998) for the exhibition held at the Katonah Museum of Art (US). Carl People is the exception whose works I have not found referenced.

20 Wall text, Art Without Precedent: Nine Artists from the Musgrave Kinley Outsider Art Collection.

21 Wall text, ibid.

22 Wall text, Madge Gill.

23 Wall text, Oswald Tschirtner.

24 Wall text, John 'J.B.' Murry.

Bibliography

Alexander, V.D. 1996. *Museums and Money: The Impact of Funding on Exhibitions, Scholarship and Management* (Bloomington and Indianapolis: Indiana University Press).
Allied Irish Bank, 1995. *AIB Art* (Dublin: AIB Group).
Alsop, J. 1982. *The Rare Art Traditions: The History of Art Collecting and its Linked Phenomena* (New York: Princeton University Press).
Anderson, R. 1986a. 'Whistler: An Irish Rebel and Ireland', *Apollo Magazine,* April, 254–8.
— 1986b. 'Whistler in Dublin, 1884', *Irish Arts Review*, 3(3):45–51.
Archer, M. 1990. 'A new necessity. Declan McGonagle talks on art outside the gallery', *Artscribe*, summer, pp. 63–58.
Bailey, C.B. 2002. *Patriotic Taste: Collecting Modern Art in Pre-Revolutionary Paris* (New Haven: Yale University Press).
Barrett, C. and Sheehy, J. 1996. 'Visual Arts and Society, 1850–1900', in W.E. Vaughan (ed.), *A New History of Ireland: Ireland Under the Union II, 1870–1921*, vol. VI, pp. 436–74. (Oxford: Clarendon Press).
Bauman, Z. 1987. *Legislators and Interpreters: On Modernity, Post-Modernity and Intellectuals* (Cambridge: Polity Press).
— 1992a. *Intimations of Postmodernity* (London: Routledge).
— 1992b. 'Love in Adversity: On the State and the Intellectuals, and the State of Intellectuals', *Thesis Eleven*, 31(1):81–104.
— 1995. *Life in Fragments: Essays in Postmodern Morality* (Oxford and Cambridge: Blackwell).
Becker, H.S. 1982. *Art Worlds* (London: University of California Press).
Bennett, T. 1995. *The Birth of the Museum: History, Theory, Politics* (London: Routledge).
Best, S. 1998. 'Zygmunt Bauman: Personal Reflections Within the Mainstream of Modernity', *British Journal of Sociology*, 49(2): 311–20.

Bhreathnach-Lynch, S. 'Louis le Brocquy's *A Family*: An unwholesome and satanic distortion of natural beauty', http://www.recirca.com/articles/LeBrocquy.shtml

Black, E. 1998. 'Practical Patriots and True Irishmen: The Royal Irish Art Union 1839–59', *Irish Arts Review Yearbook*, 14: 140–6.

Bodkin, T. 1956. *Hugh Lane and his Pictures* (Dublin: The Stationery Office).

Bourdieu, P. 1969. 'Intellectual Field and Creative Project', *Social Science Information*, 8 (2): 89–119.

— 1977. 'Symbolic Power', in Gleeson, D. (ed.), *Identity and Structure: Issues in the Sociology of Education*, pp. 112–9. (Driffield: Nafferton Books).

— 1984. *Distinction: A Social Critique of the Judgement of Taste* (London: Routledge).

— 1988. *Homo Academicus* (Cambridge: Polity Press).

— 1993a. *The Field of Cultural Production: Essays on Art and Literature* (Cambridge: Polity Press).

— 1993b. *Sociology in Question* (London: Sage).

— 1996. *The Rules of Art: Genesis and Structure of the Literary Field*. (Oxford: Polity Press).

Bourdieu, P. and Wacquant, L.J.D. 1992. *An Invitation to Reflexive Sociology* (Cambridge: Blackwell).

Bowler, A.E. 1997. 'Asylum Art: The Social Construction of an Aesthetic Category', in V. Zolberg, and J.M. Cherbo (eds), *Outsider Art: Contesting Boundaries in Contemporary Culture*, pp. 11–36. (Cambridge: Cambridge University Press).

Boylan, P. 1988. *All Cultivated People: A History of the United Arts Club, Dublin* (Gerrards Cross: Colin Smythe).

— 1996. 'Mrs Duncan's Vocation,' *Irish Arts Review Yearbook*, 12: 98–101.

Carden, S. 2001. 'Alderman Tom Kelly and the Municipal Gallery', *Dublin Historical Record,* vol. LIV (2):116–38.

Castle, F.T. 1991. 'Irish Museum of Modern Art', *Art Magazine, 55* (2):107–10.

Clifford, J. 1988. 'On Collecting Art and Culture', in *The Predicament of Culture: Twentieth-Century Ethnography, Literature and Art* (London: Harvard University Press).

Coulter, R. 2003. 'Hibernian Salon des Refusés', *Irish Arts Review,* 20(3):80–5.

Crane, D. 1987. *The Transformation of the Avant-Garde: The New York Art World 1940–85* (Chicago: University of Chicago Press).

Crookshank, A. 1986. 'The Visual Arts, 1740–1850', in T.W. Moody and W.E. Vaughan (eds), *A New History of Ireland: Eighteenth-Century Ireland, 1691–1800,* vol. IV, pp. 499–54. (Oxford: Clarendon Press).

Crookshank, A. and the Knight of Glin. 1994. *The Watercolours of Ireland: Works on Paper in Pencil, Pastel and Paint c. 1600–1914* (London: Barrie and Jenkins).

— 2002. *Ireland's Painters, 1600–1940* (London: Yale University Press).

Curtis, L.P. Jr, 1971. *Apes and Angels: The Irishman in Victorian Caricature* (Newton Abbot: David and Charles).

Danto, A.C. 1997. 'Introduction: Modern, Postmodern and Contemporary', in *After the End of Art: Contemporary Art and the Pale of History,* pp. 3–20. (Princeton: Princeton University Press).

Dawson, B. 1993. 'Hugh Lane and the Origins of the Collection', in E. Mayes and P. Murphy (eds), *Images and Insights: Hugh Lane Municipal Gallery of Modern Art,* pp. 13–31. (Dublin: Hugh Lane Municipal Gallery of Modern Art).

Dawson, G. 1987. 'The Douglas Hyde Gallery', *Irish Arts Review,* 4 (4):39–42.

Dean, D. 1994. *Museum Exhibition: Theory and Practice* (London: Routledge).

de Courcy, C. 1986. 'The History of the Royal Hibernian Academy of Arts', in A.M. Stewart, *Royal Hibernian Academy of Arts: Index of Exhibitors 1826–1979; vol. 1 A-G,* pp xi–xix. (Dublin: Manton Publishing).

DeNora, T. 2003. *After Adorno: Rethinking Music Sociology* (Cambridge: Cambridge University Press).

Denvir, B. 1993. *The Chronicle of Impressionism: An Intimate Diary of the Lives and World of the Great Artists* (London: Thames and Hudson).

Douglas, R. *et al.* 1998. *Drawing Conclusions: A Cartoon History of Anglo-Irish Relations 1798–1998* (Belfast: Blackstaff Press).

Duncan, C. 1995. *Civilizing Rituals: Inside Public Art Museums* (London: Routledge).

Duncan, C. and Wallach, A. 1980. 'The Universal Survey Museum', *Art History,* 3 (4): 448–69.

Dunn, A. 1998. 'Who Needs a Sociology of the Aesthetic? Freedom and Value in Pierre Bourdieu's *Rules of Art*', *Boundary 2,* 25(1): 87–110.

Dunne, A. 2000. 'Art, Hauteur and Lucre', *Circa,* no. 94, winter, p. 13.
Edelstein, T.J. *et al.* 1992. 'Introduction' in T.J. Edelstein (ed.), *Imagining an Irish Past: The Celtic Revival 1840–1940,* pp. ix–xiii. (Chicago: The David and Alfred Smart Museum of Art).
Fallon, B. 1994. *Irish Art 1830–1990* (Belfast: Appletree Press).
— 1998. *An Age of Innocence: Irish Culture 1930–1960* (Dublin: Gill & Macmillan).
Fallon, C. 2000. 'The Royal Hibernian Academy and What it is About', *Art Bulletin*, December/January, pp. 11–3.
Ferriter, D. 2004. *The Transformation of Ireland 1700–2000* (London: Profile Books).
Foster, R.F. 1993. *Paddy and Mr Punch* (London: Penguin).
Fowler, B. 1997. *Pierre Bourdieu and Cultural Theory: Critical Investigations* (London: Sage).
Frazier, A. 2000. *George Moore 1852–1933* (New Haven, CT and London: Yale University Press).
Frow, J. 1995. *Cultural Studies & Cultural Value* (Oxford: Oxford University Press).
Fyfe, G. 2000. *Art Power and Modernity. English Art Institutions, 1750–1950* (London: Leicester University Press).
Gamboni, D. 1997. *The Destruction of Art: Iconoclasm and Vandalism Since the French Revolution* (London: Reaktion Books).
Glandon, V.E. 1985. *Arthur Griffith and the Advanced-Nationalist Press, Ireland 1900–1922* (New York: Peter Lang).
Gordon Bowe, N. 1999. 'Art and the Public: The Friends of the National Collections of Ireland', in The Friends of the National Collections of Ireland, *75 Years of Giving*, pp. 11–30. (Dublin: The Friends of the National Collections of Ireland).
Gregory, Lady. 1973. *Sir Hugh Lane: His Life and Legacy* (Gerrard's Cross: Colin Smythe).
Grunenberg, C. 1994. 'The Politics of Presentation: The Museum of Modern Art, New York', in M. Pointon (ed.), *Art Apart: Art Institutions and Ideology across England and North America*, pp. 192–211. (Manchester: Manchester University Press).
Hartigan, M. 1987. 'The Irish Exhibition of Living Art', *Irish Arts Review,* 4(4):58–9.
Haskell, F. 1976. *Rediscoveries in Art: Some Aspects of Taste, Fashion and Collecting in England and France* (New York: Cornell University Press).

Hennion, A. 2003. 'Music and Mediation: Toward a New Sociology of Music', in M. Clayton *et al* (eds), *The Cultural Study of Music: A Critical Introduction,* pp. 80–91. (London: Routledge).

Hennion, A. and Grenier, L. 2000. 'Sociology of Art: New stakes in a Post-Critical Era', in S.R. Quah *et al* (eds), *The State of the Art in Sociology,* pp. 341–55. (London: Sage).

Herrero, M. 2002. 'Towards a Sociology of Art Collections: Irish Intellectuals, Modernity and the Making of a Modern Art Collection', *International Sociology*, 17(1):57–52.

— 2005a. 'Jeremy Tanner 2003. The Sociology of Art: A Reader', *European Societies*, 7(3):493–500.

— 2005b. 'Encounters with Postmodern Art: Zygmunt Bauman, Sociology and Art', *Irish Journal of Sociology*, 14(1): 134–40.

Hetherington, K. 1999. 'From Blindness to Blindness: Museums, Heterogeneity and the Subject', in J. Law and J. Hassard (eds), *Actor Network Theory and After,* pp. 51–73. (Blackwell: Oxford).

Hooper-Greenhill, E. 1989. 'The Museum in the Disciplinary Society', in J. Pearce (ed.), *Museum Studies in Material Culture*, pp. 61–72. (Leicester: Leicester University Press).

— 1992. *Museums and the Shaping of Knowledge* (London: Routledge).

— 2000. *Museums and the Interpretation of Visual Culture* (London: Routledge).

Howe, S. 2000. *Ireland and Empire: Colonial Legacies in Irish History and Culture* (Oxford: Oxford University Press).

Hutchinson, J. 1987. *The Dynamics of Cultural Nationalism: The Gaelic Revival and the Creation of the Irish Nation-State* (London: Allen and Unwin).

Hutchinson, J. 1991. 'On the Record', *Circa*, no. 57, May/June, p. 21.

Johnson, R. 1993. 'Introduction: Pierre Bourdieu on Art, Literature and Culture', in P. Bourdieu, *The Field of Cultural Production: Essays on Art and Literature*, pp. 1–25 (Cambridge: Polity Press, 1993).

Kachur, L. 2001. *Displaying the Marvellous: Marcel Duchamp, Salvador Dalí, and Surrealist Exhibition Installations* (London: MIT).

Kavanagh, G. (ed.), 1994. *Museum Provision and Professionalism* (London: Routledge).

Kelly, N.A. 1999. 'The Creation of an Irish Visual Heritage: The Collection at the Irish Museum of Irish Art', masters dissertation (Dublin: The National College of Arts and Design).

Kellner, D. 1995. 'Intellectuals and New Technologies', *Media, Culture and Society*, vol.17:427–48.

Kennedy, B.P. 1990. *Dreams and Responsibilities: The State and the Arts in Independent Ireland* (Dublin: the Arts Council).

Kennedy, S.B. 1991. *Irish Art & Modernism 1880–1950* (Belfast: Institute of Irish Studies at Queen's University).

Kilminster, R. and Varcoe, I. 1996. 'Addendum: Culture and Power in the Writings of Zygmunt Bauman', in R. Kilminster and I. Varcoe (eds), *Culture, Modernity and Revolution: Essays in Honour of Zygmunt Bauman,* pp. 215–47. (London: Routledge).

Laermans, R. 1992. 'The Relative Rightness of Pierre Bourdieu: Some Sociological Comments on the Legitimacy of Postmodern Art, Literature and Culture', *Cultural Studies*, 6(2):248–60.

Lambert, G. 1983. 'In Pursuit of Excellence', *Art and Artists*, October, pp. 23–4.

Larmour, P. 1992. *The Arts and Crafts Movement in Ireland (*Belfast: Friar's Bush Press).

Loesberg, J. 1993. 'Bourdieu and the Sociology of Eesthetics', *ELH*, 60(4):1033–56.

Lorente, J.P. 1998. *Cathedrals of Urban Modernity* (Aldershot: Ashgate).

Lyons, F.S.L. 1982. *Culture and Anarchy in Ireland, 1890–1939* (Oxford: Oxford University Press).

Marshall, C. 1999. 'A Quiet National Treasure: Gordon Lambert and the Making of a Collection', *Irish Arts Review Yearbook*, 15:71–9.

Maizels, J. 1996. *Raw Creation: Outsider Art and Beyond* (London: Phaidon).

McGonagle, D. 1991. 'The Necessary Museum', *Irish Arts Review Yearbook*, 8:61–2.

Moody, T.W. and Vaughan, W.E. (eds), 1986. *A New History of Ireland: Eighteenth-Century Ireland, 1691–1800*, vol. IV (Oxford: Clarendon Press).

Moore, J. 1998. 'Art in State Buildings 1970–1985', in Office of Public Works, *Art in State Buildings 1970–1985*, pp. 13–15 (Dublin: Stationery Office).

Moulin, R. 1994. 'The Construction of Art Values', *International Sociology*, 9(1):5–12.

Mulcahy, J. 2002. 'Arthur Gibney and the Future of the RHA', *Irish Arts Review,* 19(1):42–7.

Murphy, W. M. 1978. *Prodigal Father: The Life of John Butler Yeats (1839–1922)* (London: Cornell University Press).

O'Byrne, R. 2000. *Hugh Lane, 1875–1915* (Dublin: Lilliput Press).
O'Doherty, B. 1999 [1976]. *Inside the White Cube: The Ideology of the Gallery Space* (London: University of California Press).
Office of Public Works, 1997. *Art in State Buildings, 1985–1995* (Dublin: Stationery Office).
— 1998. *Art in State Buildings, 1970–1985* (Dublin: Stationery Office).
— 2000. *Art in State Buildings, 1922–1970* (Dublin: Stationery Office).
O'Grady, J. 1996. *The Life and Work of Sarah Purser* (Dublin: Four Courts Press).
O'Kane, M. 2000. 'An Insight into Private Patronage in Ireland', *Circa*, no. 91, spring, pp. 36–9.
O'Toole, F. 1999. *The Irish Times Book of the Century* (Dublin: Gill and Macmillan).
Osborne, T. 1997. 'The Aesthetic Problematic', *Economy and Society*, 26(1):126–46.
Outhwaite, W. 1999. 'The Myth of Modernist Method', *European Journal of Social Theory*, 2(1):5–25.
Pearce, S. (ed.), 1989. *Museum Studies in Material Culture* (Leicester: Leicester University Press).
— 1992. *Museums, Objects and Collections: A Cultural Study* (Leicester: Leicester University Press).
— 1995. *On Collecting: An Investigation into Collecting in the European Tradition* (London: Routledge).
Pomian, K. 1990. *Collectors and Curiosities: Paris and Venice, 1500–1800* (Cambridge: Polity Press).
Price, S. 1989. *Primitive Art in Civilized Places* (Chicago and London: The University of Chicago Press).
Putnam, J. 2001. *Art and Artifact: The Museum as Medium.* (London: Thames and Hudson).
Rhodes, C. 2000. *Outsider Art: Spontaneous Alternatives* (London: Thames and Hudson).
Robbins, D. 2000. *Bourdieu & Culture* (London: Sage).
Ruane, F. 1995. 'The Collection in Context: Over a Century of Irish Art', in Allied Irish Bank, *AIB Art*, pp. 5–13 (Dublin: AIB Group).
Russell, J. 1981. 'Introduction', in D. Walker, *Louis le Brocquy*, pp. 9–18. (Dublin: Ward River Press).
Ryan, V. 2003. *Movers & Shapers. Irish Art since 1960* (Cork: The Collins Press).

Seidman, S. 1994. *Contested Knowledge: Social Theory in the Postmodern Era* (Oxford: Blackwell).
Serota, N. 1996. *Experience or Interpretation: The Dilemma of Museums of Modern Art* (London: Thames and Hudson).
Sharp, N. 2003. 'The Wrong Twigs for an Eagle's Nest? Architecture, Nationalism and Sir Hugh Lane's Scheme for a Gallery of Modern Art, Dublin, 1904–13', in M. Giebelhausen (ed.), *The Architecture of the Museum: Symbolic Structures, Urban Contexts,* pp. 32–53. (Manchester: Manchester University Press).
Smith, A. 1994. 'The New Directors', *Irish Arts Review Yearbook*, 10:72–84.
Staniszewski, M.A. 1998. *The Power of Display: A History of Exhibition Installations at the Museum of Modern Art* (London: MIT Press).
Stewart, A.M. 1997. *Irish Art Societies and Sketching Clubs: Index of Exhibitions 1870–1980, vol. II, M-Z* (Dublin: Four Courts Press).
Stewart, S. 1993. *On Longing: Narratives of the Miniature, the Gigantic, the Souvenir, the Collection* (Durham and London: Duke University Press).
Strickland, W.G. 1969. *A Dictionary of Irish Artists, vol II, L-Z.* (Shannon: Irish University Press).
Swartz, D. 1997. *Culture & Power: The Sociology of Pierre Bourdieu* (London: University of Chicago Press).
Tanner, J. 2003. *The Sociology of Art: A Reader* (London: Routledge).
Taylor, B. 1999. *Art for the Nation: Exhibitions and the London Public, 1747–2001* (Manchester: Manchester University Press).
Turpin, J. 1991. 'The RHA Schools, 1826–1906', *Irish Arts Review*, vol. 8, pp. 198–209.
— 1995. *A School of Art in Dublin Since the Eighteenth Century: A History of the National College of Art and Design* (Dublin: Gill and Macmillan).
Vaughan, W. E. (ed.), 1996. *A New History of Ireland: Ireland Under the Union II, 1870–1921,* vol. VI (Oxford: Clarendon Press).
Walker, D., 1988. 'Emerged/Submerged', *Irish Arts Review*, The GPA Yearbook, pp. 137–41.
—1997. *Modern Art in Ireland* (Dublin: Lilliput Press).
Walsh, G. and Bouchier, K. (eds), 1991. *Martello: Royal Hibernian Academy of Arts* (Special Issue).
Walsh, K. 1991. 'The Douglas Hyde: A Short History', *Circa*, no. 58, July/August, pp. 20–5.

Witkin, R.W. 1995. *Art and Social Structure* (Cambridge: Polity Press).

Wolff, J. 1981. *The Social Production of Art* (London: Macmillan).

— 1983. *Aesthetics and the Sociology of Art* (London: Allen and Unwin).

Zolberg, V. 1981. 'Conflicting Visions in American Art Museums', *Theory and Society*, 10, pp. 103–25.

— 1990. *Constructing a Sociology of the Arts* (Cambridge: Cambridge University Press).

Zolberg, V. and Cherbo, J.M. (eds), 1997. *Outsider Art: Contesting Boundaries in Contemporary Culture* (Cambridge: Cambridge University Press).

Catalogues

1901. *Loan Collection of Pictures by Nathaniel Hone RHA and John Butler Yeats RHA.*

1905. *Catalogue of Pictures given to the City of Dublin to form a Nucleus of a Gallery of Modern Art*, exhibited at the National Museum of Ireland.

1908. *Illustrated Catalogue,* Municipal Gallery of Modern Art, Dublin: Dollard.

1967. *Rosc '67. The Poetry of Vision: An International Exhibition of Modern Painting and Ancient Celtic Art.*

1977. *Rosc '77. The Poetry of Vision: An international Exhibition of Modern Art and Early Animal Art.*

1980. *Rosc '80. The Poetry of Vision: An International Exhibition of Modern Art and Chinese Painting.*

1980. Catalogue of the 21st Anniversary Retrospective Exhibition, College Gallery.

1991. *Inheritance and Transformation,* Irish Museum of Modern Art.

1992. *Contemporary Irish Art Society Exhibition,* Hugh Lane Municipal Gallery of Modern Art.

1998. *Catalogue of the Collection,* Irish Museum of Modern Art.

1998. *Private Worlds: Classic Outsider Art From Europe,* Katonah Museum of Art.

1999. *Irish Art Now: From the Poetic to the Political,* Merrell Holberton Publishers and Independent Curators International in association with the Irish Museum of Modern Art.

2001. *Celebrating a Decade*, Irish Museum of Modern Art.

Newspapers

An Claidheamh Soluis
Dublin Daily Express
Daily Mail
Evening Herald
Freeman's Journal
Irish Daily Independent
Irish Independent
Irish Press
Irish Times, The
Leader, The
New York Times
Sinn Féin
Sunday Business Post
Sunday Times
Sunday Tribune

Interviews

Barbara Dawson, director, Hugh Lane Municipal Gallery of Modern Art, 26 November 2001.
John Hutchinson, director, Douglas Hyde Gallery, 14 November 2000.
Monika Kinley, outsider art collector, 4 July 2001.
Brenda MacParland, senior curator, Irish Museum of Modern Art, 20 June 2001.
Catherine Marshall, senior curator, Irish Museum of Modern Art, 25 June 2001.
Patrick Murphy, director, Royal Hibernian Academy, 12 April 2001.
Helen O'Donoghue, senior curator, Irish Museum of Modern Art, 17 July 2001.
Marguerite O'Molloy, assistant curator, Irish Museum of Modern Art, 27 June 2002.

Exhibition's wall text, IMMA

Art Unsolved: Works from the Musgrave Kinley Outsider Art Collection. Wall text by Declan McGonagle and Catherine Marshall, May 1998.
Art Without Precedent: Nine Artists from the Musgrave Kinley Outsider Art Collection. Wall text by Catherine Marshall, January 2000.

Irish Art Now: From the Poetic to the Political. Wall text by Catherine Marshall, November 2001.

Exhibition information, IMMA

Once is Too Much, 28 November 1997–15 February 1998.

Calendar of Events, May to August, 2002.

Press releases, IMMA

'Lafrenz Collection at the Irish Museum of Modern Art', 14 May 1992.

'Mary Farl Powers Loan and Major Acquisitions for IMMA', 27 March 1995.

'Weltkunst Collection of Contemporary British Art at IMMA', 11 April 1995.

'Ferguson Donation on Show at Irish Museum of Modern Art', 10 April 1997.

'Art Unsolved: the Outsider Collection at the Irish Museum of Modern Art', 12 May 1998.

'Outsider Art Collection to Remain at the Irish Museum of Modern Art until 2006', 22 October 1999.

'Loans and Donations from Maire and Maurice Foley at the IMMA', 9 June 2000.

'McClelland Collection on Show at the Irish Museum of Modern Art', 4 September 2000.

'The Nissan Art Project for the Millennium until December 2000', 27 September 2000.

'Winner of Glen Dimplex Artists Awards 2001 Announced', 25 May 2001.

Department for the Arts, Heritage, Gaeltacht and the Islands

Meeting of the Inter-Departmental Committee to report on possible uses of the RHK:

7 May 1980.

31 January 1984.

Department of Finance

Cultural/Heritage Tax Reliefs, TSG 98/13.

Department of the Taoiseach

Speech by the Taoiseach, Charles Haughey, 25 May 1991. Government Information Services.

Index

Illustrations are indicated by locators in **bold** type